Zombies, Migrants, and Queers

Zombies, Migrants, and Queers

Race and Crisis Capitalism in Pop Culture

CAMILLA FOJAS

UNIVERSITY OF
ILLINOIS PRESS
Urbana, Chicago, and Springfield

© 2017 by the Board of Trustees
of the University of Illinois
All rights reserved
1 2 3 4 5 C P 5 4 3 2 1
♾ This book is printed on acid-free paper.

Printed and bound in Great Britain by
Marston Book Services Ltd, Oxfordshire

Library of Congress Cataloging-in-Publication Data
Names: Fojas, Camilla, 1971– author.
Title: Zombies, migrants, and queers: race and crisis capitalism in
   pop culture / Camilla Fojas.
Description: Urbana : University of Illinois Press, [2017] |
   Includes bibliographical references and index.
Identifiers: LCCN 2016026333 (print) | LCCN 2016045180
   (ebook) | ISBN 9780252040924 (cloth : alk. paper) | ISBN
   9780252082405 (pbk. : alk. paper) | ISBN 9780252099441
   (ebook)
Subjects: LCSH: Mass media and culture—United States—
   History. | Popular culture—United States—History. |
   Mass media and minorities—United States—History. |
   Capitalism—United States—History. | Violence—United
   States—History.
Classification: LCC P94.65.U6 F653 2017 (print) | LCC P94.65.U6
   (ebook) | DDC 302.230973—dc23
LC record available at https://lccn.loc.gov/2016026333

Contents

Acknowledgments   vii

Introduction. C.R.E.A.M.:
Capitalism Ruins Everything around Me   1

1. Border Absurd:
   The End-Times and the End of the Line   16
2. Migrant Domestics and the Fictions
   of Imperial Capitalism   41
3. Zombie Capitalism: Night of the Living Debt   60
4. Queer Incarcerations   82
5. Sinkholes and Seismic Shifts:
   Ecological and Other Disasters   104
6. Imperial Ruins and Resurgence   124

   Afterword: Racial Capitalism Redux   140

Notes   151

Bibliography   157

Index   165

Acknowledgments

I have many people to thank for their encouragement and thoughtful engagement with many of the ideas in this work. This project began in a writing group with Nitasha Sharma and Frances Aparicio whose feedback and generous readings were invaluable to the shaping of it. Martin Manalansan and Bill Johnson González offered helpful insights at various stages of this project. I thank Alexandra Keller for the opportunity to explore these ideas in a public forum. Christine Holmlund is not only a good friend but a great interlocutor on all things pop culture. I am deeply grateful to Zelideth Rivas, Carolina Sternberg, Lourdes Torres, Amor Kohli, Dusty Goltz, and Jane Park for engaging my inchoate musings on things related and unrelated to the topics of this book. I rehearsed many of these ideas with my students to whom I owe a debt of gratitude. I would like to thank the society of Vincent de Paul professors for research support. Dawn Durante is a great editor whose close readings, engagement of collaborative process, and commitment to the project helped it along and moved it in a new direction. Finally, this project would not have come to fruition without the ongoing discussions, screenings, thoughtful readings, and intellectual rigor of Dacia J. Harrold. I dedicate this work to her.

Zombies, Migrants, and Queers

Introduction
C.R.E.A.M.: Capitalism Ruins Everything around Me

> Gonna free fall out into nothing
> Gonna leave this world for a while.
> —Tom Petty, "Free Fallin'" (1989)

> We have entered an era of austerity and retrenchment unlike any this generation has ever known. But not only is it in the realm of economics and politics that America appears in a downward spiral. Socially, culturally, morally, America has taken on the aspect of a decadent society and a declining nation.
> —Patrick J. Buchanan, *Suicide of a Superpower* (2011)

The pronouncement of U.S. decadence by aggrieved paleoconservative Patrick J. Buchanan captures a cultural mood and signals the emergence of a dominant posteconomic crisis storyform, one that begins with decline and ends with creative renewal. In fact, Buchanan was White House communications director for former President Ronald Reagan whose "revolution" crystallized the storyline of U.S. capitalist culture characterized by taglines like "It's morning again in America" or America will "stand tall" again meant to restore mainstream confidence in the United States after the disorienting political and economic turmoil of the 1970s. Buchanan is a highly visible political figure in his own right who made his own forays into bids for the executive office. He is also a prolific conservative author and commentator and "defender" of white America. Buchanan consistently shapes discourse that rationalizes and normalizes violence, often by denying histories of genocide and refusing to acknowledge other forms of racialized, ethnic, and migrant injury and oppression. His work supports forms of structural violence as a preemptive move to stem the decline of white supremacy or what he decries as "the end of white America." His is not an extraordinary discourse, but one that is common in times of crisis. He exploits an anxious public mood to rally his readers to action. His book about the "suicide of a superpower" ends on an exhortatory note: "The crises that afflict us—culture wars, race division, record deficits, unpayable debt, waves of immigration, legal and illegal, of peoples never before assimilated, gridlock in the capital, and possible defeat in war—may prove too much for our democracy to cope with. They surely will, if we do not act now."[1] If we take his argument to its logical end, the action Buchanan proposes is that of retrenchment and a return to superpower status, a status achieved through forms of racial capitalism that sustain and consolidate white power and privilege. The story of the waning and resurgence of U.S. power is revised after the economic crisis, creating an entirely new storyform that begins, not with decline, but with an exhilarating freefall and ends with new ways of revitalizing white America.

Starting in 2007, the U.S. economy was not just weakening, it was, according to a number of critics, pundits, and economists, in a freefall in a manner that signaled the waning of U.S. power and an unraveling of capitalism—a crisis that returned in 2013 with the government shutdown and threat of national debt default. Financialized capitalism cannibalized itself: the same bundled loans were bought and sold over and over again with ever more borrowed capital in a kaleidoscopic geometry of debt based on phantom values. As the rest of the hemisphere was working toward alternatives to the neoliberal tenets of the "Washington Consensus," the financial systems of capitalism were in swift decline. The colossus of the North experienced a momentary lapse toward parity with the global South, particularly in terms of debt and an overleveraged banking system. While this lapse was temporary, it opened up a chasm within the structures of capitalism that exposed the violence that sustains it. That is, capitalism is structured by racialized inequities, evident in the geopolitical conditions in which the global North, as an outcome of legacies of colonial rule, retains privilege and power over the global South. For Cedric Robinson this form of "racial capitalism" emerged out of European feudalism as premised on the inequities and violence of imperialism, colonialism, slavery, and genocide. Capital relations are fundamentally racialized and unequal.[2] Violence is also part of the logic of capitalism and the form this violence takes is structural, even systemic. For Žižek, systemic violence is not racially based but describes the "catastrophic consequences" of the "smooth functioning" of the economic and political system that enacts more violence than it prevents.[3] Structural violence is an outcome of a social system that advantages some at the expense of others. Capitalism targets the poor in the global South, exploits land and resources, and results in what Garry Leech describes as "death on a genocidal scale."[4] After the Great Recession, when the global North began to head south, the former devised innovative ways of leveraging its position by recolonizing the global South and ceding its actual and representational spaces. Racial capitalism foregrounds European or white domination and includes the proliferation of diverse forms of racial domination and non-European imperialism in the neoliberal era. Racial hierarchies are supplemented by other typologies, ones that are racialized but contain different symbolic capacities, particularly that between migrant or refugee or displaced person and citizen and global North and global South. Racial capitalism creates new tributaries of oppression in its neoliberal imperial form.

Freefall Capitalism

The lessons of capitalism's inevitable doom, as foretold by Marx, went unheeded in this hemisphere when the "miracle" of the neoliberalized Argentine economy collapsed into ruins in 2001 at the same time that the U.S. economy was in a recession. Nobel laureate Joseph Stiglitz, former Obama advisor and former World Bank Chief economist, blamed the entire financial system for the 2007 global catastrophe—including the ideology and policies that subtend it—as being in a state of rot. Stiglitz recapitulated the cultural rhetoric of the day, asking how the largest global economy could drop into a freefall, a rapid descent distinct from the boom and bust cycles of capitalism.

Freefall means that the fall is longer, more intense, more devastating, and unfettered; it is total and final and the return to the top, to stability and lost social and cultural standing, is difficult or even impossible. Freefalling is frightening, evoking a fall from great heights resulting in certain death. It recalls planes nosediving or skydivers and BASE jumpers without functional parachutes and, recently, terrified men and women leaping to escape the burning embers of the twin towers in lower Manhattan on September 11, 2001. The latter is beautifully captured in Tom Junod's description of the photograph of a man departing "from this earth like an arrow" who "if he were not falling, he might very well be flying." The falling man emblematizes the spectacle of the freefall as a terrifying form of pure negation: "In the picture, he is frozen; in his life outside the frame, he drops and keeps dropping until he disappears."[5]

The falling body as a trope in popular culture emerged during another time of crisis, from the rumor and hearsay about widespread suicide of financiers—

tacitly coded as mostly male—plunging from skyscraper windows following the 1929 stock market crash. Thomas Stubblefield finds the claims about people lining up to jump from windows to be utterly false; in fact, there were very few such leaps. Yet, the number of leaps is less significant than the symbolic resonance of the imagined jump. The falling body emblematizes the economic freefall. It captures a number of fears about rapid and unstoppable descent as a bodily experience, as a sign of the social life of capital or how the structures of capitalism shape experience. For Stubblefield, the falling body is the key nodal point in the memory and recollection of disaster. He links this to dreams of falling discussed by Freud—particularly the way that such dreams transform enjoyment into anxiety, that is, the pleasure of the childhood game of being tossed into the air becomes the anxiety of an unassisted and unprotected fall. For Freud, the dream of falling captures the pleasure of childhood memories of various airborne games—including that of flying, being thrown in the air, or tumbling and romping—while it contains the foreboding that emanates from the actual outcome of the childhood romp that "ends in squabbling and tears."[6]

Freud admits to being unable to account fully for falling in dreams and offers only a schematic and inchoate impression. He does admit the sexual sense of dreams of falling in the example of a woman taking a tumble that evokes the resonance of the "fallen woman" who violates the sexual propriety of normative womanhood. Stubblefield occludes Freud's particularizing of the experience of falling by coding the subject as male. In his account, women do not signify as "falling bodies." Instead, the slip from "falling man," in the classic examples from Icarus to Dante to James Stewart's character in *Vertigo*, to "falling body" universalizes the male experience of unfettered descent and raises the subsequent trauma to the level of an existential crisis of social dimensions within the racially unmarked norm of whiteness. The appearance of this falling body during times of financial turmoil yokes the white male subject it denotes to capital. His demise is the very demise of the white and masculinist culture of capital.

Richard Drew's photograph of the falling man, mentioned earlier, whose body is framed by one of the twin towers, key nodes of U.S.-based capitalism, is the iconic symbol of the empire in freefall. It is an image that memorializes those who died as volitional agents whose leap into the air, lateral to the viewer, elicits identification. His position is so disorienting that, as Junod notes, he could be flying. The photograph offers the viewer a perspective imbued with optimism, of disavowal, in which falling signifies escape, an alternate path out of a terrifying experience. Falling is a form of liberation. In the photograph, he falls forever, his movement is a kind of stasis, an image that crystallizes the moment of the internal rupture of U.S. self-identity as a liberal democratic and nonimperious state, a moment suspended and abstracted from all temporal flow. The image connotes Wall Street in freefall and its capitalist subject too. Yet his arrested fall is hopeful, an uncertain future that has yet to be written—in contradistinction to the hyperdeterminism of social life for those outside of the frame.

In Tom Petty's song of the same name, freefalling is both an experience of freedom and an abnegation of a good life represented by the love of a "good girl." The subject of the lyrics freefalls into "nothing" and undergoes an ecstatic disappearance into the vanishing point of being. This void at the end of the freefall is an aporia, a gap in meaning from which new thought emerges. Freefalling is distinct from the freefall, not just for the difference in tense, but in the suggestion, evident in the song, that "freefalling" is a philosophical disposition signaling a series of choices away from the safety and solidity of a mainstreet lifestyle. For Tom Petty, the experience of liberation and complete abandon takes place in the fantasmatic zones of Ventura Boulevard and Mulholland Drive in Los Angeles, sites of numerous stories of loss, ruin, and reinvention. As the subject of the song explores his freedom, he knows that others like him have left the comfort and stability of a domestic life to pursue the same uncertain but liberated course; like him, they are freefalling.

A freefall might evoke both the rapturous state of capitalist freedom and a frightening consequence of its inevitable ruin. It marks a radical yet momentary rupture from forms of institutional power. The abyss we imagine at the end of the freefall is replete with meaning; its various tributaries are charged with fantasies and fears about loss of identity, absolute freedom, the vacating of social difference and inequities, and the elimination of social hierarchies. The freefall generates a great leveling subsequent to crisis or disaster. It marks the beginning of a new storyform for the global North.

Crisis Capitalism

The storyform of capitalism has a uniquely U.S. provenance based in a history of boom and bust cycles. The narrative follows a similar pattern; it begins with a period of economic boom and wanton profligacy, followed by an overleveraged position of imperial overreach, and ending with hope for renewal. The economic boom following World War II coincided with incredible global influence or what Joseph Nye describes as soft power or the power of attraction and persuasion rendered by a complex of popular, mass, entertainment, and consumer cultures that convinced the rest of the world to follow and endorse U.S. hegemony.[7] U.S. power is bolstered and fortified by its security and intelligence forces that comprise the largest global matrix of military bases of operation and powerful leadership positions in various international coalitions and organizations such as the International Monetary Fund (IMF) and the World Bank. The U.S. storyform of crisis capitalism is equally hegemonic, shaping global narratives about crisis as inevitable and ultimately productive in a manner that further consolidates U.S. power.

The crisis capitalist storyform has a short timeline; one of its major signposts is the great depression of the 1930s and the fall from economic heights after the 1929 stock market crash—emblematized, as Stubblefield argues, by the falling man jumping from the height of success to his demise. These boom and bust cycles continue after World War II, but none are so severe as to disrupt the continued growth of U.S. power until most recently. The story of U.S. capitalism is dynamic and often described as following organic cycles and natural vicissitudes. Economist Nouriel Roubini and economic historian Stephen Mihm argue that crisis is a permanent condition of capitalism, likening it to the appearance of a storm as a readily scientifically monitored event: "Though crises are commonplace, they are also creatures of habit. They're a bit like hurricanes: they operate in a relatively predictable fashion but can change directions, subside, and even spring back to life with little warning."[8] They apply the language of natural disaster to human-made phenomena, which suggests that crises are inevitable conditions to which we must adjust and acculturate. Roubini and Mihm are part of a cadre of popular economists who draw lessons and remedies from the crisis—most notably Paul Krugman, Alan Greenspan, and Joseph Stiglitz. They seek ways of interpreting the crisis to find the silver lining of the dark cloud of catastrophe. Partly instructive and partly bromide, their work is practical, intended to develop remedies to alleviate the disturbances of crisis.

Roubini and Mihm critique current methods of doing business and analyze the dramatic unfolding of the crisis masterplot in order to write a new ending for it. Rather than restoration or rejuvenation of the toppled order, they argue for wholesale reform. They write of the "script" of the crisis that begins with the ballooning of the bubble of speculation:

> Like all bubbles, this one eventually stopped growing. And as in most bubbles, the end began with a whimper, not with a bang. Prices moved sideways; a strange sort of stasis came over the markets. The bubble boosters insisted this lapse was momentary; prices would rise again soon. But they did not. At this point in the drama, they rarely collapse overnight. They simply stall.
>
> Then they collapse, a few institutions at first, then many. The effects reverberate throughout the financial system. Fear and uncertainty grip the markets, and while the price of the bubbly asset crumbles, the real action lies in the financial

institutions that provided the credit behind the bubble. Deleveraging begins, and faced with overwhelming uncertainty, investors flee toward safer, more liquid assets.

The recent crisis stuck to this script.[9]

Banks do not fold all at once but mark the story of economic freefall with spectacular and dramatic collapses, like smaller conflicts that accrue to a crisis point, "setting the stage for even more dramatic failures." Thus crisis is evident not as a single crash but in economic fluctuations, each worse than the one that precedes it. And the drama always goes global since "when it comes to financial crises, all the world's a stage."[10] Finally, crises, following Aristotelian plot, culminate in "one failure so spectacular that it overshadows all the rest."[11] And the turn to a "lender of last resort" offers a deus-ex-machina plot device rendered in the bailout. For Roubini and Mihm, this final dramatic turn points to the need for systemic reform. They take the drama of crisis to impose a different ending, one that turns ruin into an opportunity for revision. The dramatic arc of crisis, its climax, leads not to dismantling of the system but measures that will diminish the impact of cyclical crises. Again, using the language of natural disaster, they intone, in the book's final statement:

> As we contemplate the future of finance from the mire of our own recent Great Recession, we would do well to try to emulate that achievement. Nothing lasts forever, and crises will always return. But they need not loom so large; they need not overshadow our economic existence. If we strengthen the levees that surround our financial system, we can weather crises in the coming years. Though the waters may rise, we will remain dry. But if we fail to prepare for the inevitable hurricanes—if we delude ourselves, thinking that our antiquated defenses will never be breached again—we face the prospect of many future floods.[12]

This sentiment is a commonplace of the popular discussion of economic crises, one that deploys the crisis as the inciting event of a cautionary tale and that uses metaphor and analogy to associate capitalism with the natural world within a plot structure that terminates with a clear and coherent resolution.

Debt Capitalism

Imperial capitalism is the final and highest stage of capitalism. For Vladimir Lenin it turns economic divisions and disparities into a global imperative.[13] It describes the ever-expanding and deepening forms of interdependence and interchange across geographies and species. It is voracious, co-optive, and capacious. Imperial capitalism operates and circulates via the oldest form of exploitation, the debt economy and its symbolic tributaries: speculation and risk, public debt, social debts, personal debts, moral debts, racial debt, bodily debts. Debts demand repayment and recompense with time, money, bodily exertion, and other forms of symbolic exchange. Creditors are subjects of exchange, and debtors, to varying degrees, are objects of exchange. And all of these relations are rendered visible in crisis, during moments when the smooth functioning of ideology is interrupted by catastrophe. Silvia Federici notes that debt has always been a means of subjugation, exploitation, and enslavement but cautions against conceiving of it as a "political universal" for its continual and, more recently, significant transformations. The debt crisis of 1979 restructured global debt dynamics, which was triggered by the Federal Reserve's interest rate increase on the dollar and subsequent structural readjustments by the World Bank and International Monetary Fund. This initiated a recolonization of the global South as the former colonial world plunged deeper into debt and was forced to sell off its resources to Europe and the United States and, later, to China. Federici argues that the debt crisis caused the rollback of the gains of anticolonial struggles.

The new "debt economy" emerges with the "neoliberal turn in capitalist development" that made debt ubiquitous, marking what Maurizio Lazzarato calls the rise of "indebted man." And debt shapes the entire global order with international, national, state, and municipal debts and individual forms of indebtedness from student loans, mortgage and credit card debt, and microfinance debt. Individual and group debt, Federici argues, amplifies "the economic effects of state debt" and changes the relation between workers, "making exploitation more self-managed and turning the communities that people are building in search of mutual support into means of mutual enslavement."[14] Indeed, Federici's insights about the impact of the debt economy on social dynamics are everywhere apparent in postcrisis culture. She might have been describing the social interactions of characters in a popular TV show about a group of people trying to survive after the zombie apocalypse.

Popular culture responded to the anxieties and disorientations of the economic crisis with diverse storylines. Some of these stories found culprits for the economic freefall with tales of the cruel machinations of the financial elite—the bankers and politicians that enabled widespread ruin—and stories of typical Americans struggling to keep afloat. Hollywood gave us epic stories of the bad guys of capitalism and presented the crisis as a consequence of aberrant behavior and the perversions of Wall Street; *Capitalism: A Love Story* (2009), *Wall Street: Money Never Sleeps* (2010), *The Other Guys* (2010), *Inside Job* (2010), *Margin*

Call (2011), and *The Wolf of Wall Street* (2013). Other stories thematize the impact of the crisis on "main street" as it unfolded in a number of TV storylines: *Girls, Two Broke Girls, Undercover Boss, Arrested Development, Weeds, Undercover Millionaire, Breaking Bad, Desperate Housewives, The Simpsons, South Park*, and *Hung*, among many other shows and programs. A number of fiction and nonfiction books about the economic elite explored the culture of the ultrarich in works like Chrystia Freeland's *Plutocracy*, Wednesday Martin's *Primates of Park Avenue*, and *The Unfortunates* by Sophie McManus.

Stories from the top and middle of the economic order narrate the experience of freefall, a sharp downturn in status and circumstance. Taking some of these texts as points of departure, Kirk Boyle and Daniel Mrozowski explore the landscape of film, television, and literary culture of the Great Recession along **diverse lines of inquiry and across multiple genres and topoi to exam**ine "bust culture" or media "inflected by diminishment, influenced by scarcity, and infused with anxiety."[15] Their work confirms the interconnection of the cultural and the **economic, particularly through the industrial formations of** multinational media conglomerates that, by tapping into the cultural moment, sought profit from crisis. Boyle and Mrozowski take a diagnostic approach in which popular culture of the Great Recession exhibits symptoms that demand ever more recursive forms of interpretation. The prevailing trope in "bust culture" media is a dialectical opposition between postmodern obscurantism—emblematized by the derivative—and plain speak as "common sense." The former indicates a linguistic split between the signifier and that which it is meant to signify—in this case, financial operations with no actual referent. And this linguistic obscurantism may veil a lack of knowledge. To fully decode the culture of the crisis is nearly impossible since "with the Great Recession it appears that creative destruction has become so creative as to have outwitted itself."[16] Some of the stories of popular culture suggest a return to pragmatism, to common sense, as a possible remedy for all that ails bust culture. Boyle and Mrozowski et al. document the various traumatic signs and symptoms of the Great Recession to uncover the fears, anxieties, and fantasies upon which they are based.

While the crisis generated anxiety and fear, these affects energize a spirited entrepreneurialism that turns ruin into forms of cultural capital. The Great Recession created new opportunities in popular culture for white subjects to refashion and reconstitute their social subjectivies. These subjects would adapt to these new economic conditions by adopting survival strategies associated with a racialized underclass. In popular cultural storylines, white protagonists cede the representational territories of the global South. This is the story for those that experience crisis as episodic, emerging only along with global economic trends. It is not the story for those for whom everyday is a crisis, those who exist in the persistent crises of racial capitalism: dispossession, economic oppression, imperialism, and small and large forms of violence that accrue to genocide. In the dominant postcrisis storyform, a simple return to normalcy or even reform is a desirable resolution. For those at the bottom of the economic order, this outcome means only more violence.

Zombies, Migrants, and Queers examines how the popular cultural artifacts of the global economic crisis shape social dynamics, ultimately giving rise to a cultural mood of U.S. indomitability vested in a renovated form of racial capitalism. These popular cultural stories instrumentalize marginalized populations—the poor, racialized underclasses, migrants, trans/queers, prisoners, and other institutionalized peoples—to fortify fallen mainstream populations. The economic crisis reshuffled capitalism, creating a new social order with different opportunities across redrawn economic and racial lines. Demise and failure became mutable forms of social capital that might be resignified to new ends. The ideological banner of neoliberalism, austerity, became the cardinal virtue of mass culture as if it were a liberating intervention into the denaturing forces of capitalism. This became evident in every corner of popular culture, iconized by white rapper Macklemore's popular 2013 single, "Thrift Shop," in which the subject boasts of "savin' money" and partaking in a recycled and vintage aesthetic as a refusal of being "swindled and pimped" by corporate consumer culture and its homogenizing name-brand apparel.

The devastation of the U.S. economy rendered visible what had been previously offscreen, in the margins, or along the sidelines. The excluded outside is not legible in itself but through the form and character of the mainstream, that is, the misfortune wrought by an unstable financial system is most evocative when it hits the white middle class. These stories engage public sympathies for the transformation upon which they turn. They recall that of Michael Gates Gill, who lost his job at an advertising agency and chronicled his new line of work in the book *How Starbucks Saved My Life: A Son of Privilege Learns to Live Like Everyone Else* (2007). From his freefallen position, he re-creates his story, becomes someone new, more aware of social and racial inequities. The fall from heights opens up a new class and race consciousness from which accrue new forms of capital in a reconstructed sense of social subjecthood, one that is more versatile and adaptable to altered social and economic conditions; all of which are readily exploitable for lucrative mass media contracts, from book deals to television shows. There are a number of television shows about the same phenomena, where the fall from position for the white middle class is the stuff of pathos and increased empathy and understanding and, subsequently, social savvy: *Undercover Boss* (CBS 2010-) where bosses experience the world of the common worker, or being broke is a sad but enabling condition that inspires white characters' desire to remake their lives, *Two Broke Girls* (CBS 2011-), or *Secret Millionaire* (ABC 2008-), in which millionaires live temporarily in a world of racialized poverty. These protagonists of hegemonic culture stand in for the marginal, occupying the same economic ruins and rubble as the racialized populations at the bottom of the socioeconomic strata: immigrants, impoverished, dispossessed, trans/queer, and institutionalized (mainly in prisons and psychiatric wards). Such is the case in the popular Netflix series *Orange Is the New Black* (2013) about a white yuppie doing time for the misdeeds of her younger days and cavorting uneasily with prison's diverse racialized and queer social underclass. This series is based on the memoir by Piper Kerman, who, during her prison stint, gained new knowledge, a book, and a Netflix deal, and increased her social and economic capital in the process.

There are numerous stories of freefall and abandon, of departure from the course of upward mobility followed by creative ways of rebounding from a state of economic and social ruin for mainstream white protagonists. The series *Weeds* (Showtime 2005–2012), *Breaking Bad* (AMC 2008–2013), and *Arrested Development* (Fox 2003–2006 and Netflix 2013) are all stories that, at some point, take place in proximity to the border separating the United States from Mexico. In these series, crossing the border means breaking boundaries to create new freedoms and entrepreneurial opportunities for the white characters—through either traffic in drugs or involvement in the building of the wall between the United States and Mexico. These shows partake in a cultural mood of cynicism to critique the order of things, although black humor is also a sign of exhaustion and lack of political stakes in issues related to social and economic inequities. Instead, the main characters of these shows inhabit a morally skewed world in which self-interest and the pursuit of profit guide their actions. They co-opt the social roles and cultural modes associated with peoples of color and turn their own personal freefall into dizzying profits.

The economic freefall occasioned the arrest of all development and the rapid contraction of the economy. Housing projects were put on hold, humorously displayed in the TV show *Arrested Development* or dramatically in *The Queen of Versailles* (2012) and in the shift in the tone of the numerous house and home shows on the Home and Garden television network. There are also houses that collapse into ruin, abandoned in foreclosure or literally collapsing from the industrial remaking of the geological order that results in sinkholes and other disasters that destroy cities. Entire cities filed for bankruptcy—Detroit, San Bernardino, Stockton—and brought their citizens down with them. The impact of the financial operations of the economic elite of the United States could be felt on a global scale, particularly in the global South both in the United States and its client and colonial states. *The Queen of Versailles* and the first incarnation of the *Real Housewives of New York* (Bravo 2008-) show another side of the extravagance and obscenities of extreme wealth highlighted and undermined by the presence of the migrant Filipina domestic.

In the United States, the housing market is pivotal to the economy and its implosion rocked the global economic order and changed the social and cultural significance of home ownership and the status of the home. The crisis made clear who bore the brunt of the failures of the U.S. private financial markets: the marginal, the poor, women, people of color, trans/queers, migrants, and unskilled labor. In short, all vulnerable populations at the bottom of the labor market who are the first to lose jobs in an unstable economy. Those lured in by the easy access to loans found themselves overleveraged and their homes "under water" with the collapse of the mortgage industry. The government bailout of this decimated industry meant that big banks and big business emerged even bigger in the mergers and buyouts bolstered by the state. This cultural condition resonates with the paradoxical mantra of entrepreneurial capitalism: individualize the profits and socialize the losses or capitalism on the way up and socialism on the way down. The end result is resurgence and revival of a defunct system and the idea that capitalism follows a "natural" boom and bust cycle based on biological metaphors. The documentary about the king of timeshares, David Siegel and his profligate wife Jacqueline, *The Queen of Versailles*, illustrates the lifecycles of capitalism. Just as the Siegels hit economic rock bottom, they are bailed out by a bank loan. Their story of "rags to riches" and "riches to rags" takes another turn on this cycle and, subsequently, faith in the system is renewed.

Another postcrisis storyline is that of the disaster film in which economic ruin is imagined and experienced as large-scale ecological destruction and the two are linked as consequences of human action. Disaster films present crises as spectacular events that cannot be readily incorporated into daily experience. They are so extreme as to elicit and encourage disavowal of the potential reality of the outcome of ecological and other disasters. Audiences are rescued from the ravaging course of natural disaster by a deus ex machina in the form of space shuttles, distant planet habitation, rescue ships, and the like. As disaster stories engaged audiences, another species of disaster entered the news cycle: the sinkhole. Sinkholes appeared the world over consuming people, pets, cars, and houses and seemed to more readily capture the inchoate fears associated with the freefall of the financial markets and ecological disaster. The sinkhole appears at random and puts intimate domestic spaces and objects at risk. It emblematizes the impact of the economic crisis on individuals, literally bringing it home. And in this way, the sinkhole offers a manageable symbol for working through individual rapport to global crises, opening up a space for imagining possible remedies and solutions to ecological devastation.

The Great Recession found its emblem in the zombie apocalypse. Yet unlike the ecological disaster film and its sinkhole kin, the zombie film evokes fears and anxieties about the indebted life and of life in debt as a form of indentured servitude unto death. Zombie stories like *Dawn of the Dead* (2004), *The Walking Dead* (AMC 2010-), and *World War Z* (2013) are about proto-communal alliances across gender, racial, and class lines that form in response to a zombie threat. This remaking of the social order after the total destruction of its major institutions, primarily capitalism, is not imagined differently. Many of these stories are **fundamentally conservative, reproducing the hierarchies and social** ordering of capitalism without capital. Zombie stories like *World War Z* restore the social order to a more militarized form of heteropatriarchal capitalism, reanimating **a system of debt through repayment and recompense.**

Like zombies, inmates evoke the social dynamics attendant to life in debt in biopolitical terms in which social debts are tendered by bodily freedom. Prison stories, in particular women in prison stories, are a popular form for exploring issues related to freedom and un-freedom in homosocial communal spaces imagined as an alternative to living in capitalism. While the actual prison is not this ideal space, these stories contain moments of communal solidarity and offer glimpses of a different mode of living without the mediations of capital. These stories frame the prison as a queer space yet one based on white supremacy.

Orange Is the New Black (Netflix 2013-), based on Piper Kerman's memoir of the same name, is part of an archive of white women writing about their prison experience as an "accidental" inmate who must acculturate to the disorientations of incarceration. The Netflix series based on the memoir draws on a history and contemporary context of women in prison stories like *Caged* (1950), the series *Lockup* (MSNBC 2005-) and *Capadocia* (HBO Latino 2008-). In these stories, the protagonists become accustomed to prison life and what is initially terrifying becomes a matter of course. The queer aspects of prison life—lesbianism, criminality, female homosociality, gender nonconformity— are normalized for the protagonist who is a proxy for the viewer. These queer inmates are unrepentant. They refuse to pay their debt to society. They refuse to be normalized. These stories offer a different crisis capitalist plotline.

The postcrisis stories of class descent, sexual deviance, ruination, and disaster explore the contradictions and tensions exposed by the economic freefall.

Postcrisis stories give shape to capitalism as the very experience of capitalism, profoundly impacting public mood and providing the affective tonality of social life. These stories imbue social life with meaning and circulate as capital. These constitutive parts of the world of capitalism, the stories we borrow and trade, create and sustain our social lives, making neoliberalism and the debt economy seem inevitable and self-evident, without alternative. These pop cultural stories thematize the insecurity of living in a neoliberal order while they also explore ways of surviving and even thriving in social and economic conditions of ruin. Popular culture of the Great Recession contributes to a social order shaped by economic precariousness and generates stories that encourage and enable publics to adapt to this new condition. And, for Isabell Lorey, precariousness is the basis for governmental control, one that coincides with neoliberal principles of capital accumulation and social regulation. Disorder and insecurity are not an exception, but the rule; they are the primary modes of governing in crisis capitalism.[17] For Lorey, insecurity is a way of life and crises generate more, not less, social control:

> Contrary to the old rule of a domination that demands obedience in exchange for protection, neoliberal governing proceeds primarily through social insecurity, through regulating the minimum of assurance while simultaneously increasing instability. In the course of the dismantling and remodeling of the welfare state and the rights associated with it, a form of government is established that is based on the greatest possible insecurity, promoted by proclaiming the alleged absence of alternatives. The way that precaritization has become an instrument of government also means that its extent must not pass a certain threshold such that it seriously endangers the existing order: in particular it must not lead to insurrection. Managing this threshold is what makes up the art of governing today.[18]

Popular culture aids and abets in this work, dramatizing ways of living in ruin that manage disorder, promoting adaptation and assimilation along with the quarantining of the trans/queer and the outcast, the repatriation of unwanted migrants, and denial of hospitality to refugees. These stories limit critical awareness of and resistance to the violence of capitalism by pointing, optimistically, to a future beyond crisis and instability, while occluding the extent to which this future is shaped by its past, beholden to it. These stories must not, using Lorey's language, cross a certain threshold, one that would lead to insurrection. Perhaps all it takes is a little nudge to push these stories over the line, to reinterpret them and reframe their revolutionary and liberatory potential.

Financial and moral ruin and rot plagued the world over as people lost their jobs, houses, and savings in a turn of events that seemed to augur the very end of capitalism. For cultural critic Slavoj Žižek, it is the "end times" caused, in the language of Patrick J. Buchanan, by the "suicide of a superpower."[19] When the economy shows signs of recovery, the cultural memory of the demise of capitalism wanes. Yet, the massive chasm in the structure of neoliberal capitalism remains. Its fault lines reveal the cultural undertide of race at the limit and in the margins of the national story. We are living in times of upheaval, less the end-times than the end of denial, when we can no longer ignore the gulf between the economic ruling class and those dispossessed by economic and other crises. We can no longer disavow state-sponsored racialized violence against people of color, migrants, indigenous peoples, and those considered sexual and gender dissidents. Some of this violence is direct and some is the consequence of neglect and lack of effective response to economic and other disasters enacted upon marginalized communities.

CHAPTER 1

Border Absurd

The End-Times and the End of the Line

> Hegel remarks somewhere that all great, world-historical facts and personages occur, as it were twice. He has forgotten to add: the first time as tragedy, the second as farce.
> —Karl Marx, "The Eighteenth Brumaire of Louis Bonaparte"

> Sometimes the repetition in the guise of a farce can be more terrifying than the original tragedy.
> —Slavoj Žižek, *First as Tragedy, Then as Farce*

The postcrisis flattening of the social order spurred a flurry of anxiety-ridden stories of extralegal endeavors to maintain a middle-class lifestyle against further ruin. Middle-aged white suburbanites resort to the drug trade, and entire families engage in untoward and extralegal activities to make ends meet. Many of these stories have some reference to limits symbolized by the U.S.–Mexican borderlands as the arena at the end or limit of the nation and a theater of ruin and loss at the end of capitalism. And many use a tone of cynicism, the absurd, and dark or black humor to send up the ridiculousness of maintaining appearances and to defuse the grimness of violence and moral distortions. In *Arrested Development*, the Bluth family lost their wealth through illegal dealings and so began developing homes in the Los Angeles basin and, more lucratively and extralegally, in Iraq, eventually becoming involved in a political bribe to erect a wall between the United States and Mexico. In *Weeds* (Showtime 2005–2012), a single white mom loses everything and sets up a cross-border drug ring to maintain her affluent lifestyle, eventually marrying Esteban Reyes, a Mexican drug kingpin and mayor of Tijuana. In *Breaking Bad* (AMC 2008–2013), a nonsmoking white man is diagnosed with lung cancer and his inadequate health insurance inspires him to join the drug trade in the Southwest, taking over a market left by a Latino operative he murdered and putting him in direct competition with Mexican cartels. For these white protagonists ruin and personal devastation put them at the limits of the United States in proximity to the U.S.–Mexican border where crossing over is the final stop on their personal freefall. The border is the end of the line. The southern frontier offers ready symbols for the end of capitalism, signified as a geographical limit. Capitalism reaches its limit when it no longer serves white supremacy, when whiteness loses its value as capital and needs new forms for survival.

The freefall activates a rush, euphoria, and the limit experience of absolute freedom wrought by breaking boundaries, breaking bad, and falling out. For **these white protagonists, rock bottom is the source of new forms of freedom** and possibility, where criminality signifies as entrepreneurialism, determination, and grit. The same is not true for racialized outsiders at and beyond the borders of these stories. Racialized characters are ancillary but useful; their histories and social worlds are exploited and extracted as resources. White characters co-opt racialized borderland survival strategies and aesthetic forms for the reinvigoration of whiteness. Their access to border cultures makes them adaptable, flexible, and savvy. The renewal of capitalism begins with the renewal of whiteness; it is revised and reconfigured through adaptation to and appropriation of racialized forms. The inversion of the racial order is treated with black humor as part of the absurd upheaval that accompanies the demise of racial capitalism. The joke belongs to the white characters who, once ridiculous, turn ruin into profit and revitalize the cultural capital of whiteness.

The Social Life of Capital

While there are numerous examples that might elucidate the current structure of capital in the end-times, I turn to the industrial and storyline routes of the development of the television show *Arrested Development* for its political allegories, timely focus on the housing and construction industry, and cynical treatment of the ideal white family in relation to a racialized outside within the global dynamics of U.S. imperialism. The show aired on the Fox television network for three seasons (2003–2006) and was resurrected as a digitally streamed program through Netflix in 2013. It is a drama about a family populated by good and bad people, mostly bad, who are characterized primarily in relation to their sense of entitlement evident in their lack of fiscal discipline. The "arrested development" of the show has multiple meanings referring to both psychological immaturity, again evinced in part as financial illiteracy, and to the family business,

Figure 1.1. *Arrested Development*, ship of fools with Michael Bluth (Jason Bateman) at the helm.

a real estate development firm that, through nefarious international dealings leading to major losses, is in a holding pattern brought about by the arrest and imprisonment of the family patriarch and company CEO, George Bluth (Jeffrey Tambor)—an obvious homonym and reference to then president George W. Bush (2001–2009); the show makes oblique reference to the Bush doctrine of at-will intervention exercised in Iraq. The series takes place, as with many of the disaster and doomsday stories and stories about ruin and freefalling— *Battle: Los Angeles* (2011), *2012* (2009), or *This Is the End* (2013)—in Los Angeles, border city and locus of U.S. soft power as the epicenter of the Hollywood film and television media empire.

The political allegory of the show regarding Bluth business in Iraq and the construction of the border between the United States and Mexico is paradoxically heavy-handed and subtle, in keeping with the tenets of farce. Through financial mismanagement and the illegal dealings of George Bluth, the family loses everything and is forced to live in their sole remaining asset, the model home that served as the prototype for a development in Iraq. George is married to the profligate social climber Lucille (Jessica Walter) and they have four adult children: Michael (Jason Bateman), the only "sensible" son, Gob (Will Arnett), characterized by his flight from all things difficult, Buster (Tony Hale), the infantilized mama's boy, and Lindsay (Portia de Rossi), a self-absorbed narcissist married to Tobias (David Cross), a former psychiatrist in talentless pursuit of an acting career. In an inversion of the familial order, it is Michael who yields authority and manages the family, assuming the role of patriarch, while the rest are beset by their immaturity and unrepentant displays of self-interest.

Arrested Development is popular and entertaining for its self-reflexive cynicism about its political and social context along with its play with the plasticity of language and semantic ambiguity. For example, there is a lawyer called Bob Boblaw who has a law blog. Or the matriarch Lucille is confused with a "loose seal" and her best friend and nemesis of the same name. Or Gob, pronounced like the biblical Job, is the opposite of his heroic namesake. The wordplay underscores the general mood of ridicule and ridiculousness permeating the series. In fact, the Bluth family dramatizes the absurdity of capitalism or what Gilles Deleuze and Félix Guattari call the "rationality of the irrational" in which capitalism is "delirious" or "mad" but completely functional.[1] It functions because it is based on individual investments and desire; it flows with and through desire. For Deleuze and Guattari, the libidinal economy uses the same circuitry as the political economy to animate the corpus of capitalism. Desire infuses the social order, whose primary unit is the family, and is directly implicated in, rather than outside, it. On the show, individual desires are fundamentally egocentric and self-serving, enacted via the social roles of each character within a functionally dysfunctional family unit. In this capitalist farce, each character's desires are frustrated and impossible, that is, none evinces any productive potential or meets its intended outcome. This is evident in Lindsay's failed attempts to garner male attention to compensate for the lack thereof in her marriage, to her husband Tobias's unacknowledged homosexuality and Michael's dating catastrophes. Like the shortcomings of the family business plan, the frustrations of desire in the show highlight the failures, contradictions, and dead ends of imperial capitalism.

The only person with any financial strategy in the Bluth family, Michael, imposes an economic austerity program to stabilize its position, to the utter disapprobation of the rest of the family who are unable to curb their profligacy. The cornerstone of Michael's economic plan, austerity, is one of the myths of liberal economic policy that only produces more poverty and does not remedy stagnation. Michael is the comedic "straight man," as the reservoir of cynical realism amid the ridiculousness and self-absorption of his family. He is the ultimate instantiation of the cynic who must negotiate the antics of an imperious and arbitrary state. Cynicism is the perfect mode to connote the affective vacuity of the show. For Lyotard, the moral of capitalism is cynicism for its emptiness; it offers nothing to believe in, no redemption.[2] It is the cardinal quality of late capitalism.

Figure 1.2. Michael Bluth aggrieved by his family's antics.

For Peter Sloterdijk, cynicism is the only reasonable response to the broken promises of the era of ideological critique and the failures of its attendant critical theory. Writing in 1981 in Munich, Sloterdijk responds to the prevalence of cynicism in German culture as a form of disillusionment with the unfinished utopian global movements of the 1960s and '70s. Cynicism is "chic bitterness" that expresses discontent with the social order in a form of, citing Marx, "enlightened false consciousness," as an outcropping of the Hegelian "unhappy consciousness."[3] Political disillusionment finds expression in a stagnated form of critique, one that goes nowhere, in which there is no moral high ground and everything is a target and source of discontent in the recognition of the inevitable "eternal return of the same." Sloterdijk's critique of cynical reason is once again very timely in a manner that follows the cycles of a capitalist social order. That is, there are historical moments that allow openings for the critique of hegemony followed by the sealing of such fissures. Cynicism is the mood evoked by the recognition of this futile and endless cycle of optimism and doom.

Henry Giroux updates this analysis to a neoliberal frame. Cynicism signals a lack of trust in the validity and utility of politics and a subsequent lack of "social vision" regarding equity or civic engagement. It is a sign of exhaustion. As the public sphere depoliticizes, the private sphere is co-opted by consumerism and its conservative ideology in which participation in a consumer market is a viable expression of citizenship.⁴ And this neoliberal brand of cynicism means a retreat into the private, into the family and other privatized spheres. *Arrested Development*, *Weeds*, and *Breaking Bad* share a cynical outlook and all are premised on an alibi of familial cohesion behind which egoistic and individual desires obtain. They dramatize the absurd social life of capital, taking the premise of neoliberalism to its logical extreme, where self-serving antics, contradictory beliefs, bankrupt moral worlds, and dark urges are given full sway. The protagonists of each series is an antihero or antiheroine, driven more by passion than ideals, whose main desire is to accumulate capital at the expense of the family each purports is his/her motivation.

In these series, cynicism is expressed via black humor as a sign of the "absurd tragedy which has trapped us all" and that is "savage, brooking no compromise with its subject."⁵ As critic Richard Schickel wrote in 1963, it is a curious mix of anger, disillusionment, and merriment and the only viable mode with which to treat serious existential crises without pretension.⁶ It emerges in the United States as a consequence of post–World War II cultural exhaustion with a social order in upheaval, or as Conrad Knickerbocker describes it in 1964:

> Bitter, perverse, sadistic and *sick*—as the righteous defenders of a sick society aver—the new humor is black in its pessimism, its refusal of compromise and its mortal sting. Its adherents are few as yet but increasing. Bored beyond tears by solemnity and pap, an increasing audience finds in black humor no tonic, but the gall of truth. There are no more happy endings. A cheery wave and a fast shuffle no longer leave them laughing. New for us, black humor has been part of the response of wiser peoples in other times.⁷

Black humor signals an abyss of meaning occasioned by crisis or major social transformations. Writing in the 1960s during a mood of social unrest, Knickerbocker argues that black humorists are the keepers of the social conscience who, "amid the banality, the emptiness, and the excess . . . offer the terrors and possibilities of self-knowledge."⁸ Within the absurdity and illogic of each of these TV and Netflix series about individual self-interest is a social critique of the vacuity of moral social being in neoliberalism. And the proximity to the border signals the global, cross-border impact of the pursuit of profit.

State of Austerity

The first epoch of *Arrested Development* parodies the economic principles of the neoliberal state while it indulges fantasies about an indestructible "American way of life" premised on family. It allows audiences to enjoy a playful critique of

Bluth imperiousness, arbitrariness, and even "perversion" to ultimately valorize the primacy of family above all other matters. The family, and its ideological basis, is the kernel of the state. The Bluths experience a freefall from their social and economic position but land in the security of a normative, if dysfunctional, family.

Arrested Development immerses viewers in the logical impasses and ludicrous arbitrariness of Bush-era neoliberal policies and rhetoric. The family is in complete disavowal about its circumstances, having no money but acting as if they do, while Michael Bluth scrambles to cut their spending and forces each person to enter the unskilled labor market. Their inability to adapt to this new lifestyle of austerity and the increasingly baroque strategies they devise to avoid it make them ever more ridiculous. Mark Blyth calls austerity a "dangerous idea," not simply because it is ineffective but because the policies around it use a rhetoric of "payback" or retribution for overspending and general profligacy. On the state level, austerity is a "form of voluntary deflation in which the economy adjusts through the reduction of wages, prices, and public spending to restore competitiveness, which is (supposedly) best achieved by cutting the state's budget, debts, and deficits."[9] In the language of retribution, the implied target is the state, but austerity measures impact the poor and marginal, leaving them further dispossessed and without recourse. On the show, the family simply refuses to adapt to the austerity measures that Michael imposes, their resistance to be inculpated and act accordingly registers as a critique of his policies. In a send-up that exposes the contradictions of his measures, Michael violates his own austerity plan when he buys an expensive sports car as his "company car."

The show might be read as an allegory of the state and its economic and political principles while it casts a broader drama about the social life of neoliberalism. The show's cynicism, presented through the critical distance and logical bearing of Michael Bluth, veils the reality of its recapitulation of the dominant order and the "American Way" in which the nuclear family is the basis of capitalism. This idea is dramatized in the show *Modern Family* (ABC 2009-) in which the characters are beset by their failure to adhere to social norms, yet real success is measured by family coherence and integrity, and all other "aberrations" of a norm are tolerated if they consolidate rather than dissolve the family—e.g., interracial marriage, gay marriage, transracial gay adoption. In *Arrested Development*, the white family closes ranks to stabilize and strengthen its economic position and those marginal to this narrative remain in their position as adjuncts.

In the shadows of the bright spectacles of the U.S. empire lurk untold stories of dark figures haunting the margins and threatening the stability of the state.

In *Arrested Development*, it is a Korean adoptee, African American characters like Carl Weathers (playing himself) and Latina/o workers who shore up the ridiculous antics of the Bluth family but remain nonetheless on the sidelines. For example, Lucille Bluth treats her staff, in particular her Latina maid, Lupe (B. W. Gonzalez), with cruel arbitrariness and suspicion, which is meant to reflect poorly on her. She also adopts a Korean boy (Justin Lee) to appear sympathetic but he never really accedes to a name and is called by the first word he utters—*Annyong* (*hello*)—and, in keeping with the status of Asian Americans, he is paradoxically a target of resentment and indifference, accused of usurping Buster's infantilized role in the family just as Asians and Asian Americans are accused of quietly appropriating that which belongs to white Americans in the national imaginary. Similarly, in *Margin Call* (2011), about the antics of a financialized banking system that led to the 2008 crisis, a Latina janitor is invisible in plain sight; she is presumably too unimportant to heed for the executives who flank her and talk over and through her in the cramped space of an elevator. These examples reflect the arrogance of the economic ruling class and their utter disregard for those most affected by their decisions and actions. Arguably, these stories are critical of the dominant order, and those most culpable for its excesses are thus protagonists of these imperial allegories.

The spectacle of ruination of the entire system and structure upon which capitalism and its neoliberal principles rest is performed by a mainstream cast of characters in both the news and entertainment media: elite to middle-class, mostly Anglo, figures. These are figures who experience a freefall in economic circumstances—Bernie Madoff—or political regard—Anthony Wiener or Eliot Spitzer—whose abjection is the stuff of pathos. Like the Bluths, their transgressions are multiple and repeated, which elicits no sympathy. These are the new moral stories in the down cycle of capitalism.

Double Crossers

In 2012, the once defunct show, *Arrested Development*, was reanimated and sent back into the U.S. ether through digital media. The ruined family was resurrected in a new post–economic crisis development model premised on diversification of individual investments. There is a curious ideological shift between the first era of the show in the early 2000s, and its postcrisis return. The latter era finds the family fragmented in a manner that is reflected in the framing and setup of the show, where each episode is devoted to individual family members. The Bluths are atomized and separate in a scenario much different from the former centrality of the family as a coherent unit. This highlights each person's social role and significance in the political allegory. For example, earlier gestures to Tobias's dubious sexuality are, in the new season, overtly signaled and marked as gay; that is, what was ambiguous becomes certain, more visible, thus undermining the family's coherence around a heteropatriarchal structure.

A major plotpoint of the second incarnation of the show is the Bluth company's involvement in promoting the building of a wall between the United States and Mexico in order to profit on the sale of land that is purportedly on the border but is actually 50 miles south of the border. George Bluth seeks support from conservative African American candidate Herbert Love for the project of building a wall between the United States and Mexico—an idea that his wife claims to have originated. Love's other political platform is to oust President Barack Obama from office, an expression of his complete lack of solidarity with African Americans and all those out of step with his conservative ideology. George tells the political candidate that if he supports the wall, he'll give Love "a piece of the action," but Love demands his bribe in the form of a campaign contribution. In the era of the prophesied end of capitalism, the creation of a wall recalls other politically charged bulwarks that separate nations and peoples. As the Berlin wall marked the end of communism, the wall along the U.S.-Mexico border is a symbolic gesture marking the defense against a similar fate for capitalism; it was built to fend off the threatening incursion of the global South into the unstable center of empire.

As the Bluths become ever more fragmented and treacherous, the racialized social movements against their reactionary political moves become more visible. In a political rally, a large Latino protest against the wall merges with that of Latinos protesting the Bluths' intervention into city politics to change the Cinco de Mayo holiday to "Cinco de Cuatro"—the Bluths' attempt to orchestrate a citywide change to the holiday so that their domestic workers would not take the day off from work. The reinvented series revises the power structure in the family; the absurd and contradictory rule of the parents holds less sway. The Bluth adult children present a concerted if disingenuous and temporary front against the conservative ideology of the political candidate, Love, who, acting on a bribe from George, is responsible for fomenting resentment toward Mexico and Mexicans that results in support for building a wall along the U.S.-Mexico border. This wall, meant to block off and foreclose entry into the United States, is a barrier erected to protect against and contain the contaminating strains of migration.

Yet Bluth political affiliation shifts arbitrarily. Lindsay is committed to the cause against the wall until she falls for Herbert Love, at which point she makes an ideological about-face. She changes her political position again when he

Figure 1.3. Lindsay Bluth (Portia de Rossi) falls for conservative political candidate Herbert Love (Terry Crews).

breaks it off with her. This privatization of social struggle is posed against images of the shared space of communal life of the rally or protest. Lindsay Bluth's fake political stand is a potent reminder of how social movements are readily co-opted in neoliberalism. Each character's political investments are potentially redirected according to individual interest and desires.

The cynicism of *Arrested Development* in season four, where the family is no longer coherent or allied against the world beyond it, is a productive point of departure for examining the dead ends of capitalism. That is, the show bears out Marxian ideas about how capitalism addresses the family, instrumentalizes it, but ultimately tears it asunder, leaving it as morally bankrupt as the state to which it refers. In the first incarnation of the show on cable television, Michael represents the law; he is the privileged outsider who is above the law of the family while imposing law and order upon them in a manner that is ultimately ineffective. Yet, through him we are able to gauge the absurdity of the Bluth "family values." In the Netflix version or the latest incarnation of the show, all family relations are leveled and there is no longer any illusion that there is a moral point of reference or privileged moral center. The Bluth family antics reveal the moral vacuity of state policy with regard to Iraq, Mexico and the wall along the border, immigration, and migrant labor.

In this postcrisis historical frame of reference, the family is rendered asunder even while a few of the adult children share the temporary phantom link of a social movement. In the logic of the freefall into nothing and nothingness, in the second incarnation of the show, the characters had to begin anew, without safety nets, and strike out on their own without the cover of the family business. The business continues to shape their maneuverings but offers no stability. The structures of capitalism no longer promise security for the white middle class. In fact, the fourth and final season opens with an introduction that elides the family's future with that of the show, both subject to market forces, calling *Arrested Development*, "the story of a family whose future was abruptly cancelled." This show, and others like it, presents storyworlds that offered clues about the possible outcomes for U.S. capitalism at the end of the line.

After the financial collapse of the family company and the various individual disasters, each Bluth child, in both incarnations of the show, returns to, or never left, the family home. This was not just the result of a "failure to launch," the title of a film of the same name released in 2006, but a prevalent cultural condition for many adult children after 2008. *Failure to Launch* tells the story of a son who chooses to live with his parents and who, to all appearances, is thriving and not beset by either psychological or economic woes. It is the story of a quirky and exceptional situation that, following the financial crisis, is less quirky and much more commonplace. In *Jeff Who Lives at Home* (2011), the title character is unemployed and unable and unmotivated to find work and, as the title indicates, lives in his mother's home. His situation strikes a cultural cord. The combination of mounting interest on massive student loans, a downturn in the economy, and lack of jobs created a scenario that sent many postcollege adults back to their parents' homes. Aptly called the *boomerang generation*, dwindling career options have resulted in a cultural form of arrested development.[10] Katherine S. Newman finds that these "structural barriers to independence" emerge from global economic dynamics, particularly globalization, and are intensified by the Great Recession.[11] The boomerang kids reflect changing cultural ideas about mobility and the "American Dream," particularly for the mainstream for whom this condition is new and unanticipated. The story arc and mythos of the American way is that of betterment, to supercede previous generations, particularly that of your parents. For the middle class, downward mobility is the new way forward. The boomerang kids are part of a generation undergoing arrested development and a failure to launch in which the economic circumstances offer cover for the refusal to accept the responsibilities of adult life—again nicely dramatized by all the adult Bluth children as quirky in the first incarnation of the series and in a situation that is more commonplace in the Netflix variation. The boomerang phenomena is portrayed as part of an upper-middle-class entitlement and coded as white. In *Weeds*, there is a similar character, Andy Botwin (Justin Kirk), who lives in his sister-in-law's house and, at one point, is caught (albeit dozing off) with a book that captures the ethos of this generation, *Rejuvenile*, by series creator Jenji Kohan's husband, Christopher Noxon—he later embraces the term and refers to himself as "rejuvenile."

Following the economic crisis, many faced an uncertain future when the typical ways of securing a better future are unavailable. The family business of *Arrested Development* involves manipulative if not extralegal and protolegal attempts to remain economically solvent though the family members continue to be constrained by their underdevelopment. Other shows that capture this cultural moment of economic stasis and insolvency involve fantasies of economic resurgence through means typically associated with marginalized populations: people of color, immigrants, and migrants. Their schemes include extralegal activities and participation in informal economies associated with the border between the United States and Mexico in the cross-border trade in contraband. Shows such as *Weeds* and *Breaking Bad* are part of the border genre and show how the leveling of the social order puts U.S. Anglo protagonists on par with their southern Latina and Latino counterparts—that is, as the latter are construed in the Hollywood film and media imaginary.

Suburban Drug Lord and Single Mom

Weeds predates the economic crisis but takes place at a time leading up to it and continues in production during and after it. It captures aspects of the postcrisis culture in its later seasons. And the series is often compared to *Desperate Housewives* for spoofing suburbia but with more of an edge, or, as one critic opines "it makes those broadcast 'housewives' look as calm and rational as monks."[12] Nancy Botwin is a recently widowed mother in her forties with two sons: a preteen, Shane; a teenage son, Silas; and a freeloading brother-in-law (mentioned earlier), Andy. They live in a palatial home in a suburban San Diego community called Agrestic that is populated by white families and their Latina maids. The proximity to the border and to Mexico is hinted at in the dual cultures of this divided community. In other adjoining neighborhoods are the African American family of small-time dealers comprised of matriarch Heylia James and her daughter Vaneeta and nephew Conrad; Armenian immigrants who are in direct business competition with Nancy; and a Latino drug ring for whom Nancy will work, bringing her closer to the border that she will eventually cross.

Weeds exposes the dual realities experienced by white America and its racialized others. In the first season, Nancy, while visiting her dealer, is caught in a drive-by shooting of the house. The African American occupants treat this as a matter of course and go back to their business when the assault ends, while Nancy goes into shock and experiences posttraumatic stress—she ducks for cover, reliving the moment, when a passing car backfires. Her dealer, Heylia, and the other members of the household, including Conrad and Vaneeta, continually call attention to her ignorant and sheltered attitude, sometimes in jest but often with spite, and are no less critical after the shooting. The normalizing of catastrophe for communities of color emanates from a long arc of experiences of racialized violence: from large-scale historical atrocities in the Anglo settling of Native territories, to proto-police or Texas Ranger violence, to the outcomes of chattel slavery and Jim Crow laws, to anti-immigration policies, and to ongoing police violence resulting from racial profiling. After the drive-by shooting, Nancy suggests calling the police and the response that the police are the culprits shocks her as much as the shooting. Outright and direct violence from competing operatives and the police is a means of control and deemed part of the cost of doing business. In these stories, drug culture is the domain of communities of color who are acculturated to its unwritten rules. The middle-class white protagonist ventures into this other worldly domain and must learn how to operate in a new cultural context. And learn she will. The next time there is a drive-by shooting, Nancy is the driver—and she participates unwittingly in a manner that maintains her status as only ever-naively criminal.

Nancy's acculturation to the drug trade mirrors that of the mainstream white viewer. She is an ingénue like Piper Chapman of another series created by Jenji Kohan, *Orange Is the New Black*, in which a white character is introduced to a new culture and eventually comes to dominate it. Both women, Nancy and Piper, will learn from less privileged characters and develop the skills to operate in a criminal underworld. Nancy is under the protective care of Conrad, a benevolent African American dealer, and Latino operative, Guillermo, and she is served by a South Asian college student, Sanjay, who flexibly accommodates her labor needs as she outsources her drug dealing. The irony of Anglo American outsourcing to a South Asian labor market is played for dark humor. Cynicism and "black humor" signal the accumulation of white cultural capital. These characters rebound from being the butt of the joke to having the last laugh. That is, they become powerful players in a world to which they were once incompetent outsiders—and through their association with the racialized populations that degrade them, eventually learn the business and assume the positions of their overlords.

Weeds is also about female empowerment through the development of a woman-owned business. Nancy takes a different approach to business practice, one that might be described, however problematically, as a feminized one. She is the clear focus and center of the show, which is primarily about her ability to commandeer the community around her for her own edification, acculturation, and support—from a DEA agent to the multiracial gaggle of male business associates to the African American household of small-time dealers. She is industrious and inventive, co-opting everyone around her to do her bidding, from caring for her brood and her business to caring for her bodily needs. Unlike the male drug lords, her body and sexuality are continual points of reference in the series.

Nancy's sexuality and white femininity are key tropes of the storyline. Her business is premised on her femininity and feminine bodily contours; all of her business affiliations are formed from personal and often sexually charged relationships. She leverages male sexual attraction and romantic interest into business associations even to the point of marrying DEA agent Peter Scottson, whom she is dating as a "business arrangement" that provides her with legal cover. Her femininity is controlled and regulated through heterosexual masculinity—e.g., she "needs" male protection, she conforms to a version of femininity that highlights subordinate sexuality, and she is held to a standard and expectation of maternal care. An example of the latter is her strict maternal moral code that precludes harm to youth, from the sale of drugs to kids—she severely punishes one of her dealers for doing so—to the sexual traffic in children—though she puts her own children in considerable danger. This code includes a refusal to trade in anything other than marijuana as a relatively benign drug, framed in reference to its legal medical uses. She deems cocaine, heroine, and methamphetamine to be "dangerous" and destructive, while marijuana is a softer more feminine drug that causes lethargy and reduces stress. Kohan, the show's creator, calls this a "post-conventional morality," or the development of a unique and self-guided morality, one prevalent in neoliberalism in which moral issues are subordinated to individual interest and profit margins:

> I love the notion of a character having her own morality. I had to find my issue or the establishment that I would be up against, and drug dealing seemed like a really good premise. Pot was in the air in California with the passage of Proposition 215, the medical marijuana initiative. I came up with a one-line pitch about a suburban widow pot-dealing mom. I decided to make her a widow because it would make it easier to sympathize with her, and set it in suburbia because I was fascinated with the suburbs—my mother always said all of the interesting stories are in the valley. Pot was the perfect vehicle for the show because, while it is a Schedule I narcotic, it's not taken seriously, and it crosses every boundary. Every political affiliation, every gender, every class, every family has a pot smoker—it's all access.[13]

For Kohan, pot captures a multitude of social and political issues in California, crossing a number of "boundaries," particularly between races, and ultimately crossing the boundary between nations.

In the first few seasons of the show, the men of color who work for Nancy, Conrad and Sanjay in particular, are subordinate adjuncts of the storyline in keeping with an interracial dynamic inaugurated by *I Love Lucy* (1951–1957). Like Ricky Ricardo (Desi Arnaz), the "straight man," in comedic terms, to Lucy, the men of color around Nancy support and sustain her. They are rendered ever more submissive by virtue of their unrequited affection for her and their subsequent desire to please her. Conrad and Sanjay are rendered docile, conciliatory, and attentive to Nancy's demands. This makes them do irrational things and become sullen with rejection; fiercely embodied, they are civilized only by Nancy's presence. Nancy will eventually find her way into drug trade in Mexico and secure this affiliation again through the legal bounds of marriage and under the protective care of her Mexican husband, Esteban Reyes, a politician who traffics in contraband.

Nancy is a tourist to "ethnic" cultures who never really fully crosses over into "drug culture" until she crosses the border between the United States and

Figure 1.4. Nancy Botwin (Mary Louise-Parker), suburban drug lord.

Figure 1.5. Nancy Botwin and Tijuana mayor and drug kingpin Esteban Reyes (Demián Bichir).

Mexico—though when she does, she does so imperiously, rising to the top of the drug-trafficking chain of command through her affiliation to Esteban combined with her avowed grit and determination. The series puts the suburbs in visual proximity to the border, not only through Nancy's business links to Mexico, but in the her eventual displacement to Mexico. Nancy's operations cause the town of Agrestic to burn to the ground, thus initiating her migration to the border town of Ren Mar and finally to Tijuana. This move marks the end of her long mentorship with local men of color and the beginning of her serious pursuit of global profits. For David Gillota this "ethnic education" transforms Nancy's whiteness from "fixed" to fluid though it remains her most important and valuable commodity. Gillota describes whiteness as "another ethnic construct, subject to its own reductive stereotypes."[14] She is able to traffic in her whiteness to gain forms of international mobility across the border in a manner not accessible to the people of color around her. In fact, she is employed to smuggle drugs from Mexico into the United States since, as a white woman, she is less likely to appear suspicious. She is also part of a reverse flow of migration, marked by Anglo business migration to the South, rather than northbound Mexican migration. As Deborah L. Jaramillo notes, in an ironic reversal, Nancy Botwin and Walter White of *Breaking Bad* are "stealing Mexican character jobs" in a media context where the "Mexican drug dealer is a narrative and symbolic goldmine on U.S. television."[15]

Weeds is a white and feminized version of drug trade on the cusp of and after the economic crisis. It is a show that targets a female audience of suburban white women who seek the fantasy of personal empowerment and of a circumscribed self-determination in relation to white men—her power derives from manipulation and feminine wiles, not direct power. Nancy accrues direct power through her relation to men of color. Her power emanates from white entitlements and privilege over people of color and migrant labor from Mexico. She uses her white, maternal femininity to corner a drug market, branding her superior product "MILF weed" (Mothers I'd Like to Fuck), and targeting an all-male African American market emblematized by popular rapper and marijuana advocate Snoop Dogg. Snoop appears as himself on the show and delivers a rap about MILF weed and Nancy that intertwines the effects of the drug with sexual pleasure and gives her product street cachet that enhances its value.

Weeds went into eight seasons, lasting longer than the popular *Breaking Bad* series, which lasted only five seasons. The format of each show is slightly different, with *Weeds* following a format of a dramatic comedy in a shortened time slot of about 30 minutes, while *Breaking Bad* is a drama characterized by longer, more cinematic takes. The former set the terms of the suburban drug lord storyline and garnered an audience for the latter. While *Weeds* is about white female empowerment, *Breaking Bad* traces the evolution of a dissolved and threatened white masculinity through the rapacious business practice of trafficking in crystal methamphetamine into a reconstructed version of postcrisis neoliberal masculinity. Walter White represents the male body in neoliberalism in contrast, for example, to the male hero of the 1980s described by Susan Jeffords as the inviolable hard bodied hero, iconized by Rambo.[16] White is not a hard-bodied hero but a vulnerable body that is failing in a manner that reflects his social role as diminished, powerless, and dispossessed. His evolution and empowerment is excessive and it goes beyond the resumption of his lost social status. He becomes cruel and aggressive and assumes cold dominion over those around him. His story is about the sadism of capital accumulation, white male entitlements, and the imperiousness and impunity that emanates from the symbolic power of capital.

Meth Labs of Neoliberalism

The white male body has the allegorical power to represent the entire social order to which it refers; a single falling or failing body signifies broader social crises, in this case the erosion of the middle class, the wages of neoliberal capitalism, and the crisis of U.S. national identity. Walter White of *Breaking Bad* emblematizes the failing body of white manhood at the end of capitalism. A chemistry teacher with stage 3 lung cancer and inadequate health insurance, he has a family that depends on him to provide for them: Walter Jr., his son, is disabled and his wife, Skyler, is pregnant. Walter Jr. has cerebral palsy, evident in his slightly slurred speech and use of braces to walk. Yet these are only slight physical differences that do not limit his abilities in other ways. Likewise, Skyler's pregnancy in the first two seasons does not impact her mobility. Instead these physical "impediments" merely shore up Walter Sr.'s passivity and deficiencies as caretaker and breadwinner in his prediagnosis existence. His cancer aligns with and provides a cover for his extralegal activities, and his bodily ailment coincides with a reinvigoration of his "will" as masculine stoicism and assertiveness to the point of sadistic aggressivity.

Walter, in a fashion similar to Nancy of *Weeds*, secures his family's future by turning to extralegal activities. Similarly, the family of *Arrested Development* engages in manipulative if not proto-legal attempts to gain economic solvency, yet their quirks and incompetence in these pursuits is the source of comedy. These, and other shows, capture a cultural moment of economic stasis or insolvency while engaging a fantasy of resurgence and renewal through modes and means that have been associated with people of color, immigrants, and

Figure 1.6. Walter White (Bryan Cranston) of *Breaking Bad.*

Figure 1.7. Walter White and his wife Skyler (Anna Gunn).

migrants—that is, the cross-border trade in drugs. *Breaking Bad* takes place in the Southwest in Albuquerque in close proximity to the border and with reference to the national boundary and Mexico, particularly Mexican cartels. The show, as part of the border genre, reveals how the economic freefall, the leveling of the social order, allows U.S. Anglo subjects to cede the actual and symbolic territory of its Latino and Latina counterparts. In fact, the name "Walter White" recalls that of the former head of the NAACP (1931–1955) who, with blond hair and blue eyes, was, to all appearances, "white" but identified, under the "one drop rule," as black. The name "Walter White," in its literal symbolism and historical reference, signifies the appropriation of the social codes of peoples of color.

As part of the archive of border media, the show partakes in borderland culture, including a wide-ranging cast of Latino characters. Andrew Howe explores how the diversity and range of Latino characters (he does not discuss the women in the series) defy expectations. For instance, Gustavo Fring hails from post-Pinochet Chile and is clearly Afro-Latino yet has a comportment and demeanor typically associated with the Anglo characters in border media; he is fastidious, ordered, and neurotic. Yet, on the other end of the spectrum is the character of Tuco who is drug-addled and prone to violent rages and the Salamanca brothers who are callously violent.[17] In the middle of this spectrum is Steve Gomez, Hank Schrader's partner, who recalls Mexican adjuncts to Anglo heroes in Westerns, particularly characters played by actor Pedro González González who played John Wayne's sidekick in a number of films including border film *Rio Bravo*. Steve Gomez, who is presented as caring and nurturing, is ultimately more effective and professional than Hank—the latter recalls his namesake in the border film *Touch of Evil* (1958), in which corrupt cop Hank Quinlan (Orson Welles) acts on hunches and instinct, going beyond the law to frame men he believes are guilty. Then there is the light-skinned Latino character Combo who challenges ideas about Latinidad since he is assumed to be white until, upon his death, it is revealed that he is Latino. Jesse's girlfriend, Andrea Cantillo, has a small stock role as an ex-addict and single mom, and she plays it with aplomb and agency. The series draws on its border provenance with its ethnic and racialized typology while it revises them. It draws on the history of stereotypes—the bandit, the male buffoon, the harlot, and the dark lady—while diverging from these to add nuance and complexity that humanizes these figures and challenges audience expectations.[18]

Breaking Bad partakes of many of the images and storylines of border film and media culture, crossing actual and symbolic boundaries. Jaramillo notes that the use of the narcocorrido in a 2010 episode of *Breaking Bad* marks the series indebtedness to "Mexican drug culture," in which the *corrido* is a hypertext, following María Herrera Sobek, that mythologizes the white drug lord, metonymized by his black hat, and hopefully foreshadows his death and eventual supercession and thus reversion of control of the drug trade to Latino operators. The series co-opts Mexican cultural genres and turns the negative role of drug lord, as it is typically accorded Mexicans and Latinos, into a heroic and humane figure. The series, like *Weeds*, cedes ground accorded marginalized characters but it also revises the figure of the white outlaw of Westerns. Walter, like Nancy, instrumentalizes people and racialized ethnic communities to devise a strategy to maintain his family's suburban life into the future beyond his death. Eventually, he works more for the pleasures of capital accumulation and the power of his dominant position in drug trade. All of these characters turn failure and ruin into profit by way of the United States and Mexican borderlands.

David P. Pierson argues that *Breaking Bad* dramatizes many of the principles and policies of neoliberalism. In particular, it normalizes crime as a practice that is not a deviation from mainstream markets but merely another market among markets. Crime is a unit of exchange in neoliberalism, originating laws, policies, institutions, and other forms of discipline and punish that lubricate and energize the system of capitalism. The cost and penalty of arrest is simply part of the symbolic equivalencies of the system. This is in contrast to the welfare state and classic liberalism in which crime is an aberration that might be remedied and mitigated through socially oriented policies.[19]

Border Capital

The drug lord storyline as a "gold mine" is a major part of the strategic plan of the cable network of AMC, which, prior to the show's success, was known mainly for its period work. The network was in the market for a series that would match the popularity of *Mad Men* but take it into the present and transform its image as "classic" while maintaining a masculinist antihero ethos.[20] While AMC did not need to be saved, *Breaking Bad*, the most watched series on television, along with *Mad Men*, put the cable network in the ranks of premium channels like HBO and Showtime. The show captures a number of issues and experiences spanning the time leading up to and after the economic crisis. Like *Arrested Development* and *Weeds*, it dramatizes the social life of capitalism as and through the border economies that ultimately convey how privileged white protagonists instrumentalize marginalized populations to leverage their economic and social positions.

The border is a zone of freedom where Walter White remakes himself from beleaguered lower-middle-class cancer patient to the formidable and stoically masculine drug lord with the pseudonym of the theoretical physicist known for the "uncertainty principle," Heisenberg. The name is appropriate since it suggests that one cannot know all of the outcomes of an experiment, just as representation and interpretation are beyond the control of the author. The entity White creates takes on a life of its own in a manner he could not have predicted. In fact, he cannot escape Heisenberg; his image appears on an altar for the patron saint of drug culture, Jesús Malverde, in a desolate desert south of the border. His intention to stop manufacturing crystal meth is eclipsed by the mythology of Heisenberg, the power of which makes him a target of agents of a Mexican cartel. Likewise, his actions and inaction lead to catastrophic consequences that he could not have anticipated. His failure to save Jesse's girlfriend from asphyxiation leads to Jesse's intensified addiction, and her father's grief leads to an error that causes 162 deaths. The effects of his actions proliferate and expand in proportion to the dizzying profit he accrues in the drug trade.

The show offers few glimpses into the racialized and poor communities impacted by meth addiction. It deploys a cynical tone and black humor to obviate any pointed political critique and gloss the implications of Walter White's actions. That is, the drug trade deepens social inequities while it enhances the individual finances of a select few. It is a condensed version of the neoliberal system that initially failed White and of which he is now a major agent. The drug trade and its umbrella organizations linked to the restaurants and industrial laundry businesses—as fronts for money laundering—are major parts of the urban economy, employing a large population of workers both legally and extralegally. The failure of these interconnected economies would deepen the economic instability of the city.

With passing reference to the economic crisis, *Breaking Bad* explores how the current economic system weakens the white male body, causing ruin and offering no remedies within it. Walter must go beyond and outside it to find a solution; he must literally cross several kinds of borders and moral boundaries. The drug enterprise, dizzying returns on little investment, mimes the conditions of the financialization of capital. And, at some point, for Nancy and Walter, the original intention of drug dealing to support the family becomes the pleasure of capital accumulation combined with risk—deep into the drug trade, Nancy calls herself a "danger junky." *Breaking Bad* ends with Walter admitting that he engaged in the meth business not simply for his family but because he enjoyed doing it, thus releasing him from the alibi of altruism, or the logic that the ends justify the means. He confesses to Skyler that he not only enjoyed cooking meth, but he was good at it and it made him feel alive.

Walter evolves from an emasculated and underpaid civil servant to a hypermasculine and ruthless drug lord. Like Nancy, he learns how to operate in the drug trade and exceed his mentors to produce and distribute the best product on the market. He dominates the market and merges with a major global corporation for vaster distribution, temporarily losing his position of control to become that of a high-level worker. His face-off with one of the corporate moguls, Gustavo Fring, ends in Fring's death, liberating Walter to make a key decision about his role in the drug trade. With the demise of a high-level operator, Walter is free to escape with impunity since his involvement could be pinned on Gustavo. Yet he chooses to continue in the business and assumes the imperial role vacated by Fring, one of considerable power and potential profit. In a fascinating twist that encodes the significance of whiteness, already signaled in Walter's surname, Walter cavorts with white supremacists and ex-cons, Jack and his crew, who save him from arrest in the desert—where his money is buried and used as bait by the DEA. The white supremacist crew appropriate the profit accrued by White—taking almost all the money for themselves—achieving, within the narrative logic, a short-lived victory. Walter's money, significantly, bankrolls white supremacy in a fitting end to a storyline that includes the colonization of the borderlands and the ceding of territory and practices associated with Latinos, and culminates in the toppling of a global business represented by its subsidiary arm, a Latino restaurant, Los Pollos Hermanos. Yet, in perhaps too pat a resolution, all the remaining characters involved in the drug trade, the white supremacists who take over Walter's business, are killed in a *Wild Bunch*-style shoot-out. Jesse, Walter's long-suffering white sidekick, is released from his enslavement by the white supremacists and is the only character that survives,

Figure 1.8. Walter White converses with white supremacist Uncle Jack (Michael Bowen).

Figure 1.9. Jesse Pinkman (Aaron Paul), Walter White's sidekick.

fleeing the scene in wild emotional abandon; he is a proxy for the audience who likewise suffers the mediated violence and cruelty of the drug trade only to be liberated from it in the final scene.

Borderline White Supremacy

The storyworlds of *Arrested Development*, *Weeds*, and *Breaking Bad* are structured around a white family orbited by racialized characters in adjunct and supporting roles as maids, workers, and petty criminals. In *Weeds*, Celia Hodes, Nancy's (former) best friend, causes a car crash when trying to pry food from a daughter she believes is overweight. Celia imperiously asks the other driver, "Are you even legal? Who's your missus? Your lady?" Her racist and nativist language suggests that the woman's value and personhood are dependent on her employer, an attitude reminiscent of the slave-holding southern attitude toward African Americans (that Celia will echo later in the series). They are the devalued members of the new global slave trade, workers from the global South in low wage labor in the global North. The undocumented woman flees the scene to avoid detection and Celia half-heartedly asks Nancy's housekeeper, Lupita, if she knows her name, as if all Latinas are part of a network. Lupita responds cynically that she knows her only as her "maid friend." Renée Victor, the actress who plays Lupita, commends the writers for giving her a sarcastic edge to deal with instances of racism and immigrant phobia. Of her character, Victor says, "I love her sarcasm. I've met people like her, who are gracious, and assertive, and comfortable wherever they are because they are comfortable in their own skin." She plays Lupita as "assertive" and "open," adding agency to the typical portrayal of the passive domestic.[21] She is the smart-mouthed counterpart to Celia Hodes and characters like her: Lucille Bluth of *Arrested Development* and DEA cop Hank Schrader of *Breaking Bad*. These characters are of a type inaugurated by the character of Archie Bunker (Carroll O'Connor) of *All in the Family*, the curmudgeon resentful of the changing cultural and racial landscape of the post-1960s United States. They represent the racist and xenophobic attitudes in the cultural landscape of the new millennium where racism is expressed and addressed cynically through dark or black humor.

Though spanning various genres, *Arrested Development*, *Weeds*, and *Breaking Bad* share a mood of cynicism and black humor that motivates a cultural sensibility of disaffection with mainstream politics and moral values, particularly as they relate to the middle-class family and the erosion of white privilege. These shows engage a racial matrix that has whiteness at its center, not as an unmarked category but as one under scrutiny that demands revision. The power and entitlements of whiteness are not constant but shifting and gradually losing power. The white mainstream, of which these protagonists are powerful totems, adapts by instrumentalizing those already living in degraded conditions for their own uplift. In *Weeds* and *Breaking Bad*, Nancy Botwin and Walter White are out of their depths as ingénue criminal operatives in a world created and defined by African Americans and Latinas and Latinos. They lack cultural competence and street knowledge, and this lack compromises their nascent businesses. *Arrested Development* is premised on vague criminality and unsavory deals as a critique of U.S. abuses of power and impunity associated with George W. Bush's doctrine of at-will intervention in violation of international law. The paradoxes of U.S. chauvinism are dramatized in the family's push to build a wall to secure the national perimeter. The end of the line for racialized populations is the beginning of new entrepreneurial possibilities for the white characters who turn downfall and ruin into new forms of cultural capital.

The border economies in which the main characters in *Arrested Development*, *Weeds*, and *Breaking Bad* participate are a consequence of the relationship of the United States to Mexico that found its apogee in post-NAFTA (North American Free Trade Agreement) globalization. Mexico was the target of a destructive and violent form of capitalism as a consequence of the border industrialization program of the 1960s and NAFTA in the 1990s that lured multinational corporations seeking undervalued and flexible workers, loose environmental and labor laws, and tax incentives. The borderlands experienced the violent outcomes and wages of neoliberalism in a manner that is contrary to, for example, NAFTA's stated aims of creating economic equity across the main signatory nations, Canada, the United States, and Mexico. The contradictions of neoliberal capitalism, one that preaches the democratic expansion of credit through microfinance—a banking alternative in the global South—and the mortgage industry, are displayed in popular culture in different ways. Rather than the comedic fictions of black humor, the stories of the collapse of the credit industry found expression in reality-based, documentary media like *The Queen of Versailles* and, to some extent, *The Real Housewives of New York*. Like their borderlands drama kin, the stories of crisis capitalism place racialized characters, migrant Filipinas, in the margins; yet it is in the margins, as the character of Lupita from *Weeds* shows, that potential forms of resistance might coalesce.

CHAPTER 2

Migrant Domestics and the Fictions of Imperial Capitalism

> Now, today, the place of political action—not that of political theory, political conceptions or representations, but political action as such—is precisely something irreducible to either law or desire, which creates the place, the local place, for something like the generic will. And, about this place, let us say, like Stevens: it is possible, possible, possible, it must be possible. Perhaps. We hope, we must hope that it will be possible to find the possibility of our new fiction.
> —Alan Badiou, *Philosophy for Militants*

In 2014, a Chinese insurance commercial was withdrawn not long after it appeared due to the outrage of domestic worker activist groups. The commercial features a Chinese actor in brownface depicting a clumsy Filipina domestic serving her presumably single and straight male Chinese boss. As she flits around the house dropping things, her boss extols the virtues of domestic worker insurance underwritten by Malaysia-based Hong Leong Bank. The use of gender and racial drag to depict the Filipina worker connotes a colonial dynamic that feminizes and racializes Filipinos in relation to East Asians, in this case, Chinese, an intraracial distinction often glossed in the West. The public outrage about the commercial focused on the "racism" of brownface and the denigration of Filipinos as inferior, infantilized, and clumsy or less competent than their Chinese superiors; age-old representations used to justify colonial denigration within a global labor hierarchy. Yet the commercial also features a mocking drag performance within a heteronormative coupling that alludes to a history of drag as comic relief and gender nonconformity as an object of derision. The racial drag combined with its gender counterpart tacitly suggests a homoerotic and colonial dynamic of the infantilized Filipina under the protective care of her imperious Chinese boss. This perception of Filipinas and Filipinos is as globalized as their labor. They are employed the world over as ready stand-ins for domestic roles vacated by their bosses for other pursuits. They occupy the domestic and social order as proto-family members and represent a potential threat to this order; they might usurp family roles to upend them. The Hong Leong Bank commercial exposes the fantasy of disruption of normative gender, sexual, and racial relations with the anxiety-provoking thrill of transgression. But, at the same time that the anxiety is indulged, it is assuaged. The Filipina is reduced to an object of ridicule and thus the threat s/he represents is neutralized. Also, s/he is an opportunity for the expansion of the global insurance market. This is an ambivalent representational move. While the insurance advertisement signals the visibility of Filipino labor as a vital part of the global economy, it also puts Filipino migrants into the market economy as an object of transaction, not an agent of investment.

The Filipino domestic labor force occupies the visible geographies of global popular culture and capitalism in ways that demand reckoning. In U.S. cultural productions like *The Real Housewives of New York City* (Bravo 2008-) franchise and *The Queen of Versailles* (2012), Filipina domestics inhabit spaces of affluence in the global North. They work in the homes of major figures who represent significant coordinates of the economic crisis of 2008: David Siegel, the timeshare king, and Alexandre de Lesseps, the global investment banker. These two examples fortuitously coincide. The Siegel story told in *Queen of Versailles* is about the credit crisis, and the de Lesseps story in *Real Housewives of New York City* exposes viewers to the profits rendered from the world of "poverty capital" or the microfinance industry, a new frontier of speculative capitalism deemed a remedy for its cyclical crises.[1] The Filipina domestics enable the everyday lives of the Siegels and the de Lesseps, cooking and cleaning, acculturating and nurturing their children—in short, flexibly occupying any and all familial roles. They are moral counterpoints to the profligacy and vacuity of the affluent classes; each has a worldview that is potentially disruptive to the overarching narrative of capitalist accumulation. They are ambivalent figures, representing many things at once, and they are also protagonists in their own alternate story of global capitalism.

In the Siegel and de Lesseps households, stories of global economic inequalities are represented in a succinct visual manner. The white elite enjoy luxury and an exclusive social circle while their migrant domestics appear on the sidelines and in the background, singular, isolated, without family or community. *Real Housewives of New York City* and *Queen of Versailles* reveal the deep inequities and racialized violence of global capitalism. These popular cultural narratives perform several duties. They convey the mythos, fantasies, and storyform of capitalism in scenarios of wealth and luxury while they expose the fundamental and irresolvable contradictions of the economic system. The migrant subplot suggests an alternate story to the myths of uplift and capitalist bounceback, one that disrupts and defies capitalism's master narrative and lays the groundwork for a new fiction, a different possible future for those at the bottom of the global labor market.

Cultures of Inequality

Popular storylines impact the form and function of capitalism in ways that align with political and economic initiatives and policies, particularly for cultures immersed in Hollywood film, television, and new media culture. In his intervention on economic thinking on inequality, Thomas Piketty turns to cultural productions as expressions of "intuitive knowledge" about economic disparities and how they impact individual lives.[2] He notes the fundamentally subjective nature of understandings of wealth distribution upon which experts do not have the final word. However, he concedes that expert opinion might inform political discussions and reframe crucial questions through insistence on critical scrutiny of the major terms of economic debate. Piketty's work revolutionizes thinking on economic history and reenergized discussions of disparities at a time when coalition-based political work around inequity, the Occupy movement, was slipping from public visibility. Mass media rhetoric about the "renewability" of the U.S. economy and its satellite economies and the inevitability of the current global capitalist system has eclipsed the Occupy movements' exhortations to contest neoliberalism.[3] Piketty cautions against optimism about economic upswings and offers a revisionist universal remedy for economic inequality through global taxation—an idealistic proposal that he admits would not likely be welcome, much less adopted.

Free market neoliberal capitalism in its current global formation creates inequity. For Piketty, it replicates the economic relation between nineteenth-century European elite and their subjects or what the Occupy movement refers to as that of the 1 percent and the remaining 99 percent of the population. Thus the return to the "Gilded Age" when the affluence of a representative few seemed to signal social progress and prosperity but actually concealed abject economic conditions for the majority of Europe. This scenario, the current state of U.S. forms of capitalism, is ludically dramatized in a number of popular stories about the super rich, including the *Real Housewives* franchise (2008-), MTV's *Cribs*

(2000-), CNBC's *Secret Lives of the Super Rich* (2013-), and the show that began the popular fascination with the ultrawealthy, *Lifestyles of the Rich and Famous* (NBC 1984-1995). These shows are what might be called affluence porn, in the sense that we are given a view of something off-scene, considered obscene, hidden, or hitherto unseen, a "secret life" in a rarefied sphere to which we would otherwise lack access and where we are given over to the pleasures of voyeurism.

Lauren Greenfield's fascinating U.S. documentary *Queen of Versailles* (2012), nominally, is part of this slate of popular stories about the super rich. It is about David Siegel, time-share mogul, and his wife, Jacqueline, and their efforts to build the largest home in the United States modeled on the French royal palace of Louis the Fourteenth. Yet what begins as a portrait of unimaginable wealth becomes a story of its unraveling when the entire financial industry upon which the Siegel wealth rests begins to crumble. Unlike its affluence porn kin, *Queen of Versailles* traffics less in voyeuristic pleasures but is critical and exposes the chauvinism and imperiousness of the Siegel clan; it also reveals the storyform of speculative capitalism, its fantasies and desiring structure.

There is no more spectacular symptom of the dizzying accumulation of wealth and the subsequent economic crisis than that presented by the Siegels. David Siegel is the owner, founder, and CEO of Westgate Resorts or the largest privately owned time-share company in the world. The Siegel story confirms Piketty's premise that when the rate of return on capital exceeds the rate of economic growth, the result is extreme divergence in income distribution. David Siegel's wealth grows geometrically, catapulting the Siegel family into old-world-style affluence as their employees, particularly the migrant Filipinas, struggle to support their families through remittances to the Philippines. The documentary examines extreme poles of wealth, beginning with the disparities evident in the home. We witness the labors of those typically marginalized in the stories of affluence, the racialized and migrant workforce that supports and enables the leisure of the wealthy classes—conveyed in scenes where the Siegel brood lazily and listlessly exercise as the domestic workers toil around the estate. The Siegel enterprise—both the Westgate Corporation and the household economy—highlights the imperial dynamic of neoliberal capitalist culture in its insatiable demand for cheap labor from former colonies. The Siegel household is a proxy for the entire U.S. financial system, exposing the economic culture of neoliberalism and the globalization of capital, goods, and labor.

The American Versailles will no doubt compete with other simulated European palaces in its hometown, Orlando, found in the Disney and Harry Potter theme parks. In a fitting portrait of the simulacra of capitalism, the design of the Florida home is mediated through the architectural style of hotels in Las Vegas, which David Siegel copied onto the back of an envelope, making the American Versailles part of a series of mediations as a copy of a copy. And, like simulacra, their wealth is speculative and transitory, a consequence of illusion and fakery. Coincidentally, this is Piketty's interpretation of U.S. prosperity, which appears to be like that of the Gilded Age but is illusory. The edifice of capitalism was bound to crumble to reveal the ruin and racialized violence within. The story of the new Gilded Age, evinced in *Queen of Versailles*, shows the production and dissolution of wealth as a consequence of the imperial career of the United States, allegorized in David Siegel's financial and political machinations.

Of his many accomplishments, David Siegel claims to have "personally" brokered the 2000 election of George W. Bush as president in a manner that "may not necessarily have been legal." Without his interference, he remarks imperiously, "there probably would not have been an Iraqi war." *Queen of Versailles* is about the rise and fall of an elite class who benefit from the Bush-era tax cuts and neoliberal culture of loose lending and easy money leading up to the financial crisis of 2008. Or, as David Siegel admits, his business is dependent on "easy access to cheap money." In the making of the documentary, the story about building the biggest home in the United States took a turn and became one about the potential loss of this home. It is also about how Siegel persists in the effort to resurrect Versailles. The story creates the mythos of the indomitability and inevitability of the economic ruling class. The Siegel scenario is a symptom of U.S.-style capitalism in the emphasis and near-delusional insistence on optimism and renewal and overweening faith in the comeback and the mythos of the phoenix that rises from the ashes. In short, it is a story of boomerang imperial capitalism.

The Siegels accrue wealth and accumulate resources, both material and labor, from all over the world—stone from China, workers from the Philippines, art from Italy and France. They colonize space, exploit the economically vulnerable within a display and discourse of paternal benevolence—Jacqueline brings fast food for everyone in a salon servicing her family, David claims to provide thousands of workers with a better life, they adopt a "poor relation" and induct her into the affluent lifestyle. Their self-regard as benevolent enables them to ignore the social impact of their actions and decisions, which are played out in their home dynamics and home ownership aspirations. The family ambition to occupy as much space as possible in the largest, grandest, and most spectacular home in the United States turns dwelling into domination.

David Siegel veils his cold efficiency and keen profit seeking, characteristics of imperial capitalism, behind paternalism and colonial benevolence. He counts among his virtues his ability to shape and transform lives: "I changed a lot of peoples' lives. A lot of people are better off for knowing me. I certainly changed my three wives' lives. I brought wonderful children into this world. I think everyone is better off for being either my children or my employee." These two categories, child and employee, are elided, both are subordinate to his paternal care and tutelage. Infantalization is a key coordinate of imperial regard and underscores the lack of agency and power that characterizes the beneficiaries of colonial largess. Yet the employees and children are not treated the same; when the market falls, Siegel's employees are terminated unceremoniously, exposing his self-interest and lack of social conscience in his business dealings.

Perhaps Siegel believes, in coordination with the president he elected, that capitalism offers remedies for the very dispossession it creates. George W. Bush, neoliberal philosopher, opines that "Capitalism is the best system ever devised. Everyone has the opportunity to pick the kind of work they want to do . . . the freedom to choose where they work, or what they do."[4] Of course, "freedom" is an unexamined value in Bush's discourse, one that doesn't account for the postcolonial condition or forces of globalization that send labor from the global South to the global North. For Walden Bello, Filipino overseas workers constitute the "new slave trade" of a labor export economy.[5] The Filipina nannies and housekeepers on the margins of the Siegel story are a symptom of globalization, and their role in the documentary highlights issues of home and belonging for global migrant communities in the United States. They are part of a network of female and feminized domestic workers from the Philippines sent out to care for First-World families, leaving their own dependents in the care of others. This "chain of care" is not the only series of displacements featured in the documentary.[6] There is also a chain of dwelling.

There is a chain of displacements around houses and dwellings that are markers of the current state of neoliberal financialized capital, which could be called a crisis of dwelling, of homemaking, and of housing. It exposes the subprime conditions of the people, particularly migrant workers, at the bottom of the labor market. The term *subprime* has been erroneously understood to denote a type of loan; this was abetted by the mainstream media that bandied the term around in a manner that elided it with the product. *Subprime* describes the status of the loan applicant: overleveraged, undercapitalized, and economically vulnerable. The slippage of the term across the entities it denotes is a telling symptom of the social life of capital where bad loans masquerade as credit-unworthy people. Yet this population is the hidden underside of postcrisis storylines in popular culture, appearing only as adjuncts or marginal characters in stories about failure, falling, and ruin for the ruling class.

David Siegel made his fortune selling time-shares to a subprime population that he describes as vacationing in a cramped motel room, where motel is a signifier of class. His son, who manages the business, calls the clientele the "Walmart" or "Johnny lunch bucket" customer. They are lured into a seminar with the promise of tickets to expensive shows and free meals and subjected to a hard sell. The brokers are persuasive, giving beleaguered clients a taste of irresistible wealth in tours of high-end quarters that will be their vacation destination for one week a year. This is the cornerstone of David Siegel's marketing ploy, or as he remarks "everyone wants to be rich, if they can't be rich the next best thing is to feel rich," and if they don't want to feel rich, "they are probably dead." He is at the top of a chain of housing aspirations that, while appearing to be national, are part of larger imperial geopolitical dynamics emblematized by the housing aspirations of the migrant Filipinas he employs. His desire to remake Versailles in the United States is an expression of imperial American chauvinism to remake and outshine old-world wealth and glamour. His clients, mostly working poor or lower middle class, are sold access to temporary dwelling in wealth just as his migrant domestics live in the midst of affluence on the margins of his mansion.

Welcome to the Dollhouse

In *Queen of Versailles*, the most spectacular example of housing displacement is in the story of the Filipina nannies. Marissa Gaspay, one of the nannies, calls David her "idol" for his austerity and frugality, in stark contrast to the profligacy of his wife and kids. Gaspay's assertions reveal the very different economic conditions and behaviors valued by the domestic workers. Her colleague, Virginia Nebab, is highlighted and her story is like that of many Filipinas and Filipinos providing domestic care in the global North. They often leave behind dependents and family members for years to accrue enough wealth to buy land to build a house for the family that remains in the Philippines. According to Virginia, every Filipino dreams of returning to the Philippines to build their own home; but, she cautions, it is more important to go home in a better financial condition than upon leaving. She has been trying to gather enough money for eleven years, missing out on the maturation of her son and replacing her own family with the Siegel brood. She was saving money to build her father a concrete house, but he passed away before this could become a reality. His promised house, symbolically, is the tomb in which he was buried. The global economic system of wage labor puts workers in a different temporal order from owners and investors. Under wage labor, capital accrues slowly, if at all; in this case, it requires a length of time longer than one's lifespan to gather the means to achieve homeownership. However, capital for David Siegel grows rapidly and exponentially, opening up a deep economic abyss between him and his workers.

Virginia Nebab is at the bottom of the chain of dwellings that extends across a global context. She introduces us to her home, a large scale dollhouse modeled on the Siegel residence that belonged to the children but that she has occupied as her own house, or as she calls it, her "palace," yet another level of simulation of European estates. She prefers this to the maids' quarters where she lacks privacy and where one of the children has taken up refuge. The dollhouse is a sovereign kingdom apart from the fiefdom it simulates. Her dream of having her own house is only temporarily met with this toy replica. The home she would like to build in the Philippines is deferred to meet more pressing financial demands, that of supporting her immediate and extended family. Her dwelling, like the "Walmart" clients of the Westgate resorts, is transitory, and only highlights the dispossession of her daily reality and the impoverished conditions of her dependents in the Philippines, who remain an invisible backdrop to the story of U.S. capitalism in freefall. It also recalls Marx's description of the privations and discomfitures of a system that aligns work with home, a prescient description of globalized labor practices of migrant domestic workers: "It is true that labour produces for the rich wonderful things—but for the worker it produces privation. It produces palaces—but for the worker, hovels. It produces beauty—but for the worker, deformity."[7] In his discussion of the alienation of labor, Marx uses the metaphor of the home: "The worker therefore only feels himself outside his work, and in his work feels outside himself. He feels at home when he is not working, and when he is working he is not at home."[8] This indeterminate space of work, symbolic in Marx's account, is the actual condition of domestic labor, where the line between work and home has been erased and the two spaces inverted and confused. The occupation of the dollhouse, the "palace" produced by labor, is an assertion of place, of taking place and making a house and a home outside the confines of the workplace.

The dollhouse represents the simulation of home ownership. It allegorizes the role of Filipinos in the United States as subjects working in the house but living in the margins and shadows of the imperial edifice, and it offers a visual allegory of the history of racial exclusion in housing practices and policies, particularly the race-restrictive covenants that prevented the sale of homes to racial minorities. Like liberal state policies, Gaspay's transitory home ownership is an outcome of Siegel magnanimity; when she asks Jackie if she can have the dollhouse, her employer's response is incredulousness but permissive. Home ownership for a migrant and racialized underclass proved illusory and temporary at best. Mortgage finance deregulation enabled economically vulnerable populations to experience the entitlements of wealth parodied in the dollhouse palace or the transitory experience of the luxury time-share. These experiences are part of the cultural upheaval of the meaning of homeownership in which the socially oriented ideals of U.S. housing policy are in conflict with the private real estate and mortgage markets based on individual enterprise and profit seeking.

The Siegel story coincides with an era of the expanded purview of homeownership to include economically vulnerable and racialized populations as the result of a number of policy initiatives starting in the early part of the twentieth century. Housing policy would ensure homeownership and all this entails and implies within a "property-owning Democracy": stability, inclusion, security.[9] **The homeowning family is the cornerstone of the nation. Though** it fell short of these lofty goals, the 1949 Housing Act meant to ensure a "decent home" for every American family. By the twenty-first century, the broad-based **neoliberalization of markets eroded the principles of the Housing Act.** This meant a number of rollbacks of regulations protective of homeowners and an emphasis on profit over social purpose. The market grew rapacious, and homes became houses and hot commodities with increasing investment value. A home, once a source and store of wealth that would be passed down to the next of kin, was instrumentalized for its cash potential, dispensed through refinancing and equity release.[10] Moreover, the expansion of homeownership to marginalized populations is a consequence of the expansion of the credit industry. This effectively meant replacing "exclusionary racism" with "inclusionary discrimination" where access to the market is granted through deceptive and predatory means. Racialized lending practices integrated local forms of racism into a global financial market. Racial segregation in the United States, based on racial covenants and other exclusionary policies and practices, meant to protect white spaces and ensure the upward trend of property values, was reconfigured to meet the demands of the global market for greater yields on investment by increasing the volume of sales of products—primarily mortgage-backed securities. This meant expanding credit to those deemed credit unworthy, to high-risk subprime borrowers, mostly from marginalized and racialized communities, what critics have called "racialized risk."[11] This expansion in credit resulted in a reorganization of local racial spatialization enacted from afar, through global financial dynamics.[12] Virginia's inhabitation of a neighboring castle, the miniature dollhouse, in the Siegel neighborhood visually accords with the spatial reorganization of racial patterns of settlement wrought by the conditions leading up to the economic crisis.

The dollhouse also conveys the infantalization of the Filipina migrant, one that has dual transnational origins. The dual state tutelage is the result of a history of transnational networks of Filipino labor. Catherine Ceniza Choy, explores the migratory flow of nurses as a consequence of the colonial intimacy of the Philippines to the United States, one that reflects and revises a relationship of service and servitude.[13] The global circuit of the Filipino migrant dates back to the seafarers of the sixteenth century, the *ilustrados* of the nineteenth century, the *pensionados* of the late nineteenth century, and, more recently, contract labor that began to consolidate as a practice in the 1970s. Labor migration from the Philippines is a consequence of colonial and imperial relationships and of the globalization of markets and industries.

While many have argued that globalization has created a more open world and fluid borders, critics like Saskia Sassen argue that rather than the reduction or elimination of the state, state power intensifies and transforms notions of citizenship and belonging. And often, the state, like a benevolent parent, is called upon to protect its citizens from the ravages of a global economic order. Leonardo A. Lanzona Jr. calls for greater presence of the state in the advocating for Filipina and Filipino workers, likening these workers to the fanciful and perhaps delusional Don Quixote: "Like Don Quixote, the Filipino worker cannot turn back the winds of change. Yet, unlike this character who at least was able to raise his medieval lance against seemingly illusory foes, the Filipino workers lack the necessary training and equipment to protect themselves against the real dislocations and uncertainties emerging from globalization."[14] This assertion, at once, reveals a literary debt to the colonial forebear of Spain and suggests that the migrant worker is disconnected from the realities of the world, "like Don Quixote," to the point of being delusional, a dependent in need of kindly avuncular state intervention. This work falls squarely in development discourse that advocates for a strong state and protective labor market policy, one that does not impinge upon the nation's free trade policies. And it is concerned with the production of "worker quality" as a major and important part of national self-regard and as the marker of an exportable product.[15]

Filipino domestic work has long been an invisible labor sector in the liminal zone between a formal and informal occupation, promoted and protected by the state as a vital source of income in the form of remittances.[16] Rhacel Salazar Parreñas found, in her comparative study of Filipina migrants, that the low wages of domestic work in the global North and the consent of the Philippine state creates a condition of limbo and perpetual migrancy. That is, low wages mean that the migrant is not in a favorable economic position to initiate a process of naturalization and to bring her or his family, immediate or extended, to the host country. And the state, until the recent boom in call-center employment, supports this dislocation since the national economy relies heavily on the remittances of overseas workers.[17]

In terms of the sheer numbers and global scope, the Philippines exports the most government-sponsored contract labor.[18] And this labor is often feminized or represented as primarily female. *Queen of Versailles* consolidates this assumption. Robyn Magalit Rodriguez charts how the state facilitates and brokers the export of Filipino labor, casting migrants in proto-state roles as figures of nationalism and dutiful filial subjects, often along feminized lines.[19] Through analysis of the discourses of migration across various state and private agencies, employers, and migrants themselves, James Tyner excavates the ontological basis of the concept and figure of the migrant. The migrant is "made" and commodified through the discourses of globalization as a feminized figure, vulnerable to the forces of global exploitation.[20] Female migrant labor is a kind of commodity, a type of flexible and highly adaptable labor force, deemed politically neutral, a ready adjunct to the family system, a sign of a liberal state that promotes the human right of free movement. Neferti Tadiar rejects the passive objectification of the Filipina domestic arguing that "they are active producers and creative mediators of the world in which they move, the world which they in fact participate in making through the work of co-operation."[21] While both discourses are apparent, that is, the production of the migrant as a mute object of state discourse, a ready export, migrants engage these overarching discourses in various ways. In *Queen of Versailles*, the occupation of the dollhouse is an act of defiance, a claiming of autonomous space, and a significant intervention into the discourses of home and homeownership.

Capitalist Disavowal

Queen of Versailles offers an indictment of a class of people who remain afloat while the rest of the nation is "under water" because of their actions and decisions. Jacqueline's hopeful nostalgia about the possible noncompletion of the American Versailles—"I would love to spend the rest of my life here"—is followed by news that David Siegel was able to borrow a million dollars to keep the house. The central conflict around allowing bankruptcy of a major piece of the Westgate empire, the Las Vegas resort, is finally resolved by selling controlling interest to a bank. David Siegel may, it appears, return to his former position of glory and acclaim as the time-share king of the world. But the soundtrack, a circuslike tune, suggests a merry-go-round circularity and ludic quality to the entire story, reminding us of the boom and bust cycles of capitalism. David Siegel rejects the idea that his story is one of failure and filed a lawsuit against filmmaker Lauren Greenfield for defamation. He disagrees with his own words in the characterization of the documentary as a "riches to rags" tale. That is certainly the form it seems to take, but a closer examination shows that the story contains its own implicit arc around the persistence of riches and boomerang capitalism, contributing to the national storyline of a weakened nation emerging "from the ashes" of destruction. The practical conditions of economic renovation follow the speculative fiction of this emergence from crisis. These fictions go beyond the narrative form of the text—beyond even that imposed by the editors' and filmmaker's vision. The story is energized by disavowal masked as hope and faith that is particular to the privileged classes or, as Jacqueline Siegel remarks: "I'm in this fantasy world until reality hits, but I have faith." This statement is part of her closing remarks in the documentary in which she grieves the potential loss of Versailles while holding onto the building of it as a possible future.

Markets are a form of cultural signification. They are, as many economists note, a consequence of culture. Alan Greenspan notes that the United States need not worry about total economic downturns since the market will ultimately right itself.[22] The stories about the global economic market, particularly those emanating from the United States, follow an organic model of vitality and entropy as part of an infinite cycle. This boom and bust model creates an appetite for risk emboldened by the belief that loss will be followed shortly by gain. The belief and "faith" in an upswing in the idea of the "comeback"—in this case, of homes being rebuilt and vacancies filled—is the very stuff of the U.S. American way of life. The "silver lining" is key to the economic optimism that guides efforts at resurgence. In this story about houses and dwelling, the Filipinas' stories have no "silver lining," there is no sign of redemption or regenerative possibilities; their story ends pessimistically.

In *Queen of Versailles*, ruination inspires a more spirited effort to regain economic vitality, which requires a near-delusional faith in the power of the market. This story recenters the home in the mythos of capitalism as the site of the reproduction of the state on a grand scale. Versailles, the center of imperial France, marks the shift in French political structures, decentered or uprooted from Paris as a site of political unrest. Versailles represents guarded and gated power, the alignment of state power and security. The reconstruction or resumption of construction of the Siegels' Florida home is a sign of the resurgence of the state as the incarnation of corporate wealth, its return to vitality along with its isolation from the masses and ignorance of the consequences of its actions on a local level and in the global labor market. While the documentary exposes the metaphorical fissures in the posed portrait of the Siegels as they fidget uncomfortably upon their thronelike chair, they are a modern absurd and perverse aristocracy whose financial decisions impact the direction of the economy. The American Versailles symbolizes forms of U.S. hegemony; it follows the narrative arc of resurgence and renewal.

David Siegel's enterprise has global implications but is not necessarily drawn across national boundaries, except for immigrant clients with transnational ties—in one scene, his agents are negotiating debt repayment to clients in Spanish. These clients might be the same "illegal immigrant" borrowers targeted by Fox television's right-wing pundit Glen Beck as responsible for the economic decline.[23] They are certainly ready scapegoats for a culture of capitalism that, as Marx prophesied, expands rapaciously and centrifugally to all corners of the world, exposing vulnerable populations to new forms of social and personal debt. The Siegel story allegorizes a form of neoliberal capitalism as mimicry of European patrimonialism. A similar story of a U.S.-based performance of the Gilded Age with the same dramatic roles, plutocrats with long-suffering Filipina domestic labor, is found in the story of Countess Luann de Lesseps, who was married to Count Alexandre de Lesseps (they divorced in 2009) and one of the housewives featured in *Real Housewives of New York*.[24] *Queen of Versailles* is a scathing critique of the financial operations of the wealthy, while the *Real Housewives* franchise focuses on the extravagant consumer lifestyles and dramatic interpersonal relationships of rich women in major cities of the United States. The Count's occupation is mentioned only in passing, and the show's narrative does not follow the financial crisis even though the story takes place at the center of the economic upheavals in Manhattan. It is a fascinating complement to the documentary; both texts share some level of denial or, in the case of the *Real Housewives* franchise, outright disavowal of the economic crisis in their midst, and both represent the strong presence of the Filipina domestics whose philosophical worldview offers a counterpoint to that of the wealthy classes.

Count de Lesseps, like David Siegel, is a key player in the financial operations at the center of the economic crisis. He is the co-owner of a major investment firm, Blue Orchard Finance, a Geneva-based asset-managing firm and pioneer of microfinance in developing countries. Count de Lesseps is rarely on view in the show since he travels widely, but he is based in New York where he fundraises for the firm with similar endeavors in Hong Kong and various places in Europe. His work advances the integration of imperial capitalism and global security regimes or, as he stated in 2003 upon receiving the Fulbright Humanitarian award for his work in microfinancing, "The only way to solve the problems of poverty and terrorism in the world today is through investment."[25]

The microfinance market is comprised of those much like the Filipina migrants at the margins of stories like *Queen of Versailles* and the *Real Housewives* franchise; in fact, the Philippines was on Blue Orchard's 2003 list of countries receiving its microcredit loans along with other emerging nations in the global South, including Peru, Ecuador, Nicaragua, Bolivia, Cambodia, Dominican Republic, Colombia, India, Indonesia, Mexico, Bosnia, Montenegro, Morocco, Uganda, Mongolia, Kenya, Guatemala, Albania, and Kazakhstan.[26] Microfinancing typically targets the poor, particularly impoverished women, or those without collateral—except their "honor"—and thus considered unworthy of credit—underwritten by essentializing gender discourses that deem women more ethically bound. Yet women are more "ethical" or more inclined to repay their loans because they are targeted as groups of borrowers in which each member is responsible to ensure the other members' repayment. María Galindo describes how banks study women's communities and exploit their social dynamics to shape a culture of soft surveillance.[27] She argues that these microloans co-opt poor women's communal formations and their survival strategies and, rather than being a remedy for the crisis wrought by structural adjustment and subsequent male employment crisis in the 1980s, microloans constitute the expansion of the ravages of neoliberalism to all areas of the social order, including those formerly outside or beyond it: women. Women are integrated into the formal economy at a loss, they lose their freedom and become part of the cycle of debt and indebtedness that, ultimately, does not alter the larger structures of economic inequalities.

Women are targets of microloans for their vulnerability to coercion and intimidation and for their dependence on the economic resources provided by the microfinanciers to support their families. They are given loans so that they might create a sustainable business, the profits from which could be used to repay their debt. The founder of microfinance, Muhammad Yunnis of Grameen Bank, describes credit as a "human right" for its promise for economic and social uplift. In actuality, microloans integrate borrowers into a system of debt, often unto death. These programs expand the global system of debt within a network of nongovernmental organizations, national and local governments, and banks—including the World Bank—to exploit the poor of the world. Silvia Federici describes how international microfinance capital moves almost entirely unfettered, bypassing the state to ensure that "all profit accrues directly to the banks and is not appropriated by local governments."[28] The poor are identified as the next frontier for financial markets emphasizing neoliberal tenets over social justice or, as Ananya Roy characterizes it, "entrepreneurialism rather than redistribution, opportunity rather than equality."[29] The cycle of debt and indebtedness functions to discipline the poor, bring them into the logic of the market, conditioning them to the tenets of neoliberalism through "development capitalism."[30]

As de Lesseps argues, his microfinancing investment ventures are not entirely philanthropic: "The reason we lend money to poor people is not only so that they can make money, but also so our investors can make money." He also claims that while investors will not get rich with microfinance, it is "safer than the stock market." The safety of the investment derives from its low risk, premised on the idea that Third-World borrowers hold to more traditional values about repayment and presumably these various sites in twenty countries were chosen for this cultural sense of responsibility. The poor are objectified and classified according to a metric of risk assessment; his firm's "due diligence" in assessment of risk has kept its losses at near zero. He describes one such scene:

> I visited a village in Cambodia where the people used microcredit loans to buy irrigation equipment and seed, which they used to grow vegetables. They are now selling the vegetables to exporters and to a local hotel. The whole village has been transformed from dust to being productive. You don't have to ask for collateral on the loans because they don't have it. But they will die to pay you back because you are giving them a first-time chance. It's a matter of pride.[31]

In fact, his language is telling in its literalism. The code of honor that binds farmers even when their incomes are insufficient to repay their debts has led to a rash of suicides related to microfinancing. David Graeber describes how the entire project of microfinance appears to mime the subprime crisis in its process of expansion and subsequently dire outcomes in which the indebted pay their debts with their lives:

> All sorts of unscrupulous lenders piled in, all sorts of deceptive, financial appraisals were passed off to investors, interest accumulated, borrowers tried to collectively refuse payment, lenders began sending in goons to seize what little wealth they had (corrugated tin roofs, for example), and the end result has been an epidemic of suicides by poor farmers caught in traps from which their families could never possibly escape.[32]

The difference, however, is the explicit collapse of social mission with capitalist ideology—the expansion of the mortgage market was justified in some quarters as the extension of the right to home ownership to the poor and the fulfillment of socially oriented housing policy, it was never explicitly promoted as poverty alleviation in the same way that microfinance was deemed a global panacea for the impoverished.

Migrant Disaffections

Roy notes the emergence of a "geographical imagination" of sites of poverty, particularly Africa, taken as an imagined totality that evinces the negative outcomes of development policy. After 2001, the focus shifted to include development in the Arab world emphasizing the association between economic stability in the global South and security for the global North. Parts of the former U.S. insular empire might be deemed failed sites of development, particularly the Philippines and Puerto Rico. Yet these states fail to signify in the global imaginary of poverty for their proximity to the United States as patron state. The proto-colonial status of the Philippines, its persistent ties to the United States as a client state, military outpost (in the re-lease of former naval bases back to the United States), and economic and political anchor in Asia, puts the Philippines in a unique and contradictory position as visible and invisible in the political imaginary of the United States. In popular culture, Filipinos occupy the margins as domestics, sometimes entering the spotlight as performers, singers, and actors, much like the arc of visibility accorded Puerto Ricans, the most persistent U.S. colonials.[33]

Filipinos constitute one of the largest Asian populations in the United States but this is not reflected across the popular cultural or political landscape of representation. While there might be a number of minor roles accorded Filipinas and Filipinos in Hollywood film and television culture, the presence of the Filipina domestic in the reality-based storylines of these two major stories of affluence in the United States allegorize the role of Filipinos in the popular cultural imaginary as marginal. In the Siegel and de Lesseps households, the Filipina domestics are a major part of the daily functioning but often lurk silently in the background and are given very little screen time. We know next to nothing about these women beyond a few basics. They live in limbo between the families they serve in the United States and the ones they leave behind in the Philippines. Workers, like Rosie in the de Lesseps household, are depicted in their singularity, alone, without family or any other kind of network. The only reference to her life beyond work is in her monthlong trip to the Philippines; she becomes more significant and more visible in her absence.

As with *Queen of Versailles*, where the focus is on the "queen," *Real Housewives* is about the "housewives," and in this case, the Countess, Luann de Lesseps. She is conveyed via her tagline in the show's introduction of: "I never feel guilty about being privileged" and her belief, stated early in season one, that one is "born" with "class"—though she wrote an etiquette book, *Class with the Countess: How to Live with Elegance and Flair*, suggesting that "class" can indeed be learned. In an unfortunate confluence of events, she published the book at the same time that she was separated from her husband, Count de Lesseps, who subsequently left her for Ethiopian royalty, Princess Kemeria Abajobir Abajifar, known for her political activism. With the divorce, Luann undergoes her own economic downturn that results in the loss of a number of the assets that define her on the show, including her staff, most notably, Rosie.

Luann de Lesseps is very present in the social circles of the Manhattan elite, but absent in the home to the dismay of her children and Rosie. Her role is completely borne by the latter who parents the children in the absence of parental figures. Like the Filipina women in the Siegel household, Rosie is a voice of reason and a woman of logical bearing, expressing her bafflement about the lack of moral guidance for the de Lesseps children. Luann's disinterest in mothering or running a household is apparent during Rosie's absence, which leaves the de Lesseps household in a state of disarray and disorder. When Rosie returns from the Philippines, Luann immediately greets her with the unfinished work of the house with little regard for her jet-lagged state.

Upon her return, Rosie looks markedly different, her time away left her ebullient, fitter, happier. Previously, her demeanor was sullen, beleaguered, and sad, a state, given the amount of housework she faces, to which she will quickly regress. In fact, we are reminded of her unhappy past through a series of flashbacks that contrast with her current "look," which is made-over, rested, relaxed, and content. For Martin Manalansan, disaffection is a response to the conditions of migrant labor in a neoliberal order that values worker flexibility as not secure and temporary, highly mobile work. It is variously a sign of "professionalism," a strategy for survival through emotional divestment—even antipathy—and a refusal of the performance of maternal and feminized care. It signals the complex and often contradictory affects and desires that motivate and energize migrant labor.[34]

Likewise in *Queen of Versailles*, Virginia and Marissa have similar dispositions but are given more space to express their disillusionment and frustration regarding their conditions. They are forced to bear Jacqueline Siegel's excess as she spends compulsively on runaway shopping sprees. The character and quality of her spending elicits confusion if not resentment from the workers who have to corral her purchases and load them into the house. She buys the same items over and over in a repetition that registers as ludicrous as her domestic workers stand by miserably freighted with these goods. In these media, the workers resist their conditions not through struggle or confrontation but via mute expressions of disaffection and discontent. Their disaffection does not fit into the narrative arc of each story about the resurgence and revitalization of capitalism.

Sara Ahmed examines this state of discontent for the "melancholic migrant" as a refusal of the imperial logic of "liberation from abjection." Imperial expansion is justified as cultural and racial uplift and explicitly part of U.S. state discourse as the right to pursue happiness. Her analysis of the history of empire for South Asian colonials in Britain pertains in many significant ways to that of Filipino colonial migrants in the United States, as postcolonial migrants living and working in the imperial command center. The melancholic migrant refuses to make good on the promise of happiness, potentially rupturing the smooth surface of imperialism's ideological gloss.[35] The Filipina and Filipino migrants in the neoliberal global order are deemed free agents of globalization, "free," as George W. Bush opined, to work where they please. They are the recipients, according to popular fictions, of the largess of their patrons and bosses and of their sending and receiving states, all of whom expect happy gratitude, not sullen resentment.

The discourse of imperial uplift coincides with the aim of philanthropy, vaguely broached by David Siegel who "makes lives better" and more explicitly by the Count de Lesseps who is in the business of philanthropy in the global South—in its neoliberal capitalist version where altruism is only a collateral effect of self-interest and profit seeking. In these circumstances, the place of the Filipina and Filipino domestic in the home of their employer allegorizes their status in the national imaginary of the host nation as serving and servile and integral to the functioning of the household but not a member of it—permanently ancillary and adjunct. Their unhappy demeanor silently expresses this state of displacement and ill ease, forcing a rupture in the smooth veneer of the image and ideology of benevolent patronage.

Capitalism is as generative as it is denaturing, producing not its demise, as Marx predicted, but ever more stories to reshape and consolidate it. Capitalism is not doomed to fail, it suffers many failures and many downturns followed by renewed vitality. Its story is shaped by a manufactured belief in its ultimate indomitability and inevitable revitalization. The stories of economic crisis are energized by this tension between capitalism as failed and failing and capitalism as indomitable. This contradiction is part of its historical arc, part of the boom and bust cycles of capitalism, and it creates a cultural mood of disavowal about the actual conditions that gave rise to crisis, particularly of the racialization of imperial capitalism. Racial violence is a barely concealed reality in these stories of capital renewal. Popular culture orbits on U.S. myths about the unflappable and resilient "American" spirit that, unencumbered by social, cultural, or economic constraints, will rise again from the ashes and rubble of ruins.

In Richard A. Posner's handbook of the 2008 crisis, he, in characteristically U.S. American style, devotes an entire chapter to the "silver lining" of the economic devastation, pointing to the lessons and positive outcomes of disaster. Within capitalism, collapse and decline are deemed a natural part of the boom and bust cycles that coincide with the U.S. mythos of regeneration and rebirth. The idea that one might be remade or reborn, that a past could be effaced or that ruin is merely an irksome stage toward self-actualization is foundational to Americanism in the United States. Posner writes of a failure of capitalism that points to its potential to be rebuilt into a faster, stronger, more efficient system; one that is regulated, in which overconsumption and debt are curtailed and credit is less accessible. In this revised scenario, businesses would be more efficient, public and social services would be privatized, federal tax rates would decrease, and unemployment would create a demand for education.[36] All of which are deemed positive outcomes of a dire situation. Yet these renovations consolidate the current system, revitalize it, and put it back into working order. And some of these remedies serve only to intensify the social inequities that created financial collapse. The revised system of capitalism and its optimistic storyform violently erase marginal figures—a migrant and racialized underclass—found dwelling in the margins and in the ruins of the empire.

These stories impact publics and shape cultural mood, glossing social realities and turning the pessimism of ruination into the optimism of renewal. The most devastating scenes of destruction—the fall of the housing market and the bankruptcy of entire cities like Detroit and Stockton—might be restaged to reanimate the dead corpus of capitalism. The boomerang capitalist stories are based on faith and energized by the hope that the American Versailles will be built, that U.S. cities felled by bankruptcy will emerge "from the ashes," and that the U.S. economy will be renewed. The "American way" is to extract profit from crisis, to take the detritus of the past and transform it into a story of redemption. Optimism in these cases represses conflict and discontent. The affective core of these stories—optimism and hope—obviates the potential of revolutionary critique to dismantle the institutions and structures of power that create ruins, whereas catastrophes open an abyss, an aporia, from which change might emerge. Revolutionary critique refuses remedy, solution, hope, and deferral to some sunnier future. It is a pessimism of the sad order of things and the demand for another possible future, another story, or a new fiction.

The obverse of these stories of ruin for the financial elite is that of debt and indebtedness for, in the parlance of crisis capitalism, "main street." The life of ruin and ravage for those living in debt is a kind of denatured existence of the living dead and found its way into popular culture through the zombie story. And like the docudramas about the downfall of the very rich, zombie media are about human efforts, not just to survive, but to thrive and reinvigorate social life after crisis. Just as the triumphant stories of the rebirth of the elite shade and shadow those serving them in the margins, the zombie tales in the next chapter conceal a queer alternative of the story of the debt economy.

CHAPTER 3

Zombie Capitalism
Night of the Living Debt

> As the faith that gave birth to the West is dying in the West, peoples of European descent from the steppes of Russia to the coast of California have begun to die out, as the Third World treks north to claim the estate.
> —Patrick J. Buchanan, *Suicide of a Superpower*

> The debtor-creditor relationship intensifies mechanisms of exploitation and domination at every level of society, for within it no distinction exists between workers and the unemployed, consumers and producers, working and non-working populations, retirees and welfare recipients. Everyone is a "debtor," accountable and guilty before capital.
> —Maurizio Lazzarato, *The Making of the Indebted Man*

After the Great Recession, cities and towns across the United States hit by postindustrial divestiture and loan defaults were suddenly emptied of life, as if the people left to flee some menace. Such is the scene of the small rural town of Grantville, once a cotton textile town until the flight of industry, capital, and people. Parts of the town remained abandoned until the arrival of entirely new entities: television and the mediated production of zombies. For the popular AMC television show, *The Walking Dead*, Grantville is the perfect set. Its ruination and industrial decay make an ideal backdrop for postapocalyptic scenarios for "walkers" or the living dead. It is also the site of a new influx of people: industry folks working on the show and visitors from all over the world seeking the increasingly popular tours of the sights and scenes of television shows. The postindustrial ruins of the town are not refashioned or rebuilt for tourism but left in their decrepit state; visitors obsessed with zombies and zombie shows come to see these small town ruins reanimated for television. This overlay of media production and reconfigured city economies captures the current mood of postcrisis capitalism in which divestiture and debt and its symbolic counterpart, the walking dead, find recompense, and cities are reanimated to new ends. Out of the ruins of disaster emerges new capital, cultural and otherwise.

The zombie is an overarching metaphor whose presence across the popular culture landscape lends insight into our most abiding fears and preoccupations, particularly about the end-times, the apocalypse, and the current state of capitalism in crisis. The zombie, like an epidemic, is a roving and highly mobile figure. He or she transmogrifies from human to the "walking dead," from a being with "normal" appetites and desires to an unthinking figure of pure and voracious hunger for flesh. And ordinary citizens become stateless refugees as a consequence of the zombie apocalypse. Zombies initiate a remaking of the social order and elucidate the social life of capitalism in ruins, where existence is reduced to a mere struggle for survival. The zombie terror evokes the devastating impact of the economic crisis and the capitalist debt economy. The debt economy, like the zombie, is experienced as ubiquitous, ruinous, and capable of producing economic refugees the world over. The zombie apocalypse instigates the destruction of the institutions and formations of capitalism, in particular, institutional forms of power inequity and the money system.

The sentiments and meanings associated with the zombie are shifting and highly adaptable across many contexts. Zombies signify the end-times and the collapse of all that structures social relations: the state; international institutions and organizations; militaries; and forms of capitalism, consumerism, and industry. Zombie tales capture and contain audience outrage, fear, and anxiety about capitalism in crisis while they imagine the destructiveness of capitalism through debt, indebtedness, and forms of indentured servitude. These stories are replete with contradictions. They are about the end of a system and the destruction of a way of life based in capitalism, while the zombie captures a social mood about the persistence of debt—the global proliferation of debt as a viral contagion that threatens the complete annihilation of humanity.

Zombies are ciphers, mobile metaphors of disaster and crisis. Shawn McIntosh and Marc Leverette describe zombies as versatile monsters readily adaptable to any given cultural preoccupation, particularly contagion, the Other, and death.[1] The zombie is a screen for projections of the human as abject corpus and corpse, tropes that explore fantasies about the limits, boundaries, and definition of the human. Like low-wage, migrant, or adjunct labor, zombies are flexible and adaptable to any circumstance, and like global migrant labor, they are highly mobile and thus gain favor as a privileged monster trope, ready for transfer to meet diverse audience demands. They are a form of capitalism's dead labor, labor that has been so overextended and exploited that it slowly denatures. They are ready proxies for the "masses" or the "rabble," an angry mob who stages an insurrection, a primal horde bent on the destruction of society. The fears around this massified crowd, particularly in large urban spaces—Philadelphia in *World War Z* and Atlanta in *Walking Dead*—are coded with racial meanings; they might be associated with antiracist urban uprisings by people of color that have taken place in major cities, those that occurred in Detroit, Los Angeles, and Baltimore, among other cities.

For Analee Newitz, zombies are "monsters of capitalism" that manifest and express our fears about the impact of capitalism on humans and humanity. They express the inchoate and inexpressible, allowing us to see what it would be like to collapse difference and rethink the social order from the perspective of the marginalized:

> Mutated by backbreaking labor, driven insane by corporate conformity, or gorged on too many products of a money-hungry media industry, capitalism's monsters cannot tell the difference between commodities and people. They confuse living beings with inanimate objects. And because they spend so much time working, they often feel dead themselves.[2]

The capitalist monster, in this case the zombie, emerges during times of economic crisis. Though Newitz writes just prior to the catastrophic crisis that began in 2007, her analysis follows epochs of the disruption of capitalism as an "economic and moral system" that comes to bear on the historical dynamics of race and racism in the United States.[3] Zombies are racialized figures that signify a past of violence, genocide, and slavery, and that will not stay dead, repressed, or forgotten. Zombie stories evoke anxiety about disruption to the U.S. racial order based on white supremacy in a post–civil rights era—particularly evident in *Night of the Living Dead* (1968) and in the original and remake of *Dawn of the Dead* (1978, 2004). Zombies are useful tropes in antiracist storylines that show how to survive the recurrence of violent histories of racism and genocide within vengeful plots that transform race relations in the present.

The postcrisis zombie stories explore race relations through the lens of capitalism, as both a function of it while signifying a reprieve from its onslaught; race and ethnic differences are surmounted and absorbed into a primitive and utopian community formation that is outside any social ordering and institutions but remains fundamentally patriarchal, heterosexual, and white. This community is a refuge from the predations of the dead and represents the remaking

Figure 3.1. George Romero's *Dawn of the Dead* (1978).

of institutions, reforming and revising them to more conservative, autocratic, and morally rigid formations. The practical work of survival and the discourse of survivalism means reverting back to primitive forms of social organization that include essentializing ideas about gender roles that associate women with weakness and emotional vulnerability and men with brute strength and resilience.

Zombie stories in the era of neoliberalism like *Walking Dead* (AMC 2010-) *World War Z* (2013), *Dawn of the Dead* (2004), and *Land of the Dead* (2005), follow many of the same generic principles of their forebears. They are all about a diverse group of people who must band together for mutual protection and whose lives are reduced to fighting against ravenous flesh-eating zombies for survival. Most difference—racial, ethnic, linguistic, and national origin—is subordinated and neutralized to the common cause of defense. Defensive units are based on heteropatriachal formations and these units, though they function beyond any economic order, reproduce the symbolic equivalencies and hierarchies of capitalism.

The popular cultural zombie is a cultural adaptation from a racialized history that serves a western imaginary. The zombie, as a monster, does not emanate from a European or Judeo-Christian mythos or history and it derives from folk culture, unlike, for instance, the vampire that emerged in popular culture through layered mediations in literature.[4] The figure emerges in enslaved cultures in Haiti with possible roots in West Africa and takes on two separate forms: the spirit zombie and the physical zombie who has been raised from the dead, with the latter being the version that migrated into global popular culture. In his enthobiology of the zombie in Haiti, Wade Davis describes the figure as a function of social policing and restriction. To be transformed into a physical zombie—the result of a mixture of poisons that brings the person to a torpor likened to death—is a sanction and a form of social regulation and exclusion.[5] The popular cultural version of the zombie contains this repressed history of a practice of enslaved peoples and retains an ethos of social policing of deviance and enforced docility of the wayward. Zombification also suggests the process of dehumanization and reification of enslaved labor in which the walking dead are the working dead.[6]

Night of the Living Debt

The zombie is not just a "monster of capitalism" but capitalism itself. Chris Harman, once a leading member of the Socialist Workers Party, uses the term *Zombie Capitalism* to describe a system bent on death and destruction. He continues the unfinished work of Marxism to expose the ongoing instability of capitalism as it zombifies and denatures the life worlds around it.[7] The association of zombies and capitalism is as much in vogue in economic circles as zombies are in popular culture. John Quiggin enumerates the various ideas of neoliberal capitalism, like austerity policies, that continue to animate cultural and economic discourses even though they are defunct; citing Paul Krugman, he calls this zombie economics. Krugman and Quiggin are popular economists that find aspects or pieces of the capitalist system to be faulty and in need of reform and revision. By taking the system apart, there is a sense that it might be reconstituted or put back together in a manner that might better serve the entire corpus to which it refers. This optimistic take on capital is more concerned with reanimating it through improvement of the functional efficiency of the system.

To add yet another angle on the zombification of capitalism, we might associate the widespread panic about economic disaster in the collapse of systems of debt with the cultural obsession with the zombie apocalypse. In his critical history of debt, David Graeber describes how those who preached the resilience of capitalism are now "seeing apocalypse everywhere."[8] A reading of capitalism that removes capital and replaces it with debt as the basis of social life shifts the interpretation of the power relations of capital from owner and nonowner—from a hierarchical class system—to debtor and creditor; this latter relationship extends from micro to macro, from individuals, to communities, to nations, to the entire world.[9] There is no outside to the debt economy; the entire global order is implicated. In contemporary zombie films this might be read via the genre's geopolitics, in the move from the genre's early focus on specific localities as zones of zombie infestation (e.g., the eastern seaboard of the United States in George Romero's films) to the entire world, as in *World War Z*.

Zombie stories engage the tensions between freedom and enslavement, sociality and isolation, and autocracy or communitarianism. The new terror resurrected by the zombie emerges from fears of the financialization of everyday life that denatures humans, turning them into monsters of market capitalism. The only way to survive, to stave off the forces of capitalist destruction, its im**poverishing force, is through the creation of ever more debt. Debt,** for David Graeber in his vast history of the institution, is a mode of survival and social reproduction: "One must go into debt to achieve a life that goes in any way be**yond sheer survival."**[10] **Debt is a form of social life and** "ultimately it's sociality itself that's treated as abusive, criminal, demonic."[11] The commandeering of debt and of continuing to take on new debt, to seek new loans even after zombie foreclosures—when the bank has yet to strike the name of the former owner from the title—is deemed a moral outrage but also the only viable means of survival. The debtor, indebted beyond the possibility of repayment, embodies the very contradictions of capitalism. Graeber notes the paradoxes of the debt economy using symptomatic language: "debt and power, sin and redemption, become almost indistinguishable. Freedom is slavery. Slavery is freedom."[12] This confusion animates the zombie story. Caught in the endless cycle of debt, the indebted, all of us, are zombies of capitalism.

'Til Debt Us Do Part: Games People Play

Eric Berne, in his transactional analysis, popular when it first circulated in the 1960s, grafts game analysis onto social interactions to alter how we view the latter. His analysis of debt and the debtor deserves a new read in the current context of overwhelming indebtedness and servitude to the credit industries. Berne moves his discussion of the "debtor" beyond strict game analysis, claiming that it is "more than a game. In America, it tends to become a script, a plan for a whole lifetime, just as it does in some of the jungles of Africa and New Guinea."[13] From this unrepentantly colonial vantage, he traces the social contract of debt to New Guinea and the "jungles" of Africa as if to affirm its global reach and racialized roots as an enduring practice and basis of racial capitalism. This comparison is ahistorical and relativist with no regard for the intervening economic and political transformations of capitalism and its impact on the debtor and creditor dyad. In all contexts, debt is a way of life unto death:

> The big celebration, the wedding or housewarming, takes place not when the debt is discharged, but when it is undertaken. What is emphasized on TV, for example, is not the middle-aged man who has finally paid off his mortgage, but the young man who moves into his new home with his new family, proudly waving the papers he has just signed and which will bind him for most of his productive years. After he has paid his debts—the mortgage, the college expenses for his children and his insurance—he is regarded as a problem, a "senior citizen" for whom society must provide not only material comforts but a new "purpose."[14]

The discharging of all debt is the origin of the social problem, the subsequent lack of a "script" or a "purpose" and hence a place in the social order, a place that contributes to its duplication and perpetuation. Berne fortuitously intones that indebtedness is a mediated experience that is endorsed and consolidated "on TV." This analysis unfolds in the early 1960s before the rise of the credit card and the ubiquity of credit schemes. The debtor is part of an antagonistic dyad with a creditor in various games including the mildest version, "If It Weren't for the Debts," in which debtors complain about their debt obligations while fully identifying with them as their main purpose in life. Then there is the "Try and Collect" game, in which debtors launch spirited efforts to evade the creditors and accrue social status for their creative enterprise. The creditor and debtor relationship in this schema is a couple rather than a social dynamic or an institutional structure, but it highlights the actual and mediated role of debt in the constitution of social being, that is, as individual "purpose." Debt, in this game analysis, forms the very basis of social life, from which there is no outside and no alternative.

"Strike Debt," an anonymous collective in the movement of debt resistance and liberation, imagines a social life beyond debt that is less a game than a strategy for survival and a set of tactics for resistance to capitalism. In their *Debt Resistors' Operations Manual*, they outline the various steps toward freedom from the debt system, primarily through restructuring the social order. Debt shapes individual value and identity along with life opportunity and functions as a form of social control that negatively impacts those marginal to its order—migrants, women, people of color, and people who are poor, trangender, and queer. Debt controls and subjugates, immobilizing and stifling those under its burden. A world without debt is unimaginable for workers under its freight who are deprived of the luxury of leisure time to consider and theorize alternatives.

The collective research and writings of "Strike Debt" represent this nuanced and theorized work. And, though obliquely rendered, the mediated zombie apocalypse spectacularizes and dramatizes the nightmare of indebtedness and a dystopic freedom from the money system. But as an imagined universe born from anxieties and fears, rather than political ideas, the postapocalyptic social order is premised not on debt capitalism but on its symbolic equivalencies, most notably heteropatriarchy and white supremacy. The *Debt Resistors' Operations Manual* does what popular culture might only gesture toward, which is enunciate a future of liberation from the debt system.

Life and Debt

The debtor-creditor relationship is a fundamental institutional basis of global capitalism. Maurizio Lazzarato updates this dyad for the age of neoliberalism, designating Capital the "Great Creditor" before which everyone is a debtor:

> The debtor-creditor relationship—the subject of this book—intensifies mechanisms of exploitation and domination at every level of society, for within it no distinction exists between workers and the unemployed, consumers and producers, working and non-working populations, retirees and welfare recipients. Everyone is a "debtor," accountable and guilty before capital. Capital has become the Great Creditor, the Universal Creditor.[15]

He extends the analysis of debt to all levels and areas of the social order, from individual and public debt to state debt and argues that all parts of the "new economy" of information and knowledge production have been absorbed into the debt economy. This economy is emblematized by a new figure, a new totem, that of the "indebted man"—like the "falling man" mentioned earlier as an emblem of the economic crisis who also is defined as male. He elaborates Friedrich Nietzsche's analysis of the debtor-creditor relationship through the promise as the modern origin of ethical subjectivity. Debt revises the symbolic exchanges of psychoanalysis and Marxian analysis for its future orientation; debt represents a promise of future payment along with the sense that one must honor such obligations. This promise is thus imbued with memory and conscience and is a sign of psychic interiority. Debt represents the origin of guilt, blame, repression, duty, and other negative ideas and affects. A social order without debt would be rid of these notions but it would also be without a future orientation, without a sense of consequence or retribution. For Nietzsche, the promise denotes a system of moral responsibility that is the basic dynamic of the social order:

> Between the original "I will," "I shall do this" and the actual discharge of the will, its *act*, a world of strange new things, circumstances, even acts of will may be interposed without breaking this long chain of will. But how many things this presupposes! To ordain the future in advance in this way, man must first have learned to distinguish necessary events from chance ones, to think causally, to see and anticipate distant eventualities as if they belonged to the present, to decide with certainty what is the goal and what the means to it, and in general be able to calculate and compute. Man himself must first of all have become *calculable, regular, necessary*, even in his own image of himself, if he is to be able to stand security for *his own future*, which is what one who promises does![16]

In many ways, the zombie apocalypse is a way of symbolizing the end of debt as the end of the money system, but it is also the end of futurity. Yet paradoxically, these stories suggest that humans embody indebtedness and must give their flesh to discharge debt that is never really terminated, even in death. Debt persists beyond death.

Debt animates zombie economics. It keeps the economy dynamic even when it has failed, crashed, or imploded. We may not consciously acknowledge the burden of debt, indebtedness, and its logical outcomes: a life of debt, and debt until and even after death. But the psychic material of a debt economy is manifest in our popular storylines. It is no accident that zombies emerge in this posteconomic crisis moment, this moment of disorientation, when the nightmarish outcome of a debt society is garishly exposed as the collapse of a system of debts that cannot be repaid. For the system to work, the indebted must be kept alive since his or her body is an object of exchange. Debt demands the reanimated corpse of the indebted, resulting in the living death of indentured servitude. This undead state of indebtedness is associated with consumerism in the precrisis zombie films, as dramatized in the original and remake of *Dawn of the Dead*, in which humans take refuge in the U.S. temple of consumerism: the shopping mall.

Postapocalyptic zombie stories may not be explicitly about debt, but they are about the impromptu development of a social system of symbolic exchanges and substitutions basic to capitalism. There is no outside to capitalism before the apocalypse. The economic order atomizes, instrumentalizes, and denatures. The zombie apocalypse occasions an alternative, an outside to this order and its institutions. In *Walking Dead*, the ragtag impromptu community appeals to all the extant institutions that form major coordinates of the failed and broken state: the Center for Disease Control, Fort Benning in Georgia, hospitals, prisons, the National Guard, and the police—depicted by ex–police partners, Rick and Shane. None of these institutions retains any political power; they are all defunct or depopulated. Most institutions are no longer in functioning order, most apparent among these is that of the money system or that of debt expressed through promissory notes.

The idea of money is important during times of crisis as a unit of measurement and reference that destabilizes and loses value or loses its fixity as value. A social order based on this crumbling symbol is disorienting. A world without money, according to zombie stories, would have exhilarating new possibilities for interaction. The eradication of money seems to signify freedom from its structural logic of valuation. Yet debt created by the money system, its series of symbolic exchanges, is not readily dispensed. And zombie media fail to imagine a social order along radically reconfigured logical lines. The symbolic or actual capital of a system of debt becomes a social system governed by the same logic of equivalencies and substitutions; this might be delineated through Lacan's triptych of phallocentrism, logocentrism, and patriarchy along with Jean-Joseph Goux's monetarism and to which we might add empire, militarism, and white supremacy—a multiplex system of hegemony. When the economy fails to form the basis of the social order, these other forms of power take precedence. While postapocalyptic zombies and humans roam freely across borders without consequence, free of all national and international institutions, various interrelated forms of power persist. And they persist in a manner that is reactionary and conservative. In these postcrisis stories, power and symbolic power reverts to the white heterosexual male patriarch and leader from the global North.

The postapocalyptic communal formation is not one beyond capitalism or even a precapitalist form or anything approaching communism but the intensification of the logic of capitalism. In the absence of money, the social system of capitalism persists through the multilayered and interconnected symbolic economies emblematized by the white U.S.-based heterosexual patriarchs. The zombie stories engage the fantasy of escape from capitalism while entrenching the viewer, as a social subject, ever deeper into its symbolic representations. The fantasy, the scene of terror, around the zombie is not simply a wholesale transposition of the collapse of the debt economy and survival of life beyond it. The zombie is the remainder and terrifying reminder of that system, an imminent threat that cannot be fully neutralized. Zombie stories are pessimistic and share in a number of shifting social concerns. The debt crisis, credit crunch, and economic freefall are depicted as a scourge bent on destroying the entire social order. *World War Z* elicits fears of the swiftness of this collapse, its totality and explosive rendering in key sites of global capitalism, the financial districts of urban centers. The protagonists of the zombie apocalypse stories, ever part of the debt economy, embody the duty to save humanity and restore the social order.

The characters of *Walking Dead* and *World War Z* no longer live in a money system; rather, capitalism maintains a symbolic hegemony as zombies, a mobile unthinking horde bent on human destruction. The zombie, like the system of debt, seeks only to replicate itself by turning humans into the living dead, increasing its population and ensuring the expansion and continuation of zombie hegemony. The accumulation of more dead, more debt, in the symbolic exchange of life for death, perpetuates the ongoing cycle of symbolic substitutions of the debt economy. Even without money, the logic of debt adheres.

The debt economy is future oriented. It is based on the infinite production and expansion of debts, of payments owed and continually deferred. The debt society conditions and disciplines the indebted:

> Granting credit requires one to estimate that which is inestimable—future behavior and events—and to expose oneself to the uncertainty of time. The system of debt must therefore neutralize time, that is, the risk inherent to it. It must anticipate and ward off every potential "deviation" in the behavior of the debtor the future might hold.[17]

Debt demands a future; it inscribes and determines future behavior. The end of time, the apocalypse, is one way of imagining the end of a life of debt. The foreclosure of futurity, of indentured servitude, charges the fantasy of the zombie apocalypse. While it is disorienting, it is an exhilarating form of freedom.

The Living End

The collapse of the global financial system was taken as a sign of the apocalypse, foretelling the end of everything familiar and known, allegorically conveyed in the zombified end of the world. The protagonist of the popular zombie series, *Walking Dead*, summarizes his postapocalyptic experience in a single word: "disorienting." The apocalypse, from Saint John the Apostle, is the result of a revelation that causes a disorienting shift in all that is known; it tells of the end of time and the creation of a new heaven and earth. Often understood as a dark devolutionary period marked by terror and destruction, Jacques Derrida describes it not as destruction but as an unveiling of truth, following the logic of philosophical deconstruction as a similar process of revelation, of exposing the contradictions that unravel meaning and create new forms of signification.[18] Richard Dellamora links an apocalyptic mood with the upheaval of sexual norms as the source of social devastation.[19] Within apocalyptic literature, the end is associated with major shifts in religious thinking. In a canonical text of this critical oeuvre, Frank Kermode finds that apocalypse gives meaning and form to "disorganized time," thus providing a sense of ending in order to posit a new beginning.[20] Zombies figure the disorienting end of all that is known and familiar, safely encoding contemporary forms of social upheaval; again, they mark distinct transformations, from citizen to mobile and stateless refugee deprived of rights.

Zombie stories contest white supremacy and imperial chauvinism as forms of state violence that might diminish with the demise of the state. Society is remade within a revised and flattened national, racial, and ethnic order based on interracial alliances and cooperation within a model of heterosexual kinship based on gender norms. In these stories, racial equality is an alibi for heteropatriarchal political forms, and the reconstituted and racially diverse families or communities are given primacy as defensive proto-military units under white male leadership. *Night of the Living Dead* (1968), a cornerstone of the genre, released in a liberal post–*Guess Who's Coming to Dinner* (1967) context, makes interracial Black-White politics the central concern of its crisis-ridden storyline. It was released the same year as the advent of Visa and Mastercard—though American Express appeared years earlier—and the idea of virtual money, yet it is ostensibly more concerned with the Cold War and the effect of new security technologies on humans—in the form of radiation from space stations impacting life on earth.[21] The film coincides with a major transformation of social subjectivity with the inauguration of individual credit. The credit card is an artifact of the creditor-debtor relationship, metonymically defining personal identity and shaping social transactions. According to Lazzarato, the credit card encodes two major nodes of the financialization of everyday life: "the *automatic* institution of the credit relation, which thereby establishes *permanent* debt."[22] It is the sign that its owner is indebted for life. A few years later, credit-card companies targeted lower-income communities of color to expand their markets further. The 1978 *Marquette vs. First Omaha Service Corp.* Supreme Court case lifted the prohibition against usury that enabled credit card issuers to set interest rates by the state of their corporate headquarters, thereby bypassing individual state caps on interest rates. Banks sold high-fee and high-interest credit products to lower-income markets comprised most often of African Americans. Pamela Brown describes this credit transformation as one that exploited "long term credit famine in communities of color" for whom these products were "lifelines." These markets were workshops for strategies of wealth extraction, including resetting interest rates for missed payments.[23] Thus, the expansion of credit generated another form of racial oppression.

Night of the Living Dead initiates an antiracist storyline in the zombie genre; several disparate groups of people transcend racialized social divisions and band together to barricade themselves in a house against zombie attacks. These folks form an impromptu and transitional community from which they organize and plan their defense. There are two white couples, one with a young child; a single white woman; and Ben, the African American protagonist and the only character with a logical plan of action for defending the house. They must work together and overcome internal resistance within the group for their mutual protection.

For his savvy and ingenuity, Ben is the final survivor of the group, who, when approached by representatives of the state—a band of police and volunteers—is misidentified as a zombie and shot. The story ends on the frozen image of a black man gunned down by a group of white men, which registers unambiguously as racially motivated violence and injustice and the persistence of white supremacy. This idea is recast in later zombie tales. Rick Grimes, the white protagonist of *Walking Dead*, in his disoriented stumbling into the zombie apocalypse after waking up from a coma (citing a similar scenario in *28 Days Later*), is mistaken for a zombie and attacked by an African American father and son duo. Rick will later defend an African American comrade against a white supremacist to preserve the peace in his ad hoc multiracial community and defense unit. *Walking Dead*, following the genre, promotes alliances across race and ethnicity in the defense of the heterosexual human community against the zombie

Figure 3.2. Ben (Duane Jones) is misidentified as a zombie and fatally shot in *Night of the Living Dead* (1968).

Figure 3.3. White cast members of *The Walking Dead*.

scourge, though there are a couple of depictions of short-lived homonormative relationships. The series is optimistic about a postracial order in contrast to *Night of the Living Dead*, which remains pessimistic about the eradication of racial oppression. In these postapocalyptic stories, cross-racial collaborations mime proto-state formations—and the tolerance for racial difference does not diminish the symbolic power of white hegemony. These groups suggest that hierarchical state formations, aligned with heterosexual modes of association, are "natural" and inevitable forms of social congress.

The postracial zombie story often features highly mobile refugees that organize and do their work best within heterosexual couplings. This is most evident in *World War Z* (2013), in a complete departure from the eponymous novel upon which it is based. The novel is an "oral history of the zombie war" that does not focus on any single character or set of characters but shifts focus among many different oral accounts of the zombie war from across the world, never fully privileging a single nation or narrator. The film, however, is focalized through the main white male U.S.-based character played by Brad Pitt; it privileges his vantage and his predicament allegorizes that of the entire human race. Gerry and Karin Lane (Brad Pitt and Mireille Enos) and their young children are in the midst of a zombie infiltration of Philadelphia. In the film version of *World War Z*, zombies are not ambling and disorganized like their forebears; instead they are a speedy, muscular, and unified evil force bent on the destruction of the human race. The cinematic zombie scourge must be put down by a collaboration of international forces that is nominally the UN but actually a military version of this peace organization guided by U.S. security operatives and, of course, Brad Pitt's character, Gerry. The UN is one piece of a number of international organizations, including the IMF, the World Bank, and the World Trade Organization, that work together to monitor, control, and adjudicate global debt from the perspective of the creditor nations. In this case, the United States maintains controlling interest in these globally imbricated organizations that operate on the moral and legal principle that debts demand repayment.[24] Michael Hudson describes this power bloc as "debt imperialism."[25]

World War Z sets an apocalyptic mood in the opening credits with images of ecological ruin and man-made disasters from all over the world: stranded dolphins, traffic at the U.S. border, destruction of property, wildlife tearing at each other, and various images that suggest overpopulation of the world's largest cities. The zombie infestation is the apogee of these diverse forces and signs of destruction and decay. The film emphasizes key zombie tropes around movement (Brad Pitt even intones in Spanish to his Latino protectors that "movimiento es vida") and refugee status. Safe zones in zombie films are consistently referred to as "refugee camps." Social class collapses and flattens, replaced by widespread

Figure 3.4. Gerry and Karin Lane flee zombies in *World War Z* (2013).

Figure 3.5. Fleeing fast-moving zombies in *World War Z.*

global refugees. Gerry, a former U.S. government agent, is extracted from his family and called back into the field to deal with the global zombie problem. Yet we are reminded of his heterosexuality in the constant invocation of his brood—who are moved to a refugee camp—and in the proxy wife and Israeli soldier with whom he pairs. The zombie war creates a world refugee crisis allegorized by Gerry's struggle to reunite with his family. His plight invokes the heteronormative assumptions of U.S. immigration policies that emphasize family reunification over any other type of relationship, thus effectively delegitimizing queer forms of association. Our obsession with zombies is a passion for heteropatriarchal forms of organization within reimagined racial relations; these storylines reject racism through normative discourses of heterosexuality in the proliferation of heteronormative couples and families as defense units.

The family symbolically reproduces the state from which it emerges, the United States, as one that is primarily defined by military and security operations generated in and by war. In fact the entire U.S. economic order is based in military power, the expansion of which constitutes the largest share of U.S. deficit spending.[26] The global mobility of the U.S.-based character and his Israeli adjunct allegorizes the U.S.–client state relation and points to the creation of military protectorates in places like Israel. In fact, the United States, from the 1980s on, during a time of debt crises in Latin America, itself incurred huge debts through the massive expansion of bases in protectorate nations, nations that would subsequently find themselves in positions of

Figure 3.6. Jerry and Israeli soldier, Segen (Daniella Kertesz), work together.

economic and political indebtedness.²⁷ The U.S. system of debt and indebtedness is disseminated and bolstered by military power; this is spectacularly encoded in the military protection provided by Gerry in his commandeering of the World Health Organization to generate a remedy to a global threat. The spread of the zombies is curtailed and Gerry is reunited with his family, but he remarks that there will likely be no end to the zombie war—establishing not just the possibility of a *World War Z* franchise but also the continuation of neoliberal capitalism based on deficit spending for war.

In *World War Z*, Gerry is the ultimate American pioneer: resourceful and ingenious. He surmises that the best way to contain the zombie epidemic is to make humans undesirable prey by masking their health with disease, thus restoring some semblance of social order. This scenario recalls the broken yet resurrected system of capitalism as debt that energizes zombie stories. In particular, *Night of the Living Dead* and *World War Z* present the illusion of containment of the zombie threat within stories in which the social world is changed, broken, and rebuilt to a restored condition of collaboration and cooperation across ethnic and racial communities and across nations—but one ultimately led by the imperial military command of the United States. The zombie story is politically liberal, where all or almost all should enjoy formal equality under the law, locating the work of the storyline in heterosexuality, its familial counterpart, and the military empire of the United States. Zombie stories offer desirable tales of liberal forms of association and collective action, promulgating the need for local and global collaboration to defend against invasive species. But these tales fail to imagine action that might take place outside or beyond patriarchal forms of heterosexual congress and coupling.

The longevity of the series *Walking Dead* is a sign of the compelling qualities of the storyline that persists across time, addressing questions about existence, ethics, and the creation of social bonds beyond capitalism. Like *World War Z* it combines the monster or zombie genre with the apocalyptic genre, or the zombie apocalypse in which the zombie scourge forces humans to regress to a purely survival mode of living. This means a return to primitive forms of association and alliance and reliance on communal forms of decision making and policing. There are a number of scenes where the group with which the **protagonist associates, his "people," convene to settle a matter of importance** for the protection and survival of the totality—as matters of survival become ever more dire, the group shifts from a democratic to an autocratic formation. The **aberrant figure acts in a manner that is upsetting to the whole.** For example, a man who is toiling in the sun without sufficient water becomes deranged with dehydration and refuses to stop working and the group convenes making the decision to restrain him. The series presents a fantasy of return to communitarian forms of living that transcend difference, even invoking racial discourses in order to neutralize and negate them. When an African American character, Theodore "T-Dog" Douglas (IronE Singleton), claims that his situation is more precarious and dangerous because of his blackness, his white interlocutor, Dale Horvath (Jeffrey DeMunn), objects. Dale remains mystified until he discovers that Theodore is delirious with a blood infection, rendering the latter's remarks the nonsensical chatter of feverishness. Dale, voicing the liberal discourse of the series, makes clear that racial difference is not a source of political divisiveness in this community. The same is not true for gender. Early in the series, the women are relegated mostly to gender-defined roles—washing and cleaning for the group—and are often depicted as more vulnerable and less physically capable and competent. As the series evolves, women occupy roles accorded men, and few members of the group, men or women, are excluded from engaging in active defense of the community. Though, as with other zombie features, gender—alternate forms of sexuality are rare—is the primary and most significant difference among the humans and often stands in for the reproduction of forms of statehood.

Like *Walking Dead*, *Land of the Dead* (2005) begins after a zombie apocalypse but at a time much later in the evolution of the social order postdisaster. In fact, society is restored to a version with a more rudimentary money system and deeper social inequities in which the rich live cordoned off from the poor

Figure 3.7. Zombies from *The Walking Dead*.

and "walkers" alike. The new society is formed out of the very worst conditions and characteristics of the former order where the rich instrumentalize the impoverished humans, and zombies are treated like chattel for human entertainment. Human relationships are emptied of empathic connections as humans seem more like zombies and vice versa. For instance, one character remarks, in the search for marketable items in abandoned stores, that he cares more about money than love. As the divide between the rich and the poor deepens, the boundary separating the walkers from humans diminishes. The walkers are beginning to evolve to exhibit anger, moving from the base instinct of pure hunger to the outrage of the oppressed.

The imperial center of the story is Kaufman (Dennis Hopper) who created and controls the secured tower of "Fiddler's Green," an affluent residence that boasts fine restaurants and shopping. He heads the committee that controls occupation of the elite residence and created the "games" and "vices" that would keep the rabble occupied and content with their conditions. Although the film was released prior to the financial crisis, it follows the development of globalization and imagines the conditions that would result from taking its practices and policies to the logical extreme. The poor live in service to the rich, gathering goods and things that they need and working to secure the border of "Fiddler's Green" from the rabble beyond its perimeter. *Land of the Dead* is the most overt about its critique of forms of capitalism that denature humans and cause social divisions. It is a story of revolution and the emergence into consciousness of the rabble or the massified horde of zombies whose evolution includes tacit recognition of their enslaved condition. "Skyflowers" or firecrackers subdue the walkers; they become so dazzled by the play of light in the sky that they are paralyzed in position. Their evolution is marked by their immunity to the skyflowers and their determination to continue their march to the center of the empire controlled by Kaufman. The zombies, in an organized communal formation, storm the towers carrying the implements of common workers—drills, shovels, and so forth—and tear down the edifice of the affluent and thus the social order that creates inequity. The story is a clear indictment of capitalism and its subsequent forms of enslavement while it allegorizes the revolutionary approach to freedom. With the demise of the rich, there is a return to the leveled social conditions that zombie media imagine as the way things are just proceeding: the zombie apocalypse in which capitalism and the money system might be replaced by different forms of association. Or, as one of the rabble-rousers opines, they may turn the place into what they want it to be, perhaps even what the story's hero Riley Denbo hopes for: "a world with no fences."

The postcrisis storylines are imbued with hope and faith in the survival and regeneration of humanity, and this ethos sustains the popular appeal of the zombie tale. It offers solutions for living in crisis, not simply about how to survive crisis but how to cultivate a way of being beyond capitalism—that is, how to reevaluate the social world beyond or outside of the mediations of capital and the money system. This is expressed in *Walking Dead* in the allegorical tale that the main character tells his wife after their son is shot in a hunting accident. She wonders aloud whether it is not best for the son to not survive and inherit a world in which he faces relentless hunger, danger, and fear. The son wakes from his unconscious state, and one of his first remarks is his recollection of the doe that occasioned the shooting incident. The son had been admiring the deer for its majesty and grace. And the father interprets his fascination as a sign of hope, of the small gestures and symbols of the importance and value of life and a sign that it is indeed worth living. Rick uses this anecdote to answer his wife's existential quandary. Like *World War Z*, the hope for a future is located in the family, and postapocalyptic forms of meaning and value are grounded in this iconic heteropatriarchy and its noneconomic yet nonetheless hierarchical symbology. The early seasons of *Walking Dead* are premised on this hope, which wanes as the prospects for survival diminish. The series suggests that the social order is dangerous without the intervention and social control of institutions, and this results in the ever more autocratic rule of their self-appointed leader, Rick Grimes.

For David Graeber, the only remedy to "free ourselves" from capitalist catastrophe is to "see ourselves again as historical actors, as people who can make a difference in the course of world events."[28] His solution is akin to that of Marx, even in the language of bondage, to break from ideological constraint and disavowal in order to find critical ground and consciousness in history. This is ripe for a number of viable remedies to mass objectification in neoliberalism. For those trapped in the subhuman symbologies of popular culture, they must first accede to human agency. Zombie storylines are a site for excavating the preponderant realities of life in debt. They are fundamentally neoliberal storylines that encode aspects of a terrifying social and cultural milieu and imagine ways of thinking and existing beyond zombie capitalism. In these normative storylines, heterosexual communities, as proto-state formations, bond across racial lines against a terrifying outsider while recapitulating the very forms from which they seek escape.

The zombie, according to *Time* magazine is "the official monster of the recession."[29] It is a loaded cultural figure that symbolizes a number of social fears about disaster, ruin, and dehumanization. The zombie marks the return of something long dead, something unresolved, put to rest, but never fully mourned or purged. The cultural resurgence of the zombie in pub crawls, novels, movies, television shows, and costumes is significant in the context of the economic freefall and devastation of the capitalist structure of debt economies. The zombie asserts the role of debt in public life as that which orders life and death. There is no outside to the zombie apocalypse, no redemption. Some zombie stories rejuvenate capitalism against decline and prop up U.S. power and exceptionalism within U.S.-led international cooperation. These tales are fundamentally conservative, restoring the social order in a more militarized form of racial and heteropatriarchal capitalism and restoring a system of debt through repayment and recompense. Others, like *Land of the Dead*, dramatize the possibility for political action through revolution and for freedom from the stultifying bonds of debt.

In the third season of *Walking Dead*, Rick and his squadron take over a prison from zombie inmates and staff for shelter. In the process, they discover a few human inmates barricaded in the prison pantry and awaiting rescue from the National Guard. Rick informs them that there is no extant military, police, or government and that, without any of these institutional infrastructures, they are no longer incarcerated. Yet, freedom in the zombie story is completely resignified, even meaningless. The prisoners realize that they are not free and that the prison is a site of safety and shelter where they choose to remain. This scene captures the ethos, magnified as monstrous, of a life in debt even beyond the canceling of one's debt to society. The prison allegorizes the social order shaped by debt and how the latter impacts all facets of life and shapes our unconscious, guiding our actions. And the prison story is another popular form contemporary with the zombie tale that directly signals the system of debt through biopolitics. The idea of paying one's "debt to society" is a key feature of women's prison media in memoirs, television series, films, and novels. The narrative of incarceration, particularly in the Netflix series *Orange Is the New Black*, offers a critical counterpoint to the imagined social life after crises—signified in zombie stories as an apocalypse—that is, after the failure of institutions premised on capitalism but the persistence of capitalist symbolic equivalencies, particularly heteropatriarchy and white supremacy. Women in prison stories perform very different social work. They conceive of a queer space, a female homosocial in which some inmates act out their refusal to pay their debt to society in their resistance to social reform through heteronormativity. In this way, women in prison stories, unlike their zombie kin, refuse the capitalist system of debt and indebtedness and offer different strategies for coping with life unto debt.

Figure 3.8. Prisoners abandoned after the zombie apocalypse in *The Walking Dead*.

CHAPTER 4

Queer Incarcerations

> And so I went to prison, and was freed. But I shall never really be free, for memory has built a penitentiary from which there is no escape.
> —Edna V. O'Brien, *So I Went to Prison*

> When you hit rock bottom, everything is leveled.
> —Joan Henry, *Women in Prison*

> The prison has become a black hole into which the detritus of contemporary capitalism is deposited.
> —Angela Y. Davis, *Are Prisons Obsolete?*

The song that accompanies the opening sequence of the Netflix series *Orange Is the New Black*, "You've Got Time" by Regina Spektor, describes animals trapped in cages alluding to the dehumanization of incarceration. Deprived of freedom, the captives' only remaining resource is time, time to reflect on the past. "You've Got Time" sets the mood of the series about a diverse community of incarcerated women from the vantage of a white prison initiate, Piper Chapman. The women are abstracted from social space and its movement in time. Prison is a space to think ("think of all the roads, think of all their crossings") from the original meaning of *penitentiary*, but it is also a place to remember, and each woman represents a set of memories and a cardinal crime that marks her story. The storyline of the series is spawned from the original kernel of Piper Kerman's memoir of the same name; it tells of her queer and illicit antics during a time of postgraduate confusion and aimlessness. Kerman's "unintentional" criminal past is a consequence of her immersion in bohemian counterculture, one contrary to her WASP New England upbringing. The memoir reflects nostalgically on her spirited past from the safe and nonthreatening vantage of a reformed and normative subject. Piper's story in the Netflix series departs from the memoir of the same name—which, if we follow the actual biography of Piper Kerman, ends with marriage, a lucrative book and Netflix series deal, a solid career in a public interest communications firm, and a position on the board of the Women's Prison Association.[1] The Netflix series takes liberties with its source material to weave a very different tale, that of an unrepentant and unreformable protagonist whose acculturation to prison life frees her from restrictive and banal forms of normativity while it also, as in *Breaking Bad* and *Weeds*, shows how the white protagonist turns deviance into profit. The series, drawing from the memoir, initiates public discussion about institutional forms of gender and sexual discipline and non–gender-conforming characters, including a nuanced portrayal of a trans woman depicted by trans actress and activist Laverne Cox, and self-identified "butch" woman, Big Boo, played by lesbian comedian Lea DeLaria.

Orange Is the New Black is part of the archive of white women's prisons writings. It captures many of the features of earlier memoirs on the topic that set the precedent and terms for a version of the prison narrative of the white woman and her departure from the law-abiding mainstream, particularly Edna

Figure 4.1. Big Boo (Lea DeLaria) of *Orange Is the New Black*.

V. O'Brien's post-1929 stock market crash narrative *So I Went to Prison*, Joan Henry's 1952 *Women in Prison*, Helen Bryan's 1953 *Inside*, and Barbara Demings's *Prison Notes* published in 1966. Each documents the writer's "accidental" imprisonment, difficult acculturation to institutional life, and personal take on the prison industrial complex as a member of a privileged class. They participate in the prison writing genre, critical narratives about the prison experience aimed at either reform or dismantling of the prison system. The women's prison genre in popular film and television has less overtly critical objectives. The examples entertain with salacious B-grade spectacles of female sexuality—see *Prison Girls* (1972)—sometimes encoding a critical message about prison culture within dramatic storylines. The Netflix series based on Kerman's memoir partakes in a mediated culture of women's prison stories—including *Caged* (1950), the series *Lockup* (MSNBC 2005-) and *Capadocia* (HBO Latino 2008-)—and ongoing fascination with female criminality and homoeroticism. But it is also the consequence of a postcrisis mood and fascination with ideas about freedom and social debts and obligations. Women in prison stories garner popular attention for the way that they symbolize dire and unfree conditions during cultural moments of disorder, economic freefall, and persistent social inequities; symbolized biopolitically, the inmate pays her debt to society with her trapped and caged body.

These popular accounts are part of a public archive of prison narratives that appeal to readerships and audiences for their vantage point onto a world unseen of a female homosocial, a space of women without men. Women in prison stories, reality-based and fictional, constitute a genre with its own storyform and narrative arc around transgression, repentance, rehabilitation, and—ultimately—reintegration into the social order. They invite an alternate, queer reading of the prison story for its transgressive possibilities rather than its assimilative aims. In postcrisis popular culture, the prison is not just, as Michel Foucault imagined, an allegorical order of permanent surveillance; it is a space of memory and fantasy, where the past is resignified and new forms of sociality arise out of sexual and intimate alliances and the conditions of communal living. It is a mediated space of radical political and social reordering, of the refusal to remit a debt to society, of the refusal of the entire symbolic debt economy, of the entire prison system. While they contain moments of queer possibility, these stories also contain lessons about how to turn deviance and transgression into social and real capital for the white characters. They also gloss the real conditions of incarceration—privation of rights and dehumanization—for women of color and trans/queers. In this way, they are also pessimistic signs of the enduring force of neoliberalism.

Debt to Society

So I Went to Prison shapes the storyform of the postcrisis prison story as a multiplex condition of debt and indebtedness. Edna V. O'Brien describes her arrest, indictment, and prison stay in the context of the 1929 panic and subsequently weakened and depressed economy. Her memoir shows how the stock market crash and its aftermath is glossed and misrepresented as a disaster caused by individual bankers rather than a systemic failure. O'Brien admits personal responsibility though not criminal culpability. The economic crash is a consequence, not of individual acts, but of widespread speculative mania. Goronwy Rees describes the popular mood and cultural pastimes leading up to the 1929 crash:

> The passion for speculation affected all classes. The change in figures of share prices on the ticker tape, relayed to brokers' offices throughout the United States, displaced even the World Series as an object of popular interest. And as in every form of popular sport, the great majority of those who watched, or betted on the result, were profoundly ignorant of the game that was being played; they operated on a system of tips, rumours, hints, superstitions which had no more relation to the real value of the shares they dealt in than a roulette player's hunch to the laws of chance.[2]

Speculation was rampant and pervasive and spread wildly as the market expanded. Rees does not blame the crisis on the individual investor and instead turns to those who issued financial advice. Yet, even brokers, who often followed their own advice, "could hardly be accused of deliberate deceit" since they were "self-deceived rather than deceiving." Ultimately, he concludes that those most responsible for "directing the financial affairs" of the United States failed to understand the system or were "powerless to control it."[3]

Yet, individuals like O'Brien are inculpated for the freefall of the economic order. Her "debt to society" is a consequence of a series of unpaid debts and loose interpretation of the rules and codes of the security and trade commission. O'Brien literally evokes the biopolitics fundamental to the debt society. She embodies her debt as a totem of the confusing financialization of capital; she adhered to financial regulations as poorly as she understood them. Her memoir links the economic to the carceral system and reveals fissures in both.

Indicted under the Martin Act for not complying with its codes as a "broker," O'Brien claims that she was not a broker on commission but was a partner with her friends, as equal investors, on a profit-sharing basis. She expresses a familial obligation to her "partners" in contradistinction to the atomism of the market, its cold regularity and indifference. She ushers a humanism and collaboration into financial transactions akin to noncapitalist orders. She is emphatic about her sense of responsibility to her friends, her efforts to stay the tide of ruin, and her shock at the literal reversal of her fortune. She uses the language and rhetoric of natural disaster to convey the ravaging force that lays devastating waste to the entire economic system; it is a collapse from within that could result only from large-scale failures of poor design rather than individual endeavor. She insists on her heroic but ultimately powerless efforts to fight the "avalanche":

> I bought fourteen thousand shares of Columbia at prices ranging from $60 up to $80 a share. Then I sat and waited for the killing. I didn't know I was going to be the corpse!
>
> When October, 1929, rolled around I was still holding the fourteen thousand shares of other stocks, and all superimposed on other thousands of shares of collateral securities entrusted to me by friends, and for which I felt personally responsible.
>
> Then the panic broke. Only the people who actually lived through the horror of those days in the Street can realize the mental agony of standing in the midst of crashing prices, seeing the accumulated efforts of years being swept away in a few hour[s]' time. I was helpless to stay the torrent as a person caught in a hurricane. Yet I felt personally responsible somehow! My friends had trusted me and my judgment. I should have been able, someway, somehow, to have foreseen, and sold out. So with nerves taut, lashed by my own inner reproaches, I fought the avalanche and pledged myself and everything I had to save the little domain I had built.[4]

Her ruin, initiated by the crash, deepened in the years following. Within a couple of years, her Columbia stock was at $2 a share and the chasm between security value and credit widened. As her stock fell, she moved ever closer to criminal status. And she deployed the language of natural disasters, such as "hurricane," which recalled the storms that struck Miami and destroyed many new developments, marking the final collapse of the speculative boom of the 1920s.[5]

Like the protagonists of many women in prison stories, O'Brien is an accidental criminal and an outsider to the carceral system. Her family pedigree includes those who helped settle the United States and whom she describes as its "foremost citizens."[6] Upon her arrest, she likens her surprise to that of Mark Twain who "read with astonishment his own obituary."[7] Elsewhere she describes her reaction to her new circumstances as a "mingled feeling of acute astonishment, amusement, and curiosity," mirroring readership fascination with her predicament. She adds that she is "maddingly helpless" in a manner that many of her readers, deep in an economic depression, would identify.

O'Brien is unique in a number of ways. She is a trader on the stock market at a time when the presence of women in this male domain was very rare. Her trades yield such profit that she catches the attention of her friends and colleagues who ask her to invest their funds, forming the basis of a lucrative firm that would eventually grow to occupy half of a floor of a Fifth Avenue skyscraper. Her crime is a lapse, a lack of written agreements and a casual approach to business that, after the crash, turned friendly agreements into illegal transactions amounting to "grand larceny." Hers is a mingling of moral, social, and economic debt. She is indicted for engaging an intimate rapport with other investors and for being unsystematic about her financial operations. Yet, she refuses her social debt and rehabilitation and instead demands a rehabilitation of the system. She prefaces her story with the caution to shift focus from her crime or the legal proceedings around it to the entire prison complex:

> It is not my purpose in writing this book to re-try my case. Nor to make a personal issue of an experience which was of necessity intensely personal. It is immaterial whether I was innocent or guilty, or with what crime I was charged, vicious or accidental. The procedure under the law would have been practically the same. That is the interesting thing to ponder. I was just one of the human atoms caught in the legal machinery and ground through into prison.
>
> And for what purpose and with what result? Was the object to chasten me, to humble my pride? To break my spirit? If so, it failed! Was it to reform me? Reform me of what? Was its object to send me back into the world better able to achieve business success and repay moral debts honestly assumed? Unless the degree of State Prison does this, then again it failed.[8]

Her story reveals the porousness of the imagined boundary that separates criminal from law-abiding citizen. In fact, she revises the very notion of "debt to society":

> A girl from Bedford told me, "I am a thief from necessity, not from choice!" Yet that young woman had great native talent which if discovered earlier and developed would have made her a self-supporting, self-respecting citizen, stealing neither from choice nor from necessity. And the cost to the State would have been a fraction compared to what it had already spent keeping her behind bars. She may have been "paying her debt to society," but in my opinion, it was society that was doing the "paying," not only in wasted human life, but in good hard dollars. Yet the heart-sickening business goes on, day in and day out, with the commission of crimes increasing and tens of thousands of people pouring in and out of prison yearly.[9]

O'Brien's tale ends with her release but the experience of the prison continues to resonate. She resignifies freedom, claiming that she will never be free since "memory has built a penitentiary from which there is no escape."[10] She is not reformed or rehabilitated but traumatized and restored to the social order as a critical, even cynical, subject. Her story points to the revolutionary potential of the prison as an allegorical space of social unrest during times of economic crisis.

Caged, Quarantined, Contained

O'Brien's narrative highlights the cinematic and melodramatic character of the women's prison story and thus its potential to engage audience and readership interest. She notes that the prison experience, framed by the scenario of inmates watching a film, is even more cinematic and spectacular than the film they view:

> The lights went down, the picture was on. A drama of action. But I was conscious of a curious feeling within me. While outwardly this was the commonplace audience attending a picture show, yet I had the sensation that the real drama portrayed in each life was so much more vital and living, that the action portrayed on the screen seemed flat and stale in comparison. This feeling was intensified when suddenly the girl at my side stifled a muffled scream as a killing was enacted in the picture. She, poor child, had just lived through murder in reality.[11]

As will be the case with *Orange Is the New Black*, each inmate represents a dramatic story of crime and passion that comprises the narrative. Likewise, in *Caged*, the women are watching a prison movie and the guard remarks on its lack of verisimilitude, self-reflexively gesturing to the more accurate portrayal of life behind bars in *Caged*.

Caged, one of the first films to establish the women-in-prison storyline, is a social problem film about an ingénue whose acculturation to prison life is also that of the audience, a standard of both fiction and nonfiction accounts from *Lockup* to *Capadocia* and the popular series based on Kerman's memoir. The prison is a space of disorientation from the vantage of a woman who becomes incarcerated through a single bad choice or wrong affiliation. These are stories of white, mainstream, and middle-class freefall, of a radical change in circumstance occasioned by some set of arbitrary choices, rather than institutional inequities. While inside, the protagonist discovers oppressive conditions that hinder the possibility of inmate reform and rehabilitation.

Caged sets many of the terms of the prison trope in popular culture and reflects the cultural imaginary of the 1950s United States as predominantly white. It is a post-war reminder and remainder of the era when women occupied men's roles in the social upheaval rendered by war. The mood is noir, incarnating the genre through a light and dark motif, the topos of crime and criminality, guilt and innocence, and darkly transgressive passions. Marie Allen is sentenced to ten months in the Women's State Prison for her role as her husband's accomplice in a robbery, which consisted of simply remaining in the car while he robbed a gas station. She is part of a skewed social world that puts the poor in a position without recourse, while her prison time socializes her to the life of crime, making her part of a criminal underclass.

Caged is as much about homosocial prison life as it is a cautionary tale about the failures of state institutions to reform inmates. The story begins with Marie Allen in isolation in a darkened prison cell, creating an immediate visual typology of inside versus outside. The outside is bright and sun-drenched while the prison is drab, often dark, a uniform space of indifference in which, paradoxically, the rule of law is imposed in often arbitrary and perverse ways. To signal this the warden warns Marie: "no prison is a normal place." In fact, her incarceration initiates her acculturation to the abnormal that begins with an attempted seduction by a butch oldtimer. She quickly finds that prison is a unique place, a singular space, embued with homosocial intensities, intimacies, and a different form of community and association from the world outside. Marie is told: "If you stay here too long, you don't think of guys at all, you just get out of the habit."

The female prison story persists as a cultural fixation partly in the voyeuristic exploration of same-sex intimacies but also for the imaginative potential of a space occupied and organized by women. Contemporary with *Caged*, Joan Henry's *Women in Prison* tells of her stay in one of the toughest women's prisons in England, Holloway. While the story takes place in England, it was first published in New York in 1952 by Doubleday and hit a market shaped by women's prison stories like *Caged*. It is concerned with bridging the imagined chasm between criminal and law-abiding, and it attempts to transcend the personal narrative to be one of universal dimensions, not *her* story "but the story of any woman, innocent or guilty, who has the misfortune to go to prison."[12] Like other tales of its kind, it begins with Joan Henry's sentencing and acculturation to the carceral system, one that is partly achieved through the mediation of popular culture:

> A few women were walking about with pails, and one or two were talking together. They were dressed like myself, but they all looked unkempt with straggly hair and shiny faces; and they had the incurious expression of sleepwalkers. I was reminded of the women in the film *Snake Pit*, which I had recently seen.[13]

The cross-Atlantic cultural preoccupation with women's institutions—*Snake Pit* is about women in a psychiatric institution—is part of an ongoing fascination about spaces occupied entirely by women through which we might imagine a different society. And it points to a gendered difference in forms of punishment and incarceration. Women have been incarcerated in psychiatric hospitals like that depicted in *Snake Pit* more often than in prison. Angela Y. Davis describes how mental health facilities constitute a major form of social control for women for whom deviance is more often defined as insanity.[14]

The female homosocial is fascinating for its potential to raise fundamental political questions about matriarchy and female social kinship and association. These stories explore how women address social conflict, how they negotiate social codes about sexuality, and whether gender difference underwrites moral differences. Also, the female prison is a markedly different space from its male counterpart, at least in its mediated forms, or as Sam Healy, the counselor in *Orange Is the New Black*, intones: "This isn't *Oz*, women fight with gossip and rumors" and, he warns: "there are lesbians." Unlike the brute violence attributed to men's prisons, women adhere to gender conventions, using manipulation and indirect forms of power to resolve conflicts. And, there are lesbians.

According to Joan Henry, whose memoir aspires to social commentary, the biggest problem besetting the women's prison is lesbianism as a response to the "abnormality of prison existence." And she argues, "there are a great many women who are more homosexually inclined than most people would imagine, or even that they have imagined themselves."[15] These women are "ripe for the advances of the long-term prisoner" who, sexually deprived, seek any "sexual outlet" and are also targets of the "real lesbians."[16] She tacitly suggests that prison, its special circumstances, frees women from repression and unleashes their homoerotic impulses, they are given to "imagine" this hitherto unimaginable possibility for themselves. Sexologist Frank S. Caprio finds homoerotic tendencies "dormant" in all women and liberated in prison: "That the homosexual component lies dormant in every woman and may find expression under certain conditions is substantiated by the prevalence of homosexual practices among women prisoners."[17] The social interdiction against homosexuality is lifted by context, privation, and a general lack of repression. Caprio draws on Henry's work to substantiate claims that the prison is a place of liberated homosexual desire, where women might seek a prison vocation to "encounter opportunities for their homosexual cravings."[18] Unlike the sociologists that will chime in on the topic in the 1960s, Henry suggests that the prison is an enabling context for inherent, not provisional or transitory, homoerotic desires or the stuff of what Freud called "contingent inverts."[19] Yet her work accords with the discourse about the essential and inherent weakness of women who lack the agency to commit serious crime: "The majority of women in prison are weak characters who have become the victims of circumstance."[20] Like the protagonists of all the stories mentioned here, their femininity, vulnerability, and weakness lead them to transgression of social norms around sexuality and the laws of the state. She tells of various inmates whose crimes are the result of cavorting with manipulative men, poverty, mental illness, or the violation of internalized moral codes based on gender.

In the mid–nineteenth century, there was a move to separate the formerly joined populations of female and male prisoners due to ideas about the very distinct forms of discipline and reformation accorded to each gender. Women were treated with a paternalistic attitude as vulnerable and in need of protection. Rose Giallombardo, in her sociological analysis of women's prisons, notes that "whereas male criminals are usually feared as dangerous men in the eyes of society, the disgraced and dishonored woman has always been considered pathetic . . . women who committed criminal offenses tended to be regarded as erring and misguided creatures who needed protection rather than as dangerous criminals from whom the members of society should be protected."[21] Women were under the protective care of the state, the latter often emblematized in the prison warden or matron, and treatment consisted of rehabilitation to sexual and gender norms and return to the social order as wives, homemakers, and mothers. Women's prisons recruited personnel who would best accomplish these goals through knowledge of the essentials of homemaking and the proprieties of womanhood as defined by nineteenth-century standards. Thus, women were subdued and rehabilitated by acculturating them to norms that defined them as helpless, weak, dependent, and servile. In contemporary prison stories like *Orange Is the New Black*, women congregate and work more often in occupations aligned with femininity: the kitchen, the laundry room, and the hair salon—though they also work individually as electricians at various locations, the female-defined occupations take place in communal spaces of congress associated with domestic work.

Within prison discourse real reform is marked by the return to a domestic life ("find a man, get married"). But this rarely happens in popular cultural prison stories. In the cross-border Mexican telenovela *Capadocia*, the main character, Lorena Guerra (Ana de la Reguera) accidentally causes the death of her husband's lover in a jealous rage, and she is jettisoned from her safe, banal, upper-middle-class domestic life into a Mexico City prison. Again, like other women's prison stories, she shouldn't be there; she is naive and completely unprepared for the violence, sexual exploits, and perversion of law that she will face. But, her time in prison shapes her into a competent criminal and lesbian and a major player in international drug trade directed at U.S. markets. She moves further and further from her normative domestic life in the transformation of all that she knows.

In 2013, the lesbian prison storyline returned with *Orange Is the New Black*, following the same narrative trajectory as *Caged* and *Capadocia* but with some revisions. The series emerges in an era of permanent war and advanced neoliberal forms of capitalism that link the military and the prison industrial complex—Piper is told that the prison pudding comes from cans marked "Desert Storm." The prison is the apogee of the capitalist order and one of its major nodes, often a source of extremely low-wage prison labor and an economic engine of local communities. In *Capadocia*, Lorena's work on the inside of the prison as a drug trade operative is not only endorsed by the state but buttressed by it through the privatization of the prison, a private enterprise with global economic ambitions in illegal drug trade. The operations extend into the United States; and unlike other drug trafficking media, the target is the center of global financial operations in New York City, not the border region. Likewise, Litchfield in *Orange Is the New Black* undergoes a process of privatization that renders the prison population vulnerable to violence of various kinds.

In the memoir, the prison population dwindles as Litchfield faces closure. Yet the series depicts the takeover of the prison, similar to *Capadocia*, by a private corporation, Management and Correction Corporation (MCC)—based on the Corrections Corporation of America (CCA)—which has a reputation of extracting as much profit as possible in its various investments and then moving on to the next venture, in keeping with neoliberal principles of the free market. Or, as one of the staff characterizes MCC, it is interested only in "nailing this quarter and next" before moving on. The third season of the series dramatizes the various ways that the relatively stable world of Litchfield unravels through the forces of neoliberalism. Inmates and staff alike experience the negative outcomes of austerity policies. The prison staff becomes disgruntled as their jobs are reduced to part time and their benefits are cut. The new part-time correctional officers are hired without experience and offered no official training, rendering them incompetent and reactive and putting the inmates in danger. Sophia Burset, under these new policies, is punished with segregation as the victim of transphobia, since punishment is the most expedient and cost-effective course of action according to the corporate heads of the privatized prison.

The new firm exploits inmate labor for extremely low wages to sew lingerie for a private company—also a plotpoint in *Capadocia*, although in an added twist, the inmates in this Mexico City prison store drugs in the lingerie for international distribution. And this turn of events both occasions and allegorizes Piper's new business dealings in the prison. Like Lorena in *Capadocia*, she begins a criminal operation, a cartel, in which she enlists other inmates to hand over worn lingerie that will be sold as fetish objects under the company "Felonious Funk." She works with her brother on the outside and even sets up a payment

Figure 4.2. Sophia Burset (Laverne Cox) of *Orange Is the New Black*.

system for the women for a percentage of the profit. The success of the operation turns her into a coldhearted neoliberal entrepreneur. She makes an example out of Flaca, who turns union agitator demanding a fair wage, by firing her unceremoniously in front of the other women; for doing so, other inmates call Piper "stone cold." She calls herself a "benevolent dictator" and claims that her actions are the "cost of doing business," which is the very language that MCC is using to justify its economic slash and burn policies. Her cruel efficiency recalls that of Walter White in *Breaking Bad*. In fact, while her behavior is described as cold and extreme, she is also characterized as "not Walter White yet." Piper, like White, quickly rises to the top of the prison social order and turns her acculturation to criminality into a successful capitalist venture. The changes in Piper allegorize the changes in the prison wrought by neoliberalism. And the latter represents the persistent threat of violence that hangs over the prison population even as they find moments of community and noninstitutionally mediated congress.

White Is the New Black

Orange Is the New Black is not a story about the typical inmate that populates U.S. prisons, a racialized underclass, it is about an Anglo middle-class protagonist who, almost accidentally, finds herself behind bars. Like zombie media, the storyline's racial dynamics are highlighted and then flattened from the point of view of a white protagonist. The racialized division of prison life is dismissed as defensive and "tribal" rather than a reflection of systemic racism. A white inmate tells Piper, "We look out for our own . . . it's tribal not racist." There are, as the series depicts, clear and established racially defined groups, and inmates are organized according to race just as they are housed and divided across gendered lines. In her memoir, Piper describes this highly delineated "tribal" system of categorization that generates its own "others": "When a new person arrived, their tribe—white, black, Latino or the few and far between 'others'—would immediately make note of their situation, get them settled, and steer them through their arrival. If you fell into that 'other' category—Native American, Asian, Middle Eastern—then you got a patchwork welcome committee of the kindest and most compassionate women from the dominant tribes."[22] The series highlights the troubled production of difference through cases in which racialized bodies do not fit neatly into available categories, particularly in the mixed-race Asian and white character of Brook Soso, played by Kimiko Glenn. Brook is garrulous and opinionated, but her misfit status is attributed to her racial status as "Asian" and "not quite" white. As a result, she does not have a "tribe" or group affiliation until she is accepted by the African Americans.

While the differences among inmates are considered "tribal," they are embedded in a white supremacist institutional structure that accords privilege to whiteness. Piper Kerman notes that during her stay she was granted access and rights for her whiteness that inmates of color did not receive. For instance, she was called by her first name—a humanizing gesture—permitted to have far more visitors on her approved list, and given the best jobs and bunk mates.

The dismissal of difference as tribal occludes the institutionalized racism that leads to incarceration. For Michelle Alexander, the criminal justice system is the source of the "new caste system," in which race is coded as criminal and criminals are subject to legally sanctioned forms of discrimination, denial of rights, and social exclusion that were common during the Jim Crow era of segregation. Mass incarceration is a racial justice issue of epic proportions.[23] Two-thirds of all imprisoned women are Latina or African American and the majority are poor. The carceral complex extends far beyond the prison walls and allegorizes the condition of living in neoliberalism. The slashing of funding for social programs, initiated during the presidency of Ronald Reagan, and increased funding for the military industrial and carceral complex meant that social and economic inequality would be remedied by institutionalization, primarily through incarceration. In essence, poverty is criminalized. Those without recourse and without the safety net of social services often are forced to turn to informal economies, extralegal activities, and other criminalized activities to survive. Julia Sudbury calls this social and political restructuring the "War on the Poor" in which "criminalization and warehousing were the weapons of choice for minimizing the potential for social unrest and dissent."[24] The result is a crisis of mass incarceration, intensified by the war on drugs and mandatory minimum sentencing laws, of which Piper's imprisonment is a consequence. These sentences for drug-related violations were handed down differently according to race. In the 1990s when Kerman was involved in international drug smuggling, antidrug police operations disproportionately targeted low-income African American communities.

In *Orange Is the New Black* the racial order among inmates is leveled in the production of a queer space, one in which social and intimate alliances are formed between and among women, and even the latter category is contested and expanded with the presence of the transgender character within the series, Sophia Burset, and, extratextually, by the actress who plays her, Laverne Cox—and Vanessa Robinson in the memoir. The reference to the mystical place of Capadocia in the HBO Latino series points to the imaginary of the prison as a bounded space noted for its exceptional and singular qualities—Capadocia is a region renowned for its extraordinary topography and cultural characteristics. The women's prison is a queer space that generates a singular homosocial order not found in the outside world. The prison, for the white characters, is a place where the codes and hierarchies of the outside world do not pertain; abstracted from the social, the mediated prison is a place of fantasy and queer possibility through sexual making and unmaking, notwithstanding and perhaps as a result of the strict regimenting, rule of law, and divisions according to race—that is, sexual freedom offers a reprieve from the strict carceral order. Regina Kunzel explores how social and historical understandings of sex in prison highlight fissures in the construction of modern sexual identity. Prison is a place that reproduces sexuality only to reveal the false coherence of sexual identities. Sexuality in prison is fluid and flexible.[25] Yet, while sexuality is fluid, changing over time and in space, racialization is ever more fixed in prison in a manner that intensifies and crystallizes racial categories. Race, even for racially mixed populations, does not change or shift and remains grindingly deterministic for the characters on the margins of these mainstream narratives.

Communal Living in a Capitalist State

The wish for an alternate mode of social organization is a consequence of crisis and deepening social inequities. While the prison system is a consequence of capitalism and a major part of its machinery, the narrative production of the prison space accords with a vision of a different social order. Although it is not an ideal space—inmates are permanently visible, divided along racial lines, deprived of basic rights, and oppressed by arbitrary rules and codes and various privations—many of the prison memoirists describe scenes of collaboration and express desire, generated by their proximity to other women, to transform or eradicate the carceral system. Joan Henry undergoes a radical transformation from "self-centered" comportment to a communal awareness and sympathetic rapport to others; her investment in her fellow inmates inspires her reformist activism: "I wished with all my heart that I could do something to make prisons better places, that I could take the looks of fear and despair and, in some cases, just plain hopelessness off those hundreds of faces and give them something for the future."[26] With her memoir, she passes on her "thoughts and experiences in the hope that they may be of some help to somebody."[27] Helen Bryan, a political prisoner indicted by the House Committee on Un-American Activities, also learns a new form of compassion in prison through access to populations that she, as a member of a privileged class, would otherwise never encounter. She documents her shift from free to imprisoned and the process of dehumanization that renders her changed and presents her with a new mission to gather the stories of those marginalized by the carceral system. After hearing the stories of fellow inmates, she has an epiphany:

> In some half-dreaming, half-wakening state I went back to bed, aware that I was now conscious of something that had been eluding me all along but was not as clear as sunshine. Yet, what is it? I thought. I've got to remember what it is. I've got to tell myself what it is. It's the most important thing for me to know. It centered around Ursula and Linda and Eunice and Pearl. Yes, that's it! That's it! Now I know. That's what's so important. Ursula and Linda and Eunice and Pearl. These girls, their lives and their futures, and the lives and futures of all the other girls. My present is their present, yes, but my past is not their past nor my future their future. My past is a solid past, filled with opportunities and satisfying work. And I have a future, not quite so solid perhaps, but I know I can make a future. I felt the tensions and fears of the past days draining through and out of my mind. Compassion and tenderness replaced the anxieties for myself. Compassion and tenderness and a kind of grief I had never known before.[28]

In prison, Bryan encounters those less fortunate than herself and finds compassion that turns to a renewed sense of justice. Prison is a space of a working-class and poor majority, the site of the ravages of inequality. In *Prison Notes*, Barbara Deming describes the imprisoned as repressed populations who will not be silenced, forgotten, or denied. Deming cites a fairy tale in which a man attempts to rid himself of an old pair of slippers; torn and unsightly, he wants them gone from his sight. Yet each time he throws them out the window or buries them in the garden, they return to cause him some new mischief. She uses this tale to convey how society treats the imprisoned as refuse they would will out of existence and render invisible behind prison walls. It is her intention, and that of other prison writers, to grant visibility to the incarcerated, to use the prison to illustrate ideas of collectivism. Deming, incarcerated for nonviolent demonstration, ends her story by linking her political activism to the aim of her prison notes: "Of course what we were attempting as we struggled was precisely to bind people together—or rather to bring them to recognize that we are, all of us, bound to each other and so should not deny this in our actions."[29] The idea of collectivism is difficult to imagine or conceive of within capitalism and has been co-opted in the rhetoric of corporatism. But the "leveling" of the social and the collapsing of power dynamics among inmates presents a different manner of relating for many of these prison narrators. Even Kerman notes how many times fellow inmates asked how she was doing when she first arrived, offering up commissary items and orienting her to prison life, people with whom she otherwise would not interact and who inspire her to document her prison stay and join efforts for prison reform. More significantly, Kerman's memoir initiates her interest in prison reform through her experience of the ineffectual and often violent outcomes of incarceration for inmates. She regrets her role in the distribution of drugs, not for its illegality, but for the impact of drugs on communities of color, which she sees all around her:

> Even when my clothes were taken away and replaced by prison khakis, I would have scoffed at the idea that the "War on Drugs" was anything but a joke. I would have argued that the government's drug laws were at best proven ineffectual every day and at worst were misguidedly focused on supply rather than demand, randomly conceived and unevenly and unfairly enforced based on race and class, and thus intellectually and morally bankrupt.[30]

Kerman's story is both a critique of the prison system and one that conveys how she is inadvertently reformed. Like the white memoirists that precede her, she is forced into intimate rapport with people whom she would not find in her outside life and she builds an empathic connection to them, one that changes her vantage and her ideological position:

> What made me finally recognize the indifferent cruelty of my own past wasn't the constraints put on me by the U.S. government, nor the debt I had amassed for legal fees, nor the fact that I could not be with the man I loved. It was sitting and talking and working with and knowing people who suffered because of what people like me had done. None of these women rebuked me—most of them had been intimately involved in the drug business themselves. Yet for the first time

Figure 4.3. Piper Chapman (Taylor Schilling) newly arriving to Litchfield Penitentiary.

I really understood how my choices made me complicit in their suffering. I was the accomplice to their addiction.[31]

Kerman's experience leads to her role as member of the board of the Women's Prison Association, a nonprofit that helps women adjust after incarceration. While there are moments of critique in the memoir, the storyline is that of reform rather than abolition and heteronormativity rather than queerness. In the series, the main character based on Piper Kerman takes a different course. She explores a sense of community in the prison through queer affiliation in the recourse to her relationship with her codefendant, Alex Vause. In the memoir, Piper Kerman is adamantly future-oriented, with the promise of marriage and a domestic life with her fiancé just beyond the prison walls.

Gay for the Stay

The communal life of prison includes alternate, homoerotic forms of intimacy. The "friendships" spied by Helen Bryan in Alderson defies her sense of friendship on the outside:

A girl can have several regular friends and at the same time have a special girl friend. Homosexuality, either ideological or actual, is a fact for a small percentage of the girls. This stems primarily from the situation of approximately five hundred women and girls living together, with never the sight of a man except for those who are completely removed from any possible advances. Since there are no men with whom they can have the relationships they crave, their compulsions lead some girls to form relationships with girls. When two girls have agreed to be special friends, the term used to describe their relationship is "playing." A girl may come into Alderson having been a lesbian on the outside, or a girl without such experiences may find herself drawn towards it by the dullness of the routine and by being sought by another girl.[32]

Piper Kerman and women interviewed on MSNBC's series *Lockup* describe this as being "gay for the stay," which Kerman likens to the experience of transitory lesbianism in college or "lesbian until graduation." In the series, Piper, who, like **Marie and Lorena, is naively seduced into committing** a crime by an unscrupulous **partner, Alex, will reencounter her** in prison and undergo a relapse into lesbianism. When this happens, she falls out of favor with the **paternal corrections officer and counselor and sets** in motion a number of actions and practices that mark her deviation from the life she left behind. She is not the only character experiencing this split from a "self" constituted by socialization "on the outside." For example, Lorna Morello (Yael Stone), the driver-inmate who shuttles her to the prison, is known for her fantasies about the perfect wedding and ideal domestic life with her fiancé. This devotion to normativity does not square with her sexual relationship with Natasha Lyonne's character, Nicky Nichols. The lesbian prison story is about the production of queerness from within the off-scene, unseen margins of the social order. The first few seasons of the series is not about the fictional Piper's recuperation and redemption but her acculturation to a queer social. What was once terrifying and disorienting for our prison story protagonists upon entry to the prison—Piper, Marie, Lorena—is, after a few weeks, a matter of course and a way of life. These are stories in which the queer—lesbianism, criminality, female homosociality, gender nonconformity—is normalized. The protagonists enact and dramatize the acculturation to queerness; they are proxies for the mainstream viewer who undergoes a similar transformation. Transformation is the theme of an episode of the popular MSNBC documentary series, *Lockup Extended Stay: Maricopa Country Jail*.

The episode, called "Daddy's Girl," follows the narrative arc of the women in prison genre in which a white, scared, and vulnerable ingénue, Jessica Styx, encounters the confusing space of incarceration for the first time. The documentary is narrated by a male voice-of-god narrator who introduces the inmates accused of crimes and in limbo awaiting sentencing. He notes that incarceration changes people and the dorms of the women's facility "can be as transformative a setting

Figure 4.4. Piper and Alex Vause (Laura Prepon) rekindle their relationship.

as any," particularly in the G dorm where many "unauthorized relationships" take place.

The episode follows the ingénue as she falls into the clutches of repeat offender Kelly McNaughton, "McNaughty," who is a renowned manipulator and described by a correctional officer as a "game player" and controller of a pod ("pod boss"), capable of persuading inmates to do her bidding. She is an attractive, tall and feminine brunette who recalls Alex of *Orange Is the New Black*, also dominant and charming. She "set her sights" on Jessica Styx, who defensively asserts that she does not like girls and is committed to her boyfriend—also awaiting sentencing. Styx is adamant about her "straightness" and refuses to succumb to McNaughton's advances. Styx claims to have had a "good life" as a "normal person" and claims her innocence of any crime. She wants "normalcy" with her boyfriend that includes a "house and kids and jobs" and "normal day to day things." She does not fall under McNaughton's spell, but she does undergo the transformation alluded to by the narrator. Her adamant stance against homosexuality and assertion of normalcy adjusts to include "falling in love" with of one of G dorm's biggest players, Melissa Molina, or "Daddy." She makes a major transformation, crossing racial and gender lines to form a very different relationship than one she would engage outside the jail. She revises her commitment to her boyfriend from waiting for him to uncertainty about what the future holds. She seems committed to her newfound love relationship to

Molina—sealed with tattoos of her name on both forearms, thus the name of the episode, "Daddy's Girl."

Molina and McNaughton have the attention of the correctional officers as powerful figures. McNaughton collects women who are content to serve her not through coercion but intelligent persuasion. Her power is threatening to the officers and lands her in segregation where she cannot exercise her charms on other women. She enacts a direct challenge to the power structure of the jail in a manner that is less hierarchical; though a "boss," she relates to a woman as, according to one officer, a "sister," whereas Molina's power is described as "sexual." McNaughton mentors and instructs the women on how to survive when they are transferred to prison, lessons that include instruction on sex with women. Both are powerful totems of the queerness of carceral space and the potential for defiance of the system from within it.

In these stories, the critique of the prison serves various ends. These stories locate the prison as an instantiation of the current form of global capitalism, a space of cheap labor and one site of a global security matrix that includes a number of other types of facilities, including jails, detention centers, juvenile justice facilities, border security, and secret prisons. These stories also take place during times of crisis and allegorize forms of un-freedom while they depict the crisis of mass incarceration. It is a space that is a consequence of capitalism while it might be imagined as a site of a momentary reprieve from capitalism. The women's prison is a communal zone from which new forms of association are forged. The communal is a core part of the idea of communism, which is often linked to the upheavals of revolution, suggesting the dislodging of one order for another. Yet, the revolutionary potential of the women's prison is hidden in plain view, veiled by its embeddedness in the state. These shows expose alternate forms of association and explore the meanings of freedom and collectivism during times of crisis. The inmates share the common circumstance of loss of freedom, conditions that reflect the social experience of economic servitude. This is not to say that the prison is the space of revolution; it remains a space of oppression, dehumanization, and degradation, where inmates are subject to the privation of basic human rights, medical care, proper nutrition, and forms of actual and symbolic violence. The overarching experience, described by Joan Henry, is of the trauma of the incarceration of the psychic architecture of memory. These stories about white incarcerated women move the crisis of mass incarceration into the mainstream, but they tell only part of the story. Using the prison as the social setting for drama only partially addresses the prison system, it largely glosses its systemic violence and connection to larger patterns of surveillance and the policing of the impoverished, the racialized, migrants, and trans/queers.

Rehabilitation, Recuperation, Repayment

The women-in-prison stories, while part of a larger overarching prison genre, have very specific narrative features that are as much a symptom of gender and sexual socialization and regulation as they are of the fantasies that female homosocial spaces elicit—e.g., the girl's school or the convent. These stories are cautionary, often meant to put wayward girls back on the right social track. In other words, the social life of debt demands a particular ethics and way of living. "Social rights" become "social debts." That is, individuals in a postcrisis bailout context are deemed beneficiaries of state interventions to save the economy and must repay their debt through proper living. They must exhibit a set of attitudes and behaviors that correspond to a culture of austerity and work within a normalizing process of reform and rehabilitation through heterosexual kinship. The inmate must, as is promulgated in *Caged*, get out of prison, get a job, find a husband, and live a simple life. Not, as Marie Allen, Piper, or Lorena do, cavort with or become a lesbian, learn to game the system, and enhance their criminal tendencies.

These figures are out of control, off-scene, obscene; they are beyond reform, beyond redemption. They refuse to repay their debt to society. The moral imperative of debt does not square with the economic ideas subtending the system of capitalism. That is, debts are part of a system of investment risk and speculation. The lender assumes risk and bets on the loan as an investment underwritten by a complex system of laws and guarantees. Debt is not a moral value; it is the logic of an illogical system.[33] Lesbian prison stories tacitly expose the contradictions of the capitalist order of the debt economy and offer a different, albeit sometimes dark, vision of an alternative social order. These inmates deviate from a norm and defiantly accept their exclusion and possible discontent. And this form of social unease has the potential to foment resistance and energize revolution.

Piper Kerman's account of her time in prison ends with the imminent closure of Danbury as a women's prison, the facility that housed her for thirteen months and that would later reopen as a men's prison. As the prison nears its demise the population dwindles and the space becomes the kind of ghost town reminiscent of the postapocalyptic towns of zombie films. The memoir ends with the closure of the place as a female homosocial just as Kerman's life is about to take its upward course into freedom and enjoyment of her white heterosexual entitlements. This sense of an end to the women's prison is apparent in both the memoir and the Netflix series and shifts focus from the dynamics among inmates to the larger social and physical structures they inhabit—though in the series, the prison is saved from closure via takeover by a private corporation. The ruin of individual houses, buildings, communities, towns, cities, and entire nations is the wider context of crisis capitalism during the Great Recession that occasioned stories of global disaster. But capitalist disaster stories, particularly the Hollywood version, contain unimaginable events of incredible scale that are easily dismissed or disavowed by audiences. When disaster is rendered locally, brought down to human scale, to the end of a house or a prison, the wages and ramifications of disaster are more readily assimilable. The chapter that follows compares the scale of Hollywood disaster to its local incarnation in the news cycle around sinkholes, small disasters that bring home global ideas about economic ruin.

CHAPTER 5

Sinkholes and Seismic Shifts
Ecological and Other Disasters

> We are on the edge of disaster without being able to situate it in the future: it is rather always already past, and yet we are on the edge or under the threat, all formulations which would imply the future—that which is yet to come—if the disaster were not that which does not come, that which has put a stop to every arrival. To think the disaster (if this is possible, and is not possible inasmuch as we suspect that the disaster is thought) is to have no longer any future in which to think it.
>
> —Maurice Blanchot, *The Writing of the Disaster*

In the movie *2012*, deputy geologist Adrian Helmsley storms a White House black-tie fund-raiser to deliver a report about the end of the earth while protestors clash with police at the G8 summit (now G7) of the leaders of the most advanced economies of the world. Inside the forum, the President of the United States issues the proclamation that "the world as we know it will soon come to an end." Outside protestors hold signs that read "stop toxic waste," "fair trade now," "stop outsourcing," "boycott sweatshops," "people, planet, not profits," and "drop the debt." The protestors inculpate the actions and policies of the global North that negatively impact the global South and, as the storyline suggests, will destroy the entire world system. Yet, the idea that ecological disaster originates in economic policy will be swept away by the tide of all-consuming floods that precipitate the end of the earth. Disaster films like *The Day after Tomorrow* (2004) or *2012* (2009) present a template for imagining catastrophe as total, all-encompassing, and dystopic. But, as Doug Henwood writes, "catastrophe can be paralyzing, not mobilizing" and "dystopia," he opines, "is for losers."[1]

The rhetoric of catastrophe and its narrative visualization in popular culture in disaster films and storylines function to overwhelm, shock, and immobilize publics. They offer little in the way of possibilities for social transformation or revolution. However, the individual crisis, the individualization of global catastrophe in its miniaturization in small disasters, like the sinkhole, personalizes ecological crisis and, quite literally, brings it home.

Many of the popular media stories about sinkholes describe them as unpredictable and arbitrary events in which entire houses are consumed, streets and sidewalks cave in, and people and their pets are absorbed by hollow chasms in and around their homes. The sinkhole crisis demands expediency for the immediacy of its threat. The ground gives way and everything above it is subject to a freefall into an abyss of unknown proportions. Sinkholes appear the world over and are satellites of larger global crises. They denote the reduction of the scale of crisis to a manageable level of local organization and efforts. In A. M. Homes's novel *This Book Will Save Your Life*, a sinkhole demands community action, bringing together several city agencies and neighbors and ousting the protagonist from his self-imposed isolation, cynicism, and lethargy. The real threat of a sinkhole might be more effective in changing the relationship of individuals to the environment, as allegorized in Homes's novel, in which the appearance of the sinkhole inaugurates a major transformation for the protagonist within his community.

Remaking the Geological and Ideological Order

Sinkholes are a symptom of the vast remaking of the geological order in late capitalism. Its prevalence is taken as a sign of apocalyptic and terrifying change. The sinkhole is the cardinal symbol of the new era of socioecological development, also called the *anthropocene*, a term used by a multidisciplinary and international group of scholars to describe the current globalized era of geological transformation by human intervention. The scope of human impact is unimaginable but experienced in singular events like sinkholes—often the result of the collapse of carbonite rock types eroded by groundwater—capable of swallowing up all that surrounds it. They open up an abyss and act as reminders of the potential human impact on the environment. Some might be natural occurrences but many are often a consequence of human activity. In an article for the *Independent*, James Vincent describes the phenomena in the U.K. as a "plague" in language that aligns the geologic with the epidemiological.[2] These geological deformations predate the 2008 economic crisis, but their surprising and all-consuming ethos make them ready emblems of collapse and economic freefall. In fact, these ruptures in the ground are most prevalent in places hit hardest by economic disaster spurred by the housing market crash, particularly Florida.

What distinguished the 2008 crash from others of its kind was its scale; home ownership expanded rapidly with easy and open access to mortgages in which borrowers obtained loans with no money down, no documentation, and low adjustable interest rates. These borrowers lost their homes quickly when the market, like a sinkhole, blew the ground out from under them. It is no coincidence that Michael Lewis, Wall Street trader turned nonfiction writer and journalist, titles his introduction to an anthology of economic collapse "Inside Wall Street's Black Hole," highlighting the abyss of meaning that the event generated.[3] He describes the panic occasioned by the financial crisis as "sending the market into a bottomless free fall" into which everyone might fall, from the biggest players on Wall Street to "the man on the street." Or as he describes it, the crisis makes no distinction across economic class: "Stan O'Neal, the former CEO of Merrill Lynch, was fired for the same reason the lower-middle-class family in the suburban wasteland between Los Angeles and San Diego may have lost its surprisingly nice home."[4] Homelessness is the emblematic sign of the financial crisis. The sinkhole adds a new dimension to the threat of the loss of one's home; and both of these forms of disasters, economic and ecological, are often consequences of human activity.

The sudden appearance of sinkholes in populated areas is a consequence of human demand for fresh water and commercial development. The geological survey of West-Central Florida describes the phenomena succinctly:

> Induced sinkholes are generally cover-collapse type sinkholes and tend to occur abruptly. The have been forming at increasing rates during the past several decades and pose potential hazards in developed and developing areas of west-central Florida. The increasing incidence of induced sinkholes is expected to continue as our demand for ground-water and land resources increases. Regional declines of ground-water levels increase sinkhole occurrence in sinkhole-prone regions. This becomes more apparent during the natural, recurrence periods of low annual rainfall and drought.[5]

Florida, hit hardest by real estate speculation, boasts an expansive and highly populated coastal area impacted by the twin disasters of global warming and rising sea levels and the high demand for groundwater that creates fissures in the carbonite rock land mass. In fact, West-Central Florida had been dubbed "sinkhole alley" and the rise in insurance claims means an increase in insurance premiums for already taxed homeowners.[6] These geological ruins link ecological crisis with the crises of capitalism. For Eric Zency, the "financial crisis *is* the environmental crisis," which he describes as the juxtaposition of finitude and the infinite, that is the finitude of natural resources against the ambitions of global capitalism to expand without limit.[7]

Few things are as sudden and total as disaster. The sinkhole is more targeted and specific than its disaster kin. Sinkholes personalize and individualize disaster; they appear in residential areas, in houses and yards, opening up abysses capable of consuming people, houses, pets, and cars. The sinkhole craze began in 2013 with the story of Jeff Bush who was "swallowed" by a 30-foot-wide sinkhole in his bed while the rest of his family—four adults, a child, and two dogs—slept in their home east of Tampa, in the dead center of "sinkhole alley." His brother, Jeremy, awoke to a huge chasm in the house: "We heard a loud crash. . . . I ran in there and heard someone screaming, my brother screaming. And all I see is this big hole. All I see is the top of his bed. I didn't see anything else, so I jumped in and tried to get him out. The floor was still giving in and the dirt was still going down, but I didn't care. I wanted to save my brother. I could hear him screaming for me hollering for me. I couldn't do nothing."[8] His story captured the American imagination at a time when people felt overwhelmed and swallowed up by their homes and their underwater loans. The image of someone being literally consumed while they slept unawares was the stuff of nightmares. The news media consistently used language connoting consumption—engulfed, swallowed, consumed—to describe Jeff Bush's fate. Though it should be noted that Jeremy does not use this language, he describes his brother as sinking in the hole in a manner that recalls the properties of quicksand. Yet the former, the language of total and sudden annihilation captures the public mood around the hidden danger lurking in homes.

According to former University of Florida geologist, Tony Randazzo, "losing a house to a sinkhole is very common."[9] As a result, the insurance industry lobbied to change state law to make it more difficult to recover damages from sinkholes. Jeff Bush and his family were victims of these new restrictions. Just months prior to Jeff's death, an agent of the insurance company visited their house to check for evidence of sinkholes and found nothing. Perhaps a testament to the silent and sudden nature of sinkhole appearances, the very idea of the disaster to the Bush household resounded in the entire neighborhood. Neighbor Soliris Gonzalez admits to nightmares and recurrent dreams in which she checks for cracks in her house, terrified the same fate might befall her. She relates fears associated with an experience of the unknowable: "You never know underneath the ground what's happening."[10] Michael Wines describes the scenario with equally evocative terms that he refers to as the "bizarre death of a man who vanished into a huge sinkhole" during "sinkhole season" when "homes, cars, and—rarely—people can drop into the abyss without warning."[11] The language of "abyss" and the unknowable subterranean evokes the metaphysics of some inaccessible imaginary or spiritual world. It also elicits the terror of the unleashed and unrestricted unconscious. The fears around the sinkhole—which the *New York Times* article by Wines is meant to assuage—with the evocation of homes that "drop into the abyss without warning" square neatly with Freud's characterization of the uncanny. The uncanny or the *unheimlich* derives from the rendering of that which is *heimlich*—or the familiar, the homey—into something suddenly unfamiliar, a terrifying shift of something intimately known to something alien or strange.[12] The house that once gave shelter and security suddenly swallows you alive. The stuff, as Jeff Bush's neighbors describe, of nightmares.

Geologists claim that sinkholes have appeared on a daily basis for a long time, but the death of Jeff Bush put them into the news cycle and gave them new publicity. There are a number of events and issues that coalesce into the idea of the sinkhole as a literalization of a complex of abstractions. The sinkhole encapsulates anxieties about sudden loss and powerlessness, particularly the loss of shelter though financial operations too baroque for individual borrowers to fully understand. The individual experience of the global financial crisis is neatly visually symbolized in the catastrophic engulfment of the home. The housing crisis reached epidemic proportions in Florida in a manner more far-ranging than its symbolic kin, the sinkhole. The furor and frenzy over these "natural" disasters or "sinkhole madness" is displaced from their more justifiable but inchoate and multiplex target of the mortgage industry and finance deregulation. The sinkhole is a chasm of the Real, the exposed substrate that threatens the very reality that rests upon it. The Real, for Lacan, is that which cannot be integrated into "reality" and thus is not symbolized but circulates in inchoate and disorganized affects like fears and terrors.[13] Sinkhole news stories avoid the anxiety about individual participation in the degradation of the environment. Yet, the sinkhole is a fantasmatic incarnation of unimaginable fears, suggestive of arbitrarily doled-out metaphysical punishment for human crime. This scenario conceals another possible target of inculpation, that of those at the top of the social order whose actions created the conditions of the abyss into which those in less favorable economic circumstances find themselves and their homes. The news media maintain that the sinkhole is the consequence of an undecidable mix of human and natural causes, making it difficult to locate and identify a remedy or plan of action for reducing their occurrence. Yet in Florida's sinkhole alley, human intervention through overdevelopment, primarily through increased demand for water and sanitation, intensifies the natural vulnerabilities of the carbonite rock and increases the likelihood of sinkhole occurrence.

Aporetic Topoanalysis

The sinkhole is intensely personal, a dark interior with unknown depth, and as such it closely aligns with individual psyches, with the interior and dark spaces of the mind and all that pertains to the self. Thus, its close association with the accoutrements of domestic life: family, house, dog, car, and neighborhood streets. It is often described according to the scale of domestic objects. For example, a chasm that appears in the midst of a city street in southern Illinois is called a "car-sized sinkhole" compared to the dimensions of a Volkswagen.[14] It is highly local and localized even as it points to a larger global order.

Sinkholes into which people, animals, and things meet their demise often are not able to be excavated: they create absences that cannot ever be converted into presence. In the case of Jeff Bush, search crews lowered a camera into the bedroom chasm to investigate but found no signs of life and were forced to abandon their search. Terrifyingly, sinkholes are capable of consuming and metabolizing all that falls into them in a manner that is both simple and definitive. It offers a rich metaphor that evokes a complex array of ideas and affects, particularly that of aporia in the end-times. Jeff Bush's story elicits public fascination for the idea that he was taken completely unaware from an intimate space in his home while he slept. While it was a chasm that opened up under the house that consumed him, the house conflates with the sinkhole as similar and overlapping interior spaces. The house as an outward projection of inner psychic life is the very stuff of dreams, fantasies, and fiction. In Toni Morrison's *Beloved*, the house itself, in the opening gambit, is a figure and space of the fiction. It is full of spite as the embodiment of a family and community caught in the aftermath of the violence of racial capitalism. Bachelard takes the topos of the house as a symbolic template for the integration of space and psyche. It is a space that gathers and integrates memories and fantasies or dreams; it "shelters daydreams" and "protects the dreamer." For him, "the house is one of the greatest powers of integration for the thoughts, memories, and dreams of mankind."[15] Topoanalysis, an adjunct of psychoanalysis, is concerned with how spaces are imbued with psychic meaning and thus demand hermeneutic excavation. Home and hearth delimit inside from outside in a metaphysics that encapsulates both conscious and unconscious realms. Bachelard describes this space by its "maternal features," all-encompassing and nurturing, a "material paradise."[16] By extension, in the gendered language of this characterization, the house might also be imagined as vulnerable, permeable, and in need of protection. It is imagined as a domestic space identified with femininity as its territorial and private domain cordoned off from the public life and space coded as zones of masculinity.

The sinkhole puts intimate spaces at risk. It represents a rupture in the very ground of the home. It captures the "dreams of mankind" in the contemporary era in which the house is a complex source of anxious fantasy as the sign of the end, a symbol of imminent apocalypse. The anxieties elicited by this earthly chasm are associated with a fear of absorption, inundation, and dissolution. The sinkhole threatens the house and is identified with it in a terrifying collapse of interior and exterior. It demands a rethinking of identity by tearing a hole in the fabric of known territory, suffering its residents to be engulfed, displaced, or to reinhabit the interior space of home and self.

Sinkholes Will Save Your Life

In *This Book Will Save Your Life*, divorced white yuppie Richard Novak is introduced through his home of which he is "captain, lord, master, prisoner of his own making."[17] Though the novel takes place prior to the full-scale economic disaster of 2008, it is about the personal catastrophe of a life lived in pursuit of wealth as evinced by the ultimate of consumer goods, a luxury home full of Rothkos and de Koonings nestled in the hills of a prestigious neighborhood in Los Angeles. He experiences the home as an atomizing prison from which the sudden appearance of a sinkhole liberates him, initiates a reordering of his life, and exposes him to new associations with an ethnic and racialized underclass, and with his neighbors. This is momentous, given that—as Bret Easton Ellis metaphorizes in *Less than Zero*—people in L.A. are afraid to merge.[18] The sinkhole allegorizes Richard's disorientation in his life and a sense that something has already shifted but is not consciously known to him:

> Yesterday seems realer than real, a dream, an accident, like some sort of seizure or suspension. Did something happen?
> There is a depression in the earth, a large soft circular indentation that he doesn't remember from the day before. He looks at it, mentally measuring—approximately eight feet in diameter, about fifty feet from the house. Where did it come from? How long has it been there? How would he describe it? Like the mark made by the back of an enormous ladle pressed into the earth. Do things like that happen overnight?[19]

His disorientation is symbolized by the abyss that opens outside his home and jolts him from his dreamlike existence and the unthinking pursuit of wealth and accumulation of goods. The story links the opening of the sinkhole with the emergence of the disordering of capitalism on a personal level.

Richard experiences a disorienting intellectual and physical disquiet in the form of idiopathic and generalized bodily pain that he believes is causing his death. The description of the pain is less physical than existential: "a rupture, an explosion, a slow, tortured death."[20] He is delivered to the hospital after a desperate 911 call and when they find nothing, he is released the following day with a sense of uncertainty and a mood of adventure in pursuit of an uncharted path. His first stop is at a donut shop, a strictly forbidden food in his low-carbohydrate diet. His personal freefall occasions a disruption to his habits and isolation through openness to others and a global view that decenters the United States as a point of reference. He meets the donut shop owner, Anhil, who delivers vital lessons on U.S. chauvinism. Anhil opines that "In America everybody is somebody. They have so much and they all want more. In my country we are all nobodies; it's easier."[21] This friendship is enabling and nurturing for Richard in a manner that reflects a similar dynamic of the global North to the global South. Anhil is **an instrument of his transformation and a proto-therapeutic** support; he listens to Richard's neurotic rants, makes him an off-the-menu hearty breakfast, and encourages him to relax his rules and restrictions. He urges Richard **to break from his culturally bound norms of disavowal and avoidance**, asking: "Explain, why does everyone in America pretend to be blind? They practice not seeing. They get into the car and they call someone on the cell phone. They are afraid to be alone but they don't see the people around them."[22] Richard takes in this defamiliarizing view, which triggers the series of changes that alienate him from his former life. In exchange, Richard lends Anhil access to his affluence, letting him drive his Mercedes Benz. His entire life is a diorama of wealth and affluence, his personal interpretation of "a good life," and an ordered and affectless world:

> The brushed stainless-steel kitchen gave off a modern, reflectionless, dull shine. Everything was in order, perfectly placed, perfectly clean. To the left was the living room, matching white sofas, an Eames chair, glass-topped coffee table, handmade Belgian shaggy rug. Each item chosen for its beauty, its perfection. These were the things he wanted: controlled, precise, ordered. He had bought them when he moved here. On the walls were paintings, important paintings, paintings that museums wanted. It was part of his plan when he moved to Los Angeles. He told himself he was setting up a new life, a good life, and he wanted beautiful/important things to be a part of it. He told himself that he'd worked hard and should surround himself with proof of his hard work, his assets. He should surround himself with art, so that in some way he himself would become art.[23]

Just as the art is museum-grade and a commodity, he himself sought unwittingly to become, in Marx's prophetic words, a commodity among commodities. Yet this is not the source of total devastation for him, he interprets his downward turn as propitious and promising. As the sinkhole deepens he opines: "Was it foolish to think that even when everything fell apart it was luck?"[24] He stands to gain a broader perspective from his loss of position; his downward spiral puts him in contact with people and takes him out of his habitual order. And like other white protagonists of postcrisis popular cultural productions, his downturn is a source of new opportunities.

The sinkhole becomes the occasion for community gathering as a gaggle of neighbors work together to extract a horse that has fallen into its depths. The scene is so ludicrous and spectacular that those passing by mistake it for a movie shoot. The various neighbors gathered at the sinkhole use their Hollywood industry skills—e.g., stunt director—for actual and practical purposes. The indictment of Hollywood and Los Angeles as its command center and enabling context is a staple of disaster stories. This scenario taps into a popular moral sentiment that the movie industry is the source of the ideological troubles of capitalism and generates much of its structuring fantasies. In the novel, putting the Hollywood image makers to work on an actual crisis registers as a kind of existential justice again signified and brought about by the sinkhole, which, in this case, opens a chasm in the imagoscapes of Hollywood, one that must be addressed and remedied by irksome physical labors.

The sinkhole precipitates Richard's descent and dovetails with the cultural preoccupation with the freefall as a source of sublime freedom and terror: "He dreams of falling through space. He dreams he is pulled towards a spherical surface, a horizon, a boundary. He realizes that once you cross the boundary there is no escape: it is destiny, there is no way out."[25] The sinkhole concretizes the existential abyss or aporia as a falling without limit, freefalling, popularized in Tom Petty's song by the same name, evoking both disorientation and freedom from which "there is no escape." This is the primary sense of end-of-the-world stories. The novel was published in 2006, a time leading up to the economic crisis, yet it captures the cultural ethos of the end-times and disillusionment with the culture of capitalism. Capitalism is likened to a game, a mugs game, in which winning is a kind of losing, gaining money leads to alienation and objectification. Richard describes how he accrued wealth to gain the attention of those around him, including his wife, which results in further alienation:

> She threw herself into work—determined that, one way or another, she would get exactly what she wanted—and he quickly felt left out. In an effort to do good, to get her attention, he too threw himself into work, and it became all about the money, making enough to impress her and then enough to protect himself, and then just raking it in, making money from money. There was so much money out there, money that could be his for just having an opinion, a point of view,

making a good guess. It was the game of money, the fun of money, it was addictive, and he kept winning. He'd tell himself that he'd won two million dollars, he'd won a big bonus, he'd won the admiration of all of those around him who took it to heart, who took it seriously, who got eaten up by it. It's a game, he told everyone—it doesn't mean you don't want to win, but you have to be willing to lose, you have to not take it personally. It's only paper.[26]

Richard echoes the infamous tagline spoken by Gordon Gekko in the capitalist primer *Wall Street* (1987), "greed is good," but infuses the sentiment with levity. Richard's strivings are not as much a sum zero game in which someone wins at someone else's expense, instead the wages of his ambition register in his physical body, in idiopathic symptoms and general disorientation. In fact, his musings about his success at the game of capitalism are done while he is being examined on the flatbed of a scanner in the hospital.

The novel exposes the myths of affluence as attainment by making ecological disaster symbolize personal catastrophe, issued as a kind of warning in advance of more dire events. The title of the novel—*This Book Will Save Your Life*—indicates the optimistic interpretation of the sinkhole as a personal abyss that is ultimately filled but does not conceal the larger and more pressing ecological concerns related to the sewage system in Los Angeles. Drawing out the analogy presented through Richard's story, the sinkhole is a node within a larger network and system, just as the home, the site of Richard's personal wealth, is one node in the entire faltering and rapacious system of capitalism consolidated in symbolic and actual ways in the city and its industries. He tries to define his life and save his life outside of the structures of capitalism, but he ultimately fails.

Like its disaster genre kin, the novel alludes hypothetically to the end of the world, signaled by an electrical grid failure that maroons Richard, his ex-wife, and his teenage son in their hotel room. A sense of doom draws them closer:

> "Well, I just wanted to say that if this was the end of the world, right now, it would be OK with me," Ben says.
> "If this was the end of the world, I personally would wonder what was going to happen next—the world as we know it is not all that there is; there is more, something larger than any of us," Richard says.[27]

Richard's ex-wife is resistant to his musings about the "end of the world as we know it" and is the least willing to reflect on her choices; she fills her time with endless work and is numb to the world around her. Her response to Richard is in keeping with this position: "If this was the end of the world," she says, interrupting, "I would stay up talking to you, but it's not, so I'm going to lie down."[28]

The "end" of Los Angeles is that which causes sinkholes, the demand for water and increased septic removal, an underground network of water delivery and removal. This "sense of an ending," to borrow the language of Frank Kermode's work, informs and energizes a narrative structure that arcs toward finality in the Judeo-Christian mythopoetics. It is part of a story and storied tradition that, while premised on finitude and finality, points to a tradition of immanence. The novel even ends this way. Richard is swept out to sea, marooned in the Pacific, driven out by the encroaching fires on land. He is floating free in the water: "From the beach, looking back, the sky is glowing yellow, like the end of the world." He appears in news footage on CNN watched by his wife and son, but as the cameras turn elsewhere and his family can no longer see him, he says prophetically, ending the novel, "I'll always be here, even when you can't see me, I'm still here."[29]

The sinkhole is becoming more and more prevalent the world over. It is voracious, consuming animals, cars, houses, and people: a family dog in Florida, a snowplow in New Jersey, a couple walking down the street in Seoul, an entire town in Louisiana, a building in Guatemala city, eight cars in the national Corvette museum in Kentucky, among many other occurrences. It is a reminder that the earth, even in its most industrialized and ordered zones, is not safe. It opens up the discourse of disaster; the etymology of which traces the singular event of the unraveling of a star, just as the sinkhole is a singular event of epic proportions and wide-ranging consequence. Disaster, described paradoxically by Maurice Blanchot, is something that "ruins everything, all the while leaving everything intact." And recursively, it does not impact "anyone in particular" but "threatens in me that which is exterior to me." The sinkhole is a species of disaster, total, ruinous of everything, and a terrible harbinger of devastation to come, capable of initiating a seismic shift in the ideological order. It evokes fears of sudden collapse while it opens the way for redemption from total destruction, as a warning sign of environmental degradation and the possibility of forestalling it. The car, person, or dog vanish in the sinkhole abyss as a warning, as a symbolic canary in the mine. At least this is the sentiment in Homes's story about how the appearance of a sinkhole initiates a number of changes for a mainstream white male protagonist in an abyss of stultifying affluence.

In most cases, the sinkhole is a consequence of the interaction of natural environment and human technology. It is a symptom with multiple and sometimes unlocatable origins, but it remains a sign of the collapse of the ecosystem without ever directly referring to it. The sinkhole evokes a number of fears none of which seem related to the end-times, catastrophe or large-scale crisis. This may explain its lack of appeal as disaster film fodder for Hollywood. It is not sufficiently apocalyptic and does not accrue to catastrophe. Yet, unlike stories of complete disaster oriented toward the future, the sinkhole is about the imminent present.

Global Realignment

The sinkhole is perhaps a strange bedfellow of the end-of-the-world film. It is an actual instantiation of the disavowed spectacular fantasy of capitalist-induced ecological decline. Its persistence across time, the abyss it opens up in the earth around us, in our home, turns the fantasies of doomsday stories into everyday realities, and these miniature abysses might be viewed as harbingers of global catastrophe. This is evident in the description of the sinkhole in a popular article aimed at educating and informing the public, but not before alarming them. The article is titled "Beware! You Can Sink into the Earth" and begins with the following scenario using the same rhetorical tropes reserved for horror films: "If you stand in front of a four-story building and you were praising the elegant beauty and good fortune (of) its occupants then it is not unusual, but in the very next moment if you observe the appearance of a wide and deep pit in the same place, it will definitely be very terrifying."[30]

The sinkhole brings the large-scale and overwhelming ideas about ecological disaster home, literally into our homes and neighborhoods. It opens rifts and symbolic aporias across the landscape of mass culture. It is a major coordinate in the fantasmatic appreciation of the end of capitalism in the literal ruptures in the fabric of reality, its earth cover. In *2012*, the cataclysmic prophesy of the end of the world is initially evident through the rifts in street surfaces in Los Angeles and promises the very disintegration that they presage. These earth surface ruptures are signs that there is no escape and point to the ecological limits of the expansion of capitalism; they are ruptures in its smooth veneer. Insofar as the home—one's home—is an external projection, following Bachelard, of subjective interiority and integrated into a financial market, it signifies individual intimacy with capitalism. The rupture within the home or community, at the very center of it, the threat of being consumed or engulfed without warning registers as the terrifying and arbitrary threat of the forces of capitalism. While sinkholes bring cultural fears home, disaster films provide a larger template and global structure for these concerns while offering a false remedy drawn from other disaster storylines, particularly that of the deus ex machina providing a Noah's ark for escape and survival that derives from the collaboration of various industries and institutions of capitalism—major space or seafaring ships created from the most cutting-edge technologies.

Figure 5.1. Global catastrophe in *2012* (2009).

Day after Tomorrow was released following the Argentine economic crisis within a general mood of economic instability in the Americas and increased Northerly migration and fears of a refugee crisis. It is about a shocking ecological collapse in the abrupt climate shift that puts the northern parts of the globe into an "ice age" while the southern parts maintain relatively stable conditions. The disaster creates what the main character, a paleoclimatologist, calls a "global realignment." Disasters are but a preview of a larger global collapse and cause a disorienting disruption of all that is known. This is made evident by the way that the family unit is torn asunder by the impending storm. The father, paleoclimatologist Jack Hall (Dennis Quaid), leads the team investigating the rapid climate change, while his son, Sam (Jake Gyllenhaal), flies to New York (in the worst turbulence in the history of aviation) to compete in an academic decathlon. Jack's wife, Lucy (Sela Ward), remains home. The plot is about reuniting this family, and the father goes to great lengths, traveling in subzero weather where exposure leads to immediate death, to reunite with his son. The film puts the refugee crisis in heteronormative terms—where the family is proxy for the state and its extraordinary effort to restabilize.

Day after Tomorrow is explicit in its message about debt across the hemisphere where the United States is in a position of advantage. The apogee of the climate crisis creates a flood of mass migration from the United States into Mexico to the point that Mexico has to shut down its northern border. In order to convince Mexico to open its borders, the United States agrees to forgive "all Latin American debt." This is a fascinating political agreement for a number of reasons. First of all, it imagines a totalizable and wholly integrated "Latin America" of which Mexico is a part and perhaps even a leader. It recognizes the leading role the United States has in the creation of hemispheric indebtedness and northern political advantage. It reverses the power relationship of the United States to Latin America in a way that shores up and highlights the colonial and imperial role of the Colossus of the North.

Though the environmental disaster is global, the remedy is found in the global South, and the solution engineered by the United States, allegorized by the core U.S. family and its paleoclimatologist patriarch. Those fleeing from the United States find themselves in Mexican refugee centers and the sitting U.S. president gives his national address from Mexican soil. The message is one of hemispheric integration, while the storyline is about a single Anglo and U.S.-based hero whose work leads to a (short-term) solution. Redemption via reuniting with family for the protagonists in *Day after Tomorrow*, when the paleoclimatologist saves the world and his son, sends the message that it is not too late to stop climate change and restore global order. This is a commonplace of the genre.

Disaster films constitute a genre that, while broad-ranging, overlap with other film types. Maurice Yacowar distinguishes eight basic types of disaster films that exploit audience fascination with the "vision of massive doom" and in which a "situation of normalcy erupts into a persuasive image of death."[31] The eight types he identifies along with a number of subcategories for each are: natural attack, ship of fools, city fails, monster, survival, war, historical, and comic. Likewise, Susan Sontag examines the historical shifts in genre cycles that trace cultural mood and establish the main preoccupations of a given period. Stephen Keane draws on these and other critics in his account of disaster films from their earliest appearance until 2006. He explores the complex interaction of industrial and ideological formations of the genre. For instance, the formation of a genre might follow industrial rather than cultural demands. While films tend to reflect cultural obsessions, a single successful film might inspire copycats that could create a new genre or reanimate one considered long obsolete.

Keane argues, following other film critics, that disaster films emerge and are popular during times of crisis and offer remedies or solutions for large-scale catastrophe, usually through the survival of a representative group of characters. These films raise questions of who will survive and why. The trials and tests these characters face are a sign of the major anxieties of the time. Their success at solving major problems quells fears of overwhelming social upheavals and crises.

The Ends of Capitalism

Disaster films are about the end, the end-times, and doomsday predictions. The cross-platform promotion and spin around the 2009 release of the film *2012* primed audiences for anxious anticipation of the actual Mayan calendar date of December 21, 2012. Like many other disaster films, *2012* delights in destroying Los Angeles, while its storyline is a mix of doomsday prophesy, distrust of government, U.S. imperialism, the end of capitalism, Mayan prophesy, and ecological devastation. The film combines all the eschatological theories and proto-scientific prophesies that were circulating at the time. Researcher of Mayan astronomy, Anthony Aveni, gathered many of these popular preconceptions in the following list:

> The great May lord will make everything die.
> The world as we know it will come to an end.
> Damaging sunspots will reach their peak.
> The Cosmic Shaman of Galactic culture offers us clues for healing the planet which will be destroyed if we don't act now.
> The solar system will enter an energetically hostile part of the galaxy.
> Mass extinction will take place.
> Yellowstone will explode.
> The earth's magnetic poles will reverse.
> We may get sucked into a black hole.[32]

Almost all of these ideas are manifest in the film as themes or plotpoints, thus intensifying the confusion around the meaning of the date for the ancient civilization. Instead, the film is more linked to other disaster films, particularly *Interstellar* (2014), for its preoccupation with survival and survivalism, which, for Stephen Keane, engages the ethical and political question of who gets to board the biblical ark that will people the new iteration of earth after the global catastrophe. In *2012*, the price of the ticket for entry to one of these ships is a billion euros, thus the new society is for the rich and well-connected or, as the film suggests, those with enough grit and perseverance to become a stowaway.

The Mayan story is instrumentalized as a culturally significant signpost and symbolic date that is eclipsed by Judeo-Christian myths and tropes, particularly Armageddon, Noah's Ark, and the book of Revelations. The movie constitutes a popular text for working through anxieties and fears about the end-of-the-world order based on capitalism and its forms of hegemony. The biblical storyline dovetails with the American frontier myth in which the desire for freedom is thwarted by the encroachment of big government. It adds a new-fangled idea to the mix: the complex interaction of ecological and capitalist catastrophe. Like its disaster film kin, *2012* engages new anxieties but proffers conservative and well-worn solutions through the return to the patriarchal security state.

Posteconomic crisis disaster films partake in a different sense of the endtimes for their reflection, if passing, on the end of an entire system: capitalism. These films capture the public mood about the failures of capitalism more than films that explicitly thematize these failures via the downfall of its cornerstone institutions, the banks. But in contradistinction to fictional and nonfictional **stories of sinkholes, disaster films offer a conservative and recupera**tive storyline about restoration of a better state, one with less resources but a more "pure" governmental apparatus, bounded and secure, whose citizens have less **mobility and freedom.**

Both *The Day after Tomorrow* and *2012* explore the consequences of the complete and total destruction of the earth. The *Day after Tomorrow* is an ecological disaster film that issues a warning that has more to do with the fears around climate change and less about the then-nascent economic disaster encroaching on the United States. In a study based on a survey of filmgoers in the U.K., the research group TDAT, Tyndall Centre for Climate Change Research, found that the film did change audience perceptions of climate change, but only in the short term; the film ultimately enabled an overall position of disavowal:

> Viewers were significantly more concerned not only about climate change, but also about other environmental risks such as biodiversity loss and radioactive waste disposal. However, the portrayal of extreme events in the film also confused people: they believed extreme climate impacts were less likely, and would not be experienced within their lifetime, after seeing the film.[33]

Instead viewers need "specific guidelines" and examples of what to do to mitigate climate change. While this is true and provides a reasonable remedy for changing individual behavior, ecological devastation is the result of deep and intransigent ideologically charged institutional practices rooted in capitalism. Short of a complete disruption or even termination of the system of capitalism as it is currently structured, little will change the human relationship to the environment. Disaster films are fundamentally conservative and fail to transform audience capitalist consciousness; in fact, they are enmeshed in the very institution responsible for ecological disaster, the pursuit of profit. Audience engagement and interest is proportionate to the intensity of the affect elicited by the story, which corresponds to a larger profit margin. Such was the case with *The Day after Tomorrow*, which cost $125 million to make and grossed about $187 million in the United States alone.[34] Director Roland Emmerich, who helmed a number of blockbuster disaster films, including *Day after Tomorrow* and *Independence Day* (1996), refers to other films for ideas about how to submerge New York City under water after a massive tidal wave, and yet his concerns turn to the man-made disasters besetting the city: "Of course if that much water did hit New York the city would be absolutely flattened, but you have to be a little sensitive after September 11th. I finally felt that setting the film in another city would be an even bigger problem, because then the terrorists would have influenced where the catastrophe of weather strikes." He notes that the choice of New York City is itself a sign of post-9/11 patriotism and defiance against terrorists: "One shot in our movie, where the Statue of Liberty comes out of the snow, is nearly exactly the same [as that in *Independence Day*]." But he frames this shot differently to foreground the torch in the statue that is still high in the air and thus presents an image of hope and defiance.[35]

2012 was also a box office success. The story is based on fears of the Mayan warning of a global apocalypse on December 12, 2012, and follows this ominous interpretation of the Mayan calendar, which actually indicates an end to only a significant cycle of time. The marketing campaign for the film, which issued the ominous and evocative proclamation, "We were warned," is calculated to alarm and scandalize. The storyline has several strands, but the core story is that of an absent divorced father and aspiring less-than-successful-writer. His ex-wife holds him in low esteem for his struggles to meet his parental obligations. Another storyline follows Dr. Adrian Helmsley, a geologist who is both a scientist and an everyman with little concern for the elitism of a black-tie affair held in Washington's exclusive circles. He crashes the party to bring alarming news to Carl Anheuser, a key member of President Thomas Wilson's cabinet. He becomes an immediate hero who is shown taking a stand, pleading to high-level officials to recognize that a cataclysmic event will take place to end the world. Yet, there is a state-level refusal to disseminate this information, immediately and significantly linking power with knowledge. The message is not a doomsday prophesy, as was the popular interpretation of the Mayan date in 2012; instead, it was the unassailable work of science. The storyline combines fears of doomsday prophesies and global ecological fears; the latter, unlike *Day after Tomorrow*, is not linked to human activity but deemed an "irregularity" and an atypical sequence of events. Emmerich shifts entirely away from fears of climate change and environmental damage to the mythopoetics and cycles of time typical of religious and spiritual apocalyptic narratives.

The disaster film points generally to a cultural moment of crisis. The 1970s witnessed intensified cultural anxiety about the upheavals that began in the 1960s along with the twin threats of inflation and job loss. For Michael Ryan and Douglas Kellner, disaster films were popular during this era for their moorings in traditional genre and the ritualized approach to resolving cultural crises and neutralizing anxieties, particularly those generated by social revolution in gender, racial, and sexual norms: civil rights, feminism, and gay and lesbian rights. These films typically posit a world of predisaster normalcy around a traditional patriarchal familiar order, which the disaster upends. A group of characters exhibit grit and survivalist skills to restore the social order in a narrative arc of "stasis, crisis, and resolution," which projects a "psychology of fear, disconfidence, and yearning for help."[36] The solution is engineered by a strong male leader who not only restores confidence in the U.S. political system but ensures the reproduction of its white male heteropatriarchal tenets. Keane notes that, like the 1950s, there was a spike in popularity of the disaster film in the 1970s, and again in the 1990s, noting that twenty-one films were released during the peak year of 1998. The 1990s films recycle the generic anxieties of earlier decades but are much more focused on the end-times as represented by the end of the millennium. Two more cycles of popular filmmaking would follow this trend, post-9/11, 2001, of the early 2000s leading up to 2012, and the films following the "end of capitalism" after the 2008 global economic crisis. In some cases, as with *2012*, all of these "end of time" events would coalesce into an overall sense of imminent doom.

No other director is as clued into public anxieties as Roland Emmerich. Keane foregrounds his 1996 feature, *Independence Day*, as a key feature of the 1990s disaster film that is about the end of the earth and mankind under threat of alien attack. Kim Newman, in his review of apocalypse movies, finds the film a combination of an "atrocious script," "a deadening dose of religiosity" and an "even more crippling orgy of red-white-blue pride."[37] He notes its relevance in cues from 1950s disaster films but points out that it ups the special-effects ante, delivering a spectacular anxiety-provoking ride that ends in decisive victory and patriotic chauvinism. Films that followed the attack on the World Trade Center and the Pentagon—significant symbols and targets in disaster films—were more sobering in tone and often more global in both the presentation of the impact of the effects of the catastrophe and in the collaborative efforts among nations in crisis management and remedy, though they show the United States taking the lead in these efforts—this is evident in *Day after Tomorrow* and *World War Z* (2013). *Independence Day* takes place in New York City and, according to Keane, rather than destroying iconic buildings and monuments, leaves them intact, in particular the Statue of Liberty mentioned earlier that rises out of the disaster zone as a "beacon of hope."[38]

Hollywood disaster films about ecological disasters are spectacular displays about man-made disasters that symbolize other kinds of man-made disasters, such as those generated by economic policies. These films are typically global for the international impact of large-scale disasters, while the United States remains the primary point of reference in a way that reinforces ideas about its role as the global police force. Disaster narratives in U.S. entertainment and news media produce discourses about the virtues and indomitability of imperial capitalism. For instance, in *Day after Tomorrow*, the responsibility for the effects of global warming are with the United States and Washington, and its intellectual capital must be applied to it. Disaster stories rejuvenate capitalism against decline and prop up U.S. power and exceptionalism in the face of international cooperation. They spectacularize the end-times only to offer redemption based on the rehabilitation of U.S.-based capitalism and remedies in the habitation of other planets—as in *Interstellar* (2014)—or the improbable restoration of order and stasis. They offer storylines of disavowal and denial that forestall action or enduring realizations about the role of human endeavor in environmental destruction. Whereas, the sinkhole, more prevalent in popular news media than entertainment genres, signifies a very different imagined rapport to the environment. The sinkhole is both natural and man-made, random and the consequence of human planning. It is unpredictable and thus terrifying, capable of opening an abyss in the very space of the home and of consuming domestic objects, animals, people, and cars. In Homes's story, the sinkhole metaphorizes the complete disruption of the protagonist's life and social world; it occasions a new relationship to the accoutrements and symbols of capitalism and to capitalism itself. The story ends without remedy, without recourse, with the protagonist adrift, floating toward an uncertain future beyond his home and the illusory ground of capitalism.

Disaster stories spectacularize the global impact of environmental catastrophe and elicit fears of the human precipitation of the end of the earth, and these spectacles are so terrifying, so completely overwhelming and fantastical, that they cannot be integrated into the spectator's lifeworld. These images and ideas encourage disavowal more than action and tend to occasion narratives of redemption. Yet the sinkhole, still to be fully exploited by Hollywood film and television culture, appears in personal and individuated disaster forms capable of disrupting reality, of opening up an abyss in everything we think we know. It is a potent symbol of the unimaginable consequences of the economic freefall that seemed to hail the demise of capitalism or at least capitalism as we know it.

The sinkhole is a communal event that often demands family, neighbor, community, and city involvement. This is evident in the case of Jeff Bush in an ongoing saga, whose family home was again threatened by a sinkhole in 2015 and for the protagonist of *This Book Will Save Your Life*, in which the occasion of a sinkhole drags him out of his solipsistic isolation. The sinkhole is experienced as a personal or individual crisis metonymic of ruination on a larger scale in a way that follows the course of the social impact of the Great Recession. The economic crisis intensified economic distress already set in motion by capitalist developments that caused individual ruin to domino into the collapse of entire cities like San Bernadino, Sacramento, and Detroit. And no other city was more emblematic of the crisis than Detroit. In popular stories about the economic collapse, Detroit would symbolize the rise, fall, and rise again of capitalism.

CHAPTER 6

Imperial Ruins and Resurgence

> The state of ruin is essentially a temporary situation that happens at some point, the volatile result of a change of era and the fall of empires. Ruins are a fantastic land where one no longer knows whether reality slips into dream or whether, on the contrary, dream makes a brutal return into the most violent of realities. Therefore they appear to be a natural and sublime demonstration of our human destinies and of their paradoxes, a dramatization of our creative and self-destructive vanities.
>
> —Yves Marchand and Romain Meffre, *The Ruins of Detroit*

U.S. ruins, those of pre-Columbian Native Americans and of early settler colonialists along with the modern ruins of postindustrial cities, are replaced by a new variety as a consequence of the Great Recession. These are the remains of arrested real estate development and massive foreclosures that emptied towns and cities and left behind abandoned buildings, houses, and vacant storefronts. The economic crisis was fundamentally a housing crisis. It raised questions about housing as it comes to bear on questions of dwelling and how we occupy space. It inspired the Occupy Movement that, among other things, demanded mass habitation of public space to make visible those marginalized and oppressed by decisions made by the top echelons of the economic order. These actions promoted resistance through occupation as a critique of the entire neoliberal ideological system.

In 2008, Detroit became a symbol of the economic freefall, and its ruins, deserted factories, abandoned houses, were a harbinger of the end of capitalism and a sign of "urban death." Detroit dramatizes many of the symptoms of the financial crisis, particularly as they relate to housing and dwelling. While it is known for its car industry, it is also the municipality with the highest rate of home ownership. It is the symbol of the role of housing in the United States as a city that led the nation in homeownership and, by 2008, in foreclosures. And there is no better example of the spectacle of the economic freefall than the decades-long descent of the city of Detroit into bankruptcy. The city experienced a fall from the height of wealth in the machine age to the depths of racialized poverty. The ruination of the city began in the 1967 race riots that spurred a white flight to the suburbs, thereby decimating the tax structure that sustains the services of the urban center. The signing of the North American Free Trade Agreement in 1994 set off another series of disastrous consequences in the hemorrhaging of car manufacturing jobs south of the border where the Big Three automakers fled unions, enjoyed tax breaks, exploited low-wage labor, and avoided strict environmental regulations. By 2013, Detroit became the largest municipality to file for bankruptcy. The cycle of racialized poverty and deindustrialization spiraled to its lowest possible level. These were the wages of what Naomi Klein calls "disaster capitalism."[1]

Detroit is a site that reveals the racialization of capitalism, its promise and mythos, and its global expansion and the devastation it leaves in its wake. Marginal populations are instrumentalized as totems of national blight. It is also a symbolic center of capitalism's story as one based on the cyclical patterns of nature. Organic metaphors inform and drive the story of capitalism as the natural order of things, subject to the forces of entropy but always renewable. Even without infusions of capital, Detroit's recovery was afoot, not in actual terms, but in the phantom speculations of storyville. Stories of recurrence and return are part of the mythos of capitalism. The boom and bust cycles of capitalism are merely moments in an ongoing and endless cycle of ruin and resurgence and of death and rebirth.

After the Great Recession, stories and images about the ruins of Detroit were as prevalent as the idea of the city's resurgence. From the art and writing about city ruins by Camilo Vergara and Marchand and Meffre, to autopsies of dead cities in Charlie LeDuff's *Detroit: An American Autopsy*, to the optimistic stories of urban renewal in the DIY movement, Detroit allegorizes the story of capitalism and its organic cycles of life, death, and rebirth. Jim Jarmusch's *Only Lovers Left Alive* (2013) uses the ruins of Detroit to imagine a different storyline and mythos in which the past and obsolete ideas and technologies reside in the present, albeit one populated by white characters making use of racialized aesthetic forms. It is not the capitalist story of supercession and renewal but of a supersaturated and deeply historical present that resists the linear course of progress and renovation. Likewise, the documentary *Detropia* (2012), by Rachel Grady and Detroit native Heidi Ewing, eschews the language and logic of renewal and rebirth in their account of Detroit residents trying to make their immediate conditions livable. The film documents and visually preserves abandoned spaces and the people who remain after widespread and ongoing flight from the city. *Only Lovers Left Alive* and *Detropia* refuse to accept the inevitability of the "lifecycles" of capitalism that justifies the creative destruction of the city and marginalization of the poor and people of color to make way for new developments. These stories imagine another possible storyline and future, one not based on the logic of capitalism and "natural" cycles of ruin and resurgence.

Ruin Porn

There is an ongoing cultural fascination with the ruins of Detroit as a postindustrial landscape riddled with empty lots and abandoned buildings. These zones are framed for an objectifying tourist gaze as "ruin porn," as the off-scene places exposing some intimate and obscene reality about the U.S. industrial past. They are signs of an era of overweening economic growth given way to globalization of production, the fall of the housing market, racialized poverty, and white flight suburbanization. Photographer Camilo Vergara documents ruins in Detroit and various cities in the United States over an extended period of time as spectacular signs of lapsed greatness. Other artists fascinated with the decline of the city make explicit reference to empire. The French artists Marchand and Meffre, in *The Ruins of Detroit*, argue that ruin is the consequence of the "fall of empires" and they describe the city as a "contemporary Pompeii."[2] In the introduction to their work, Thomas J. Sugrue notes: "The abandoned factories, the eerily vacant schools, the rotting houses, and gutted skyscrapers that Yves Marchand and Romain Meffre chronicle in the following pages are the artifacts of Detroit's astonishing rise as a global capital of capitalism and its even more extraordinary descent into ruin, a place where the boundaries between the American dream and the American nightmare, between prosperity and poverty, between the permanent and the ephemeral are powerfully and painfully visible. No place epitomizes the creative and destructive forces of modernity more than Detroit, past and present."[3] *Ruins of Detroit* locates the city within the global historical narrative of the ruins of empires, using Rome and European heritage sites as points of reference.

Camilo Vergara's take on Detroit is slightly different from other artistic renderings of U.S. ruins. His story of the city begins in the Americas. He tacitly absorbs U.S. cities, Detroit and other postindustrial zones, into a trans-American narrative, describing how his provenance in a small town in Chile shapes his aesthetic vision and authorial gaze. Vergara roots his fascination with ruination in the United States in his family's change in circumstance in Chile of the 1950s that left them impoverished. His family sold off their luxury furnishings and depended on extended family to fund private school and for the necessities of daily living. He attributes to this demotion in status his distaste for "objects of value" and an attraction to things that are "shunned, falling apart, and changing."[4] He omits from his story the political and cultural climate of the 1950s, particularly for a nation struggling with its relationship to the United States, a place to which Latin American elite would have ready access as part of the dynamics of U.S. imperialism. For the United States, Latin America served as a crucible of empire through military interventions and covert operations, economic coercion through aid and trade agreements, the soft power of popular culture, and collaboration and cooperation between the economic elites of the North and the South.[5]

Significantly, Vergara's vantage is that of a Chilean who, upon arrival to the United States for a university education, finds "an immensely wealthy, self-confident, and energetic nation."[6] And while he does not explicitly state his aim as such, he proceeds to expose the opposite of his original impressions of the colossus of the North. While many note that his work falls into the genre of "ruin porn," it is also work that tacitly reveals an anti-imperial gaze, one that exposes the failed ambitions of empire and the disregard for racialized populations who are marooned when the tide of industrialization recedes.

In *American Ruins*, Vergara insists on Detroit as an "American Acropolis" and proposes preserving the abandoned skyline in its current state as an "urban ruins park" and monument to the U.S. industrial past. He notes that the response to this idea is outrage: "My proposal of keeping twelve square blocks south and west of Grand Circus Park as an American Acropolis—that is, to allow the present skyscraper graveyard to become a park of ripe ruins—is seen by most as at best a misguided and at worse a cruel joke."[7] He finds no support for this idea but continues to elaborate on it: "Yet I am unable to give up the vision of an American Acropolis. . . . Why can't the planned rebuilding take place *around* the ruins, as it has in Rome? . . . In downtown Detroit, as in Rome, it is still possible to marvel at the crumbling of such essential pieces of urban history. Are these not places where we can meditate on progress?"[8] While he notes the polarized image of the United States as reflected in a city that embodies progress and decay, the two extremes are not directly linked: "While the United States remains a leader in industry and technology, it also now leads the world in the number, size, and degradation of its abandoned structures."[9] Vergara tacitly suggests the larger geopolitical implications in this analogy that would identify the United States as an empire with Detroit as its Rome at the center within a critique of ideas of "progress" and "modernity," ideas that were imported wholesale to Latin America at the expense of local and indigenous cultures and histories. Detroit is an archeological object that signifies both the end of an empire and the repositioning of the United States in the Americas, a reshuffling of the American hierarchy of nations. The display of an empire in ruins is a cautionary spectacle. It recasts the modernizing storyline of colonialism as a kind of "chronicle of a death foretold."

A Death Foretold

Urban scholars and writers use different terms to describe the city, some preferring organic metaphors that describe the dynamism of urban space. Peter Eisinger uses the organic metaphors of urban death that have fallen out of favor since Jane Jacobs's work on the life cycle of cities. He argues that the understanding of urban death might be engaged more critically since it is the prevailing trope used to describe Detroit. Urban death doesn't simply mean effacement or being rendered nonexistent; it means a change in status through the loss of characteristics that define a city. These metaphors of illness and death are used in political exhortations that urge publics to seek remedies and antidotes against the degradation of urban identity. Likewise, in his best-selling memoir about the failures and ruins of Detroit, reporter Charlie LeDuff works through his and the city's past, which he subtitles—using biological analogy—*An American Autopsy*. The memoir thematizes both the city and its author and this collapse in distinction adds to the biological resonance of urban decay.

LeDuff's story engages the urban politics and struggles of racialized populations caught in the city's death throes, a pessimistic story from which he will find an optimistic story arc. He writes in the tradition of the gonzo journalist, a male and masculinist figure who gives a world weary and singular view of life on the frontlines of disaster. His descriptions are tellingly riddled with gendered and heteronormative metaphor: "I ended up working at the Gray Lady for a decade, sketching the lives of hustlers and working stiffs and fireman at Ground Zero. It was a good run. But wanderlust is like a pretty girl—you wake up one morning, find she's grown old and decide that either you're going to commit your life or you're going to walk away. I walked away, and as it happens in life, I circled home, taking a job with the Detroit News."[10] His descent, his willful downward career move, coincided with that of the city to which he returns: "My colleagues in New York laughed. The paper was on death watch. And so was the city."[11] In 2008, Detroit became a symbol of the economic freefall, and its deserted factories and abandoned houses were harbingers of doomsday capitalism.

Detroit is the emblematic center and organizing space of a cautionary tale for the United States that, according to LeDuff, is a reminder that "we're all standing at the edge of a shaft."[12] This refers to the story of a man found frozen solid at the base of an elevator shaft. That his death is deemed unremarkable is a sign of a mood of fatigued indifference or as LeDuff describes it: "In most cities a death scene like this would be considered remarkable, mind-blowing, horrifying. But not here. Something had happened in Detroit while I was away."[13] He proposes to document the events and cultural mood that results in this generalized ennui.

LeDuff's story of Detroit is also that of a purportedly Anglo male protagonist who asserts his role as privileged insider whose grit and access to racialized communities lend authenticity to his subjective history of the city. As it turns out, Charlie LeDuff is of mixed heritage. He uncovers his racialized past through the same journalistic investigation that he applies to the city. His family's history of interracial intimacies is a vital part of the history of the city. His grandfather was "mulatto" but passed for white, hiding his racial heritage. To all appearances, Charlie LeDuff appears to be white and is referred by his interlocuters as "white." Race, in his schema, is associated with place and emplotment in the city. His access to the suburbs of Detroit and his mobility throughout the city mark him more as a nonracialized agent than a racialized one.

House Afire

Detroit is a sign of the doomed future of the U.S. economy that LeDuff describes as the "epicenter, a funhouse mirror and future projection of America."[14] It is also a place where U.S. racialized conflicts emerge and implode, apparent across its history of settlement as a free city in the north and the center of industrialism. From the 1967 race riots to the racially motivated murder of Vincent Chin in 1982, to the resentment about jobs moving to Mexico, it is a combustible cauldron of racial mixing and conflict. Beginning in the 1980s Detroit was literally a place of combustion as the capital of arson targeting abandoned and some not so abandoned buildings. The 30th of October, the day before Halloween, was dubbed "Devil's Night" and spawned the tradition of setting fires across the city. LeDuff describes this thrill-seeking degeneracy as a sign of the abandonment of the city to forces of destruction. These acts of arson might simply be "pranks," but they nonetheless recall other fires set during times of crisis. Fires, for their destructive power, demand immediate attention and have the potential for politically expedient meanings.

Fire is a common motif that comes to bear on social life in many ways, from actual to symbolic. It invites interpretation; it is an abyss of meaning that demands to be read. Fire levels a place, quickly dispensing with its past. It ignites and enrages. "Devil's Night" has a long history as a time of Halloween pranks, but, in a place like Detroit, it carries the possibility of another signification, recalling the fires of slave rebellions in the global South where fire was used in acts of vengeance and revenge and as a catalyst for social change. For enslaved peoples, fire was a sign of protest and a way to register resistance to the institutions that extract profit from labor. It spreads quickly and sets off a number of social and economic events, from firefighting efforts to insurance claims, and it signals displacement and loss. Bonham C. Richardson collates the various social connotations of fire in the history of enslaved populations in the oppressive plantation culture of the Caribbean basin: "Slavery, insurrection, threats, and planned destruction in the region all have been accented by either fire or threats of fire."[15] Oppressed workers targeted the commodities they produced, primarily crops, using fire to eliminate the very thing that signifies inequity in the social order. In many cases, the crops or other goods received far more protection and esteem than the enslaved workers who cultivated them.

The tradition of "Devil's Night" has roots far afield from the fire-based protests in the Caribbean. Halloween, the popular name for All Hallows' Eve, or the eve of All Saints' Day on the first of November has Celtic origins in the fall harvest season in Ireland and Scotland more than 2,000 years ago. It was a time to honor the recently departed spirits. Linked to the Celtic festival of Samhain, it means literally the end of summer and thus signals the beginning of a season of darkness and winter. The festival was an occasion to take stock and prepare for the months ahead and it marked a concentration of supernatural energies and the forces of darkness. Spectacular bonfires, reminiscent of the power of the sun, were built to keep dark spirits at bay. It was a time of liminality, particularly when diverse forces came into contact, when spirits came into contact with living beings. For Nicholas Rogers, Halloween is a holiday that, like other festivals, evokes practices of social disorder and cultural inversion, of the carnivalesque, transgression, and parody.[16] Halloween opens up space for the repressed of everyday life and thus might be read for its potential for social and political critique.

Irish and Scottish immigrants brought the festival to the New World, and by the mid–nineteenth century, it had moved beyond its status as an "ethnic" holiday and was popularized in the major cities in the East and Midwest. Urban youths revitalized the holiday as a time of pranks and social disorder.[17] This initiated the "trick or treat" concept of Halloween. Adults would give children "treats" to discourage them from doing "pranks" or "tricks" in the form of setting bonfires. Some children continued to play "tricks" but did so only on the eve of Halloween, on October 30th or "Devil's Night," so that they might still receive "treats" on Halloween.

In the 1960s in major urban areas, harmless Halloween pranks turned sinister in the destruction of property through arson. During the late 1970s, pranksters started fires throughout Detroit, making the city the first in the nation for incidents of arson and giving the city an appearance of ruination. By 1984, October 30th was firmly dubbed "Devil's Night," marked by three nights of arson and a record number of fires, 810. That year, Detroit became infamous as the arson capital of the world.[18]

There were numerous possible reasons for arson: insurance fraud, to shut down crack houses, to remove abandoned homes, and pyromania.[19] From the 1960s, there has been a steady out-migration of people and jobs from Detroit, leaving the city increasingly impoverished and abandoned, riddled with vacant homes and lots, and beset by diminished city services. The fires appeared to be acts of civil disregard but became forms of political action and critiques of the inaction of the state. By leveling the abandoned homes and crack houses, the arsonists wrote their message in fire and drew media coverage the world over. The fires became a national obsession and were no longer limited to Halloween. In late 1987, in one case that made its way to the *New York Times*, two men set fire to crack houses and were subsequently acquitted by a jury eager to signal to city officials that they had not done enough to curtail drug trade in Detroit communities. The two men claimed that they committed arson after registering numerous complaints to the police about drug-related activity to no avail. The men were taking back the neighborhood from the drug dealers' reign of terror.[20]

The history of fire and fire-setting in communities impacted by the history of enslavement of Africans in the Americas is key to understanding how fire functions in Detroit beyond merely signaling urban degeneracy. The fires suggest divestiture in the city and its institutions. They are powerful signs of defamiliarization and dislocation. Fire represents the power to destroy while it expresses rage, elicits terror, and has been—for colonized peoples—the final desperate act of protest. The destruction of homes and buildings might form a similar kind of protest; to destroy someone's home, as part of a community, sends a message about the disregard and devaluation of racialized parts of the city victimized by neoliberal policies. The ruins and rubble of the fire also mark a desire to erase and efface, in many cases, the homes that contribute to urban blight.

By the time that LeDuff writes, arson is no longer limited to the time surrounding Halloween, but is a way of life that bankrupts a system and accelerates its decline. He begins the story at a firehouse where one of the fireman tells him that there is no shortage of work even though there is a shortage of funds. Another fireman intones that "In this town, arson is off the hook. Thousands of them a year bro. In Detroit, it's so fucking poor that fire is cheaper than a movie. A can of gas is three-fifty and a movie is eight bucks, and there aren't any movie theaters left in Detroit, so fuck it. They burn the empty house next door and they sit on the fucking porch with a forty, and they're barbecuing and laughing 'cause it's fucking entertainment. It's unbelievable. And the old lady living next door, she don't have insurance, and her house goes up in flames and she's homeless and another fucking block dies."[21] LeDuff's fireman only recounts the senselessness and sadism of the fires and, from his social position, cannot seem to imagine their possible political or extralegal intent. Arson is a blatant and insistent reminder of state indifference. Regardless of the objective, to set a house on fire with impunity means the rule of law is not upheld and there is insufficient political will to change these abject conditions.

"From the Ashes"

In the epilogue of LeDuff's "autopsy" of Detroit, he encounters "a group of black men having a cigarette" and asks about the location of the bar where his sister spent her last hours before her untimely death in a car crash.[22] One of these men, describing the bar's attempted renovation, remarks upon its failed renewal: "But what you gonna do? You ain't gonna be reincarnated, so you got to do the best you can with the moment you got." LeDuff ponders the idea: "We are born to a time. What you do with it is on you. Do the best you can. Try to be good. And live."[23] Yet there is a marked class difference between him and that of folks he surveys. His privileged position allows him more fluidity and mobility and, consequently, more optimism about his circumstances. He interprets his interlocuters' insistence on "doing the best you can" as an exhortation to "be good," which will promise a better future. For LeDuff, the story arc ends on an upswing, opening the possibility for, as he conveys it, something else, a renewal of sorts. He presents the idea of the regeneration of the city in the section, "from the ashes," through the symbolization of a spotted fawn. In the final scene of the epilogue, he, believing that the footsteps he hears means someone is stalking him, turns and encounters a "pretty little thing" in the fawn. He takes this to be a symbol of hope and regeneration of nature.

While the account of Detroit is generally pessimistic in keeping with the mood of its attribution of "autopsy," it ends on a note of optimism and the possibility of rebirth. And the overarching story, of LeDuff's career stall back home after reaching the height of newspaper reporter success at the *New York Times*, is one of success, of a downswing followed by an upward move. LeDuff leaves the *New York Times* only to reappear on its best-seller list with his Detroit book. He, like the mayor he chides, turns misery into acclaim. While others are trying to get by, as the men are that he happens upon in the bar, he is doing more than that; he is using their stories to flourish. Like the *Queen of Versailles* and other postcrisis stories, the inexorable storyform of U.S. power is that of resurgence, return, and reinvigoration after loss.

Andrew Herscher imagines the possibility of thinking beyond the organic capitalist metaphors of renewal. Under the rubric of "unreal estate" he describes the various projects to occupy Detroit differently in order to resignify the city and cities in general from the capitalist model of expansion, growth, and economic development. He argues that a city in ruins, one that is contracting, is a site of possibility that opens opportunities not available to cities following a linear plan of development. "Unreal estate" refers to places that are literally outside of mainstream economies, with a different system of values that resists valorization or is deemed without value. Once these places no longer participate in a market system of exchange, they might be used for purposes other than the extraction of wealth and typical forms of use value.[24] They are entirely outside of a system motivated by profit. These are spaces in which the dissolution of capitalism is evident, if short-lived.

The Detroit Unreal Estate Agency is the clearinghouse of ideas that opposes the idea of Detroit as a problem to be solved and encourages new ways of inhabiting space in the city. The agency's calling card reads:

Dear Friend,
  I am not here to capitalize on the value of the real estate that you own, use, inhabit, identify with, or dream about.
    Any estates that I wish to capitalize on are wholly unreal.
                                    Thank you for your understanding.
                                    Detroit Unreal Estate Agency[25]

The Detroit Unreal Estate Agency "has been unified by an interest in animating valueless or abandoned urban property by new cultural, political, and social desires." It is a powerful indictment of an approach to the city energized by the ambition to renovate and renew through capital and corporate investment.

Projects like "unreal estate" and other do-it-yourself or DIY efforts proliferate throughout the city creating small communities and collectives. Private and individual initiatives step in where public services are defunct or ineffective. The city's low housing costs and low restrictions on business operations draw a class of creatives who might set up small-scale initiatives and create insular communities. This might be interpreted as an instantiation of Richard Florida's promulgation of gentrification through an influx of the (often white) creative classes to poor communities—a colonial settlement strategy that displaces marginalized populations. And these initiatives may not be poised to make a significant impact on local tax revenue. Instead, the story of Detroit is commandeered by another major figure in the home mortgage business, founder and CEO of Quicken Loans, Dan Gilbert. Like David Siegel, Gilbert made his fortune in the industry that brought the nation to its knees in the financial crisis. And he continues this legacy. Quicken Loans is the parent company of a new mortgage broker, Rocket Mortgage, that promises to deliver an eight-minute mortgage in a manner that recalls the easy lending of the 2008 crisis.

Gilbert is part of the economic elite that guides state policy and represents the imperial power of the United States to shape global economic events. He set up shop in Detroit and has colonized a major part of the downtown with plans for urban revival in his vision and for his corporate and personal gain. His plans include parks and condominiums and businesses that only deepen the racialized economic divide between city and suburbs, inflecting that divide back into the city. Moreover, Gilbert's development creates a fiefdom organized by and around an industry that continues to assert its power to shape local and national policies.[26] It creates an image of the "rebirth" of the city through capital investment and development—an image that is premised on effacing the urban past of decline, ruin, and the historic structures of the city's past.

Undead Urbanism

The "death" of Detroit is imagined differently in Jim Jarmusch's film *Only Lovers Left Alive* (2013), a film about a pair of vampires who bemoan the onslaught of modernity while living in urban decay that befits their need for solitude and nocturnal existence. Vibrant cities are defined as sites of the linear progression of capitalism, places that nurture modernity, industry, and technology. For Jarmusch, capitalist progress—accumulation, industry, planned obsolescence—is a force of death and the work of "zombies," or humans who participate in and perpetuate neoliberal capitalism (e.g., people in the music industry), while historical memory, creativity, literature, and the arts, is the domain of the anachronistic vampire protagonists. The "undead" occupy the ruins of Detroit and actively preserve the legacy of the city as the center of creative forces—music, architecture, art, and literature. Unlike the display of Detroit within the visual culture of "ruin porn," *Only Lovers Left Alive* puts the vacant landmarks of Detroit into their historical context and ponders the future of a city within a culture dominated by capitalist "zombies." The vampire is an apt metaphor for the city as undead or beyond the biological cycles of nature—birth, death and rebirth or renewal—and perhaps beyond similar organic notions of the functioning of urban capitalism.

The vampires of *Only Lovers Left Alive*, aptly named Adam and Eve, recall the prelapsarian myth of Eden and graft it onto Detroit. Except in this instance, the fall is not the economic freefall of the city but the threat of its capitalist remake. Adam (Tom Hiddleston) lives in Detroit while Eve (Tilda Swinton), his lover, resides in Tangiers but soon joins him. Adam is a musician who lives in a large delapidated Victorian house in a desolate area of abandoned and unoccupied buildings, a perfect refuge for a vampire. He surrounds himself with a collection of vintage instruments—Silvertones, Supros, Gibsons, and Gretsches—and, what some might call obsolete, technology—a Revox reel-to-reel, amps with tubes, and a record player. He records music only for himself, not for profit, but sometimes releases his work to the world to leave his trace upon culture.

These vampires are reminiscent of the creatures of lore. Gregory Waller describes the vampire as "Transylvanian aristocrat, seductive siren, anonymous walking dead, superior natural creature, or satanic master-villain, even as bumbling anachronism or as cultured, romantic hero or as troubled isolated victim of immortality."[27] Thus, *Only Lovers Left Alive* draws on the mythos of the vampire as cultured and anachronistic romantic hero and "isolated victim of immortality" within the context of the neoliberal version of capitalism. The vampire in its other forms has long been a figure that elicits anxieties about repressed sexuality and sexual perversion that threatens to consume humans. But *Only Lovers Left Alive* is not about the vampire threat to humans. Humans are the real threat as purveyors of capitalism and contaminants of blood, water, and culture. They are totems of capitalist obsolescence and historical amnesia while the vampires preserve and carry global cultural patrimony across generations. *Only Lovers Left Alive* recuperates the history of Detroit as a place of music, art, cultural production, and architecture that, in its ruined state, is liberated from the constraints of market capitalism.

The struggle and tension of the story is not that between vampire and human but between notions of immanence and historical memory. The fear evoked in the story has more to do with the demise of the vampire and what this means for the role of art and cultural production in capitalism. The vampires thematize the presence of art and literature; for example, they use the aliases of Steven Daedalus from James Joyce's literary work and Daisy Buchanan, the elusive female character idealized by Jay Gatsby in F. Scott Fitzgerald's *The Great Gatsby*. They bring forth the living presence of historical literary figures they knew personally, opining that Byron was "a pompous ass" and Mary Wollstonecraft, author of *Frankenstein*, was "delicious." Shakespeare was a "poseur" and the work ascribed him was really written by Adam's pal and fellow vampire, Christopher Marlowe—a theory that abides in some literary circles. And, significantly, in 1819, John William Polidori, wrote the novella *The Vampyre* that is based on a fragment by Lord Byron and would ignite fascination with the genre, inspiring, among other works, Bram Stoker's *Dracula*. Adam and Eve are symptoms and signs of an intertextual literary matrix and preservationists of this cultural patrimony. They literally transport their literature as precious cargo and invaluable artifacts, carrying personal archives of books when they travel. They identify with these classic works and their deceased authors more than living humans or other vampires just as they, as kindred spirits, are out of step and marginalized in contemporary neoliberal culture.

Adam and Eve's relationship allegorizes the central concept of "spooky action at a distance," referring to Einstein's description of the theory of entanglement in which two correlated particles are separated, and any effect upon one will simultaneously impact the other, even at a great distance. This suggests the intimate bond between these vampires while it signals the impact of actions across time and space, synchronically and diachronically or globally and historically. It is a cautioning to act carefully and with forethought—resonant in the case of the many contradictory ideas regarding the future of Detroit.

In *Only Lovers Left Alive*, Adam is suffering a sense of doom and has fallen into an existential depression and is only able to write dirges, or as he calls it, "funeral music." Eve, intuiting his despair from across the world in Tangiers, travels to his side. His crisis emanates from the threat posed by "zombies" or humans and "the way they treat the world" which makes him feel as if "all the sand is at the bottom of the hourglass." They, he claims, have contaminated blood and water and are causing decline and ruin the world over. Adam has come to the end of his immortality, a crisis that impacts Eve and for which she blames Romantic poets, Shelley and Byron. She, however, is older and wiser and cautions him that "we've been here before"; she reminds him of the Middle Ages, the Tartars, the Inquisition, the floods, and the plagues. But the current world order, we are to infer, is much more tied to the conditions plaguing Detroit, ones that emanate from the destructive onslaught of capitalist ventures and that destroy culture for profit, leaving ruin in their wake.

Ava (Mia Wasikowska), Eve's younger sister, fresh from Los Angeles, represents the invasive force of capitalism upon culture. Ava threatens to expose their protected lair to the human world by indulging the old way of obtaining blood sustenance, through preying on humans. She is a contemporary vampire,

Figure 6.1. The vampires of *Only Lovers Left Alive* (2013).

like creatures of the vampire series *True Blood* (HBO 2008–2014)—who is wild, self-absorbed, and unpredictable, exhibiting all of the deleterious characteristics of the industrial center of capitalist culture, Hollywood. She is a "tourist vampire" who visits the city but shows no interest in its historical character, its residents, or culture.

Adam, on the other hand, is aligned and allied with Detroit. His foray into the city at night to retrieve blood from the hospital, the only source of uncontaminated blood, is an evocative and somnolent tour of city history. We see the city from his vantage as he passes the luminous facades of empty buildings adorned with graffiti art. He will give a lamenting tour of the city to Eve at night, when it is most looming and ominous, in a way that captures the ethos of vampire solitude in a world that privileges the present over the discarded past. He shows her the city before its resurgent turn, before the vultures and zombies realize its lucrative potential—which she notes is its proximity to a vast supply of fresh water. The tour includes singer-musician Jack White's family home—part of the historical cultural legacies of the city—and the massive and iconic Michigan theater that was built on the same site upon which Ford built the first automobile prototype and that now, in its lapsed greatness, houses a parking lot. Adam excavates the various historical epochs evident across Detroit, noting the archeological layers that are often occluded in stories of the city as mere ruins. He points out the Packard plant "where they once built the most beautiful cars in the world." Eve, ever optimistic and contrapuntal, notes: "but this place will rise again." He is not so certain. They, like their mythical precursors, are thrown out of their Eden when Ava not only kills a human associate but destroys Adam's precious vintage 1905 Gibson. Ava's presence signals the final rupture of the protagonists from Detroit. They return to Tangiers without a connection to a black-market blood supply and resort to the old method of obtaining sustenance, feeding on humans. Their future, like that of Detroit, is uncertain. Yet, like LeDuff, they are highly mobile and have the means to move in and out of the city at will.

Detropia shows what happens when residents of Detroit remain and how they negotiate the depleted landscape of the city under conditions of deindustrialization, economic austerity, and rollback. Like *Only Lovers Left Alive* the city is conveyed in often dreamlike images accompanied by somnolent music, and the overall style is observational—we follow subjects in their daily labors—though each subject is also presented through interview. Crystal Starr, a videographer who documents the city, is reminiscent of Adam and Eve, who move through the city as the unseen undead taking in its lapsed greatness. Starr channels

Figure 6.2. Adam and Eve decamp to Tangiers.

the ghostly residents of abandoned luxury apartments and narrates what she imagines occurred in their confines; she intuits the "memory of when it was bangin.'" This is not a story of ruin and renovation, but like Jarmusch's film, a commemoration of the past and of Detroit during the boom years along with the story of the impact of the receding tide of industry. The story does not depend on a mythos of the organic cycles of capitalism, its inevitable rebirth, or the desire to be great again. Rather, from union organizers to individual business owners, *Detropia* documents the individual struggles of residents to survive and to better the city and who, despite the odds, remain. Eschewing the rhetoric of renewal and resurgence, Grady and Ewing dedicate the film to "the many Detroiters who work everyday to make the city a better place."

Camilo Vergara in his photographs of Detroit ruins deploys the image of the phoenix that rises from the ashes; likewise, LeDuff uses the same visual rhetoric, replacing the phoenix with that of the doe. Both suggest that ruin is but a necessary stage in the cycle of capitalist development. Ruins demand interpretation. In these cases, they represent a past of greatness and power, the memory of which inspires the rebuilding to return to former glory. Even LeDuff's forensics of Detroit ultimately relies on mythos, one like that of his own story in which the city's decline is the stuff of his gain and elevation of cultural capital as a best-selling writer. *Only Lovers Left Alive*, *Detropia*, and the Unreal Estate movement provides an alternate imaginary of the city beyond the regenerative tropes of capitalism. They imagine the city through different ideas about progress, futurity, and creative habitation to preserve the past and refuse the deleterious course of capitalist obsolescence and supercession. And *Detropia* shows the daily struggle of living in the city. Unlike other media about the city, it does not end with a sense of optimistic upswing, revitalization, and renewal, but of the actual and ongoing adaptation to conditions of economic ruin. Postcrisis stories of ruin, failure, and devastation contain imaginaries of new formations, of alternate ways of living in capitalism, and of refusing its storylines and rerouting its linear course.

Afterword
Racial Capitalism Redux

> There is a real possibility that the main victim of the ongoing crisis will not be capitalism but the Left itself, insofar as its inability to offer a viable global alternative was again made visible to everyone. It was the Left which was effectively caught out. It is as if recent events were staged with a calculated risk in order to demonstrate that, even at a time of shattering crisis, there is no viable alternative to capitalism.
>
> —Slavoj Žižek, *First as Tragedy, Then as Farce*

The stories about the economic crisis circulating in popular culture reveal a preoccupation with economic inequality in which spectacles of the lifestyles of the rich and famous are no longer the stuff of fantasy and escapism but menacing signs of all that ails U.S. culture. The widespread examination of the "lessons" of the economic crisis by pundits and economists is accompanied by stories about failure and how to rebuild after ruin. Many of the villainous characters of popular culture might be considered members of the plutocracy who, for financial journalist Chrystia Freeland, emerged as a visible force just prior to the economic freefall that began in 2007. As the fortunes of the plutocrats reached dizzying heights, the entire economic system collapsed into ruin and many of the very rich escaped unscathed. She notes: "If you are looking for the date when America's plutocracy had its coming out party, you could do no worse than choose June 21, 2007. On that day, the private equity behemoth Blackstone priced the largest American IPO since 2002, raising $4 billion and creating a publicly held company worth $31 billion at the time of the offering. Stephen Schartzman, one of the firm's two cofounders, came away with a personal stake worth almost $8 billion at that time, along with $677 million in cash; the other,

Pete Peterson, cashed a check for $1.88 billion and retired."[1] This is a prime example of what Slavoj Žižek characterizes as the dynamic of "risk society" in which the exploited assume the burdens of risk while those in power benefit from risky ventures. He cites the Enron bankruptcy scandal as an example:

> Thousands of employees who lost their jobs and savings were certainly exposed to risk, but without having had any real choice in the matter—the risk appeared to them as blind fate. On the contrary, those who did have some insight into the risks involved, as well as the power to intervene in the situation (namely, the top managers), minimized their risks by cashing in their stocks and options before the bankruptcy. It is indeed true that we live in a society of risky choices, but it is one in which only some do the choosing, while others do the risking.[2]

But this type of scenario does not inspire in Freeland a disillusionment with the financial system; instead, she makes clear that her book "takes as a starting point the conviction that we need capitalists, because we need capitalism—it **being, like democracy, the best system we've figured out so far.** But it also argues that outcomes matter, too, and that the pulling away of the plutocrats from everyone else is both an important consequence of the way that capitalism is working today and a new reality that will shape the future."[3] Despite the deep contradictions of global capitalism, Freeland asserts her unwavering faith in it. She, like others writing in the mainstream financial press, echoes a common demand to revise and reform the current system, not, as Left cultural critics exhort, to imagine a different economic and cultural order.

Even those marginalized within the stories of tremendous wealth, like *Real Housewives of New York City* and *Queen of Versailles*, express desires to participate in a system that excludes them. For example, Bethenny Frankel of *Real Housewives of New York City*, called by another housewife, Ramona, "the underdog" of the group of friends for her lack of affluence, will leverage her role and position within the show as downtrodden and accessible into a highly capitalized lifestyle brand. Suzanne Leonard and Diane Negra note that Frankel's success emerges during the Great Recession and illustrates a new kind of "economy of the self" that combines female self-actualization with economic mobility. "Capitalist self production" is one of the versions of work in the postcrisis form of neoliberal capitalism, where self-representation merges with a biopolitical care of the self.[4] Moreover, this "self" must necessarily be flawed or fractured to produce enough material to render in intimate narratives of self-disclosure and personal reconstruction or renewal. Thus, Frankel is continually at odds with the rest of the cast; she is always in and out of troubled relationships and suffers from parental abandonment, all of which become part of her own narrative of uplift as well as signs of personal investment in her corporate makeover story. For all her cynicism and critique of the paradoxes and contradictions of the economic elite around her, Bethenny is the most vital producer of the very capitalist dynamics that energize the plutocracy and less powerful members of the economic elite.

In the same series, Rosie, the Filipina domestic to the Countess Luann de Lesseps, expresses moments of disillusionment and critique of the world around her and lends visibility to the marginal populations that support the affluent as labor and, in the case of Count Alexandre de Lesseps's work, represent new investment frontiers in the global South through the microfinance industry. Rosie's status increases with her participation in the show as she undergoes her own process of uplift and renewal. She is given a makeover that lends her the agency of self-stylization within a narrative of self-actualization. She soon transitions from full-time domestic for the family to free agent, opting to remain in New York City as Luann de Lesseps decamps to the Hamptons after her divorce. She visits Luann in the Hamptons as a guest, having emerged completely from her appearance of domestic servitude.

These storylines of revitalization and success capture the dominant ethos of the show as reproducing global and racial capitalism. Even Luann de Lesseps thrives after her divorce, turning her story into a pop song, a book, an apparel and jewelry collection called "The Countess Collection: Styled for Living," and a continued lucrative contract with the *Real Housewives* series. Her personal story is apparent in the lesson she gives to a group of inner-city girls of color. She tells of how, despite and perhaps because of her Native American heritage, she was able to achieve personal, relationship, and economic success. She tells them that they may also achieve the same through hard work and entrepreneurial will. Her comments are rendered in a political and social vacuum without any sense of the various institutional inequities that would hinder access to the entitlements de Lesseps enjoys. This "lesson" drawn from her personal experience, if taken to its logical end, would serve to delegitimize Native claims to sovereignty and gloss continued inequality in the aftermath of racial capitalism. Her advice, like that in her etiquette book, *Class with the Countess: How to Live with Elegance and Flair*, assumes social conditions of equity and equal access across race, class, gender, and sexuality.

Stories of the super-rich reveal the chasm between the global North and the global South exposed by the economic crisis. *Queen of Versailles*, *Blue Jasmine* (2013), and *The Great Gatsby* (2013) present these contradictions as delusions of the wealthy. For example, the protagonist of *Blue Jasmine* refuses to acknowledge her fallen class and economic position, preferring deception and manipulation to accepting her fate. Likewise, in *Great Gatsby*, the titular character deceives everyone around him with illusions and tales of his aristocratic pedigree. *Queen of Versailles* ends with Jacqueline Siegel's delusion that the McMansion of American Versailles will be built even as the Siegel empire falls all around her, putting people out of work and out of their homes. These fantasies perpetuate and consolidate the power and hegemony of global capitalism and are premised on the idea, despite evidence to the contrary, that lost wealth will return and the entire financial system, like the houses and cities that lay in ruin, will be rebuilt.

Freeland finds, in her cavorting with the super-rich, that the plutocracy emerges from a concordance of money, political power, and ruling ideology. David Siegel's confession that he had a major role in illegal dealings to elect then President George W. Bush is a vital expression of the plutocratic hegemony. The idea that the ultrarich have extraordinary and economically charged political power is part of the mythos of capitalism. Indeed, Freeland's work, as she herself admits, is not a new analysis of the plutocrats; yet what marks her story as different is the incredible amount of access she is granted to this elite and highly guarded group. She tells their story from inside their ranks in unreconstructed accounts of their ideological chauvinism. For example, members of the plutocracy explain their deluded moral positions in relation to the economic crisis to Freeland:

> When I asked one of Wall Street's most successful investment bank CEOs if he felt guilty for his firm's role in creating the financial crisis, he told me with evident sincerity that he did not. The real culprit, he explained, was his feckless cousin, who owned three cars and a home he could not afford. One of America's top hedge fund managers made a near identical case to me, though this time the offenders were his in-laws and their subprime mortgage. And a private equity baron who divides his time between New York and Palm Beach pinned blame for the collapse on a favorite golf caddy in Arizona, who had bought three condos as investment properties at the height of the bubble.[5]

The plutocrats act with impunity while they are self-described victims of economic overreach by the poor. They suffer delusion and self-deception and remain completely ideologically isolated from the rest of the world.

Freeland did not gain the trust of this hermetic class overnight; she describes her role as one that developed carefully over time: "Through my work as a business journalist, I've spent more than two decades shadowing the new global super-rich: attending the same exclusive conferences in Europe, conducting interviews over cappuccinos on Martha's Vineyard or in Silicon Valley meeting rooms, observing high-powered dinner parties in Manhattan. Some of what I've learned is entirely predictable: the rich are, as F. Scott Fitzgerald put it, different from you and me."[6] Her reference to Fitzgerald is timely and fortuitous. Following the publication of her book, *Great Gatsby* returned to the silver screen with a vengeance and in a way that clearly marks the racialized heritage of capitalism while highlighting its delusions and disavowals. The novel and its filmic incarnations reflect on the culture of the plutocracy and on the division of the world into two opposing camps, those with inherited wealth and the rest. Freeland cites the language of an internal Citicorp memo from 2005 that reflects this sentiment for the new Gilded Age: "The World is dividing into two blocs—the Plutonomy and the rest."[7]

Baz Luhrmann's *Great Gatsby* (2013) captures the ethos of the era leading up to the economic crisis as a consequence and expression of racial capitalism. The story is about Jay Gatsby who goes to great lengths, veiling his ill-gotten gains and humble origins under the illusion of aristocracy to regain the love of Daisy Buchanan and wrest her from the pedigreed Tom Buchanan. It raises suspicion about the overweening ambition and invidiousness of the underclasses while exposing fears that people of color will soon storm the castle owned and operated by the financial elite. The booming 1920s stands in for a similar era in the early 2000s, revealing their commonalities and the connection between the upward cycle of capitalism and phobic racial discourses. The original novel, which the 2013 film cites faithfully, is imbued with capitalist eugenics that promulgate the policing of racial purity to ensure stability in the social order. As wealth and its entitlements spread to the middle and lower classes, the landed aristocracy hunkers down to protect its embattled position.

In the economic recovery period following World War I, a number of phobic cultural ideas converged around the "unfit" represented variously by racialized populations, immigrants, physically differently abled, the sexually deviant, the impoverished, and the mentally ill. As a result of the widespread fears about threats to the purity of the white race and its impact on the strength and solidity of national identity, a eugenics movement began to gather force. The movement, funded by corporate philanthropy, gained ground in academic, medical, and legal venues and would promote and enact immigration and marriage restrictions, sterilization of the poor and racialized populations, and incarceration of the "feebleminded" and sexually deviant.[8] Tom Buchanan in the novel (and film) expresses and represents eugenic discrimination through his clamoring about the demise of the white race. Buchanan seems to quote directly from popular eugenics texts of the era—notably Madison Grant's *The Passing of the Great Race* (1916), Lothrop Stoddard's *The Rising Tide of Color against White World-Supremacy* (1920), and Earnest Sevien Cox's *White America* (1923)—when he intones violently: "I've gotten to be a terrible pessimist about things. Have you read 'The

Rise of the Coloured Empires' by this man Goddard? . . . The idea is if we don't look out the white race will be—will be utterly submerged. It's all scientific stuff; it's been proved." When he emphatically declares his racism, the rest of the dinner party does not contest his views in tacit approval. He proceeds with ever more stridency and determination: "It's up to us who are the dominant race to watch out or these other races will have control of things."[9] Buchanan couples these concerns with a willful intent to uncover Gatsby's lack of pedigree and undeserved place among the wealthy class. Racialized peoples and the lower classes are collapsed as the invidious outsiders intent on destroying the elite and ruining the "American way of life." Echoing the eugenic ideology of the 1920s, Buchanan is preoccupied by those who are "unfit" and makes it his responsibility to ferry them out and render them neutral through death or destruction.

Buchanan's Goddard is clearly a reference to leading eugenics writer Lothrop Stoddard and his work, which was published just following World War I. Stoddard writes in reference to the crisis of war and the chasm that such violent shifts in global dynamics might occasion. Buchanan echoes his language in *Great Gatsby*, as does nativist and right-wing rhetoric in the United States following the economic crisis of 2008. Stoddard writes:

> Before the war I had hoped that the readjustments rendered inevitable by the renascence of the brown and yellow peoples of Asia would be a gradual, and in the main a pacific, process, kept within evolutionary bounds by the white world's inherent strength and fundamental solidarity. The frightful weakening of the white world during the war, however, opened up revolutionary, even cataclysmic, possibilities.

Figure 7.1. Tom Buchanan (Joel Edgerton) in *The Great Gatsby* (2013).

> In saying this I do not refer solely to military "perils." The subjugation of white lands by colored armies may, of course, occur, especially if the white world continues to rend itself with internecine wars. However, such colored triumphs of arms are less to be dreaded than more enduring conquests like migrations which would swamp whole populations and turn countries now white into colored man's lands irretrievably lost to the white world. Of course, these ominous possibilities existed even before 1914, but the war has rendered them much more probable.[10]

He describes this "spectre of social revolution" rendered by the war to be merely the "first stage in a cycle of ruin," linking the ruin of white supremacy to the ruin of the entire global social and economic order, a common refrain of nativist right-wing politics.[11] The eugenics movement set the political terms and established the language and rhetoric of the hydra of white supremacy and racial capitalism. Any glitch in the great capitalist machineries—war, globalization, financialization—might expose the vulnerabilities in white supremacist ideology. For instance, the Great War revealed the internecine conflicts among white dominant nations, thus cleaving racial unity. Stoddard writes: "The white world was tearing itself to pieces. White solidarity was riven and shattered. And—fear of white power and respect for white civilization together dropped away like garments outworn."[12] Crisis reveals the vulnerabilities of white hegemony and global capitalism. And it inspires the projection of unity and power where such things are lacking through the circulation of stories of white infallibility, entrepreneurialism, adaptability, and resurgence.

The novel grafts concerns about the demise of white hegemony onto class dynamics as divided roughly between those invidious classes from West Egg and the landed gentry of East Egg. Buchanan represents those out of step with the social and cultural upheavals of race, class, gender, and sexuality after the Great War and during the booming 1920s and the Jazz Age. Although in keeping with the contradictions of his class, he is quick to enjoy the pleasures of the era and its relaxed moral values—he takes on a lover and attends Gatsby's extravagant parties—while he maintains and asserts his dubious moral superiority.

Great Gatsby returns after the Great Recession as a permutation of the many cautionary narratives about overweening economic ambition leading to inevitable failure and ruin. And this caution targets the poor, like Gatsby in his early days, people of color, and the "unfit." While Buchanan clearly elicits animosity for his cruelty and violence, his phobic racism, and his imperiousness, Gatsby inspires ambivalence. He is the aspirational poor. He lies and conceals his past. He is deceptive perhaps because he is so self-deceptive, making up a history of pedigree to satisfy his audience and conceal the illicit origins of his wealth. Gatsby is like Walter White from *Breaking Bad* or Nancy Botwin of *Weeds*, characters who accrue incredible wealth through extralegal means in order to retain their white middle-class status or accede to more affluent stature. They do so by appropriating the means and roles typically attributed to racialized figures: gangsters and outlaws. In Gatsby's case, his wealth emanates from his relation to Meyer Wolfsheim, a clearly anti-Semitic figure in both novel and film, played by Bollywood actor and celebrity, Amitabh Bachchan—a savvy Hollywood strategy of targeting audiences in the Bollywood market but that also codes Wolfsheim as an ethnic and racialized outsider. Gatsby accrues great wealth in the method and strategy of Wolfsheim; yet unlike the latter, he is able to turn money into the illusion and performance of white Anglo pedigree. Like the racialized gangsters, bootleggers, and drug traffickers of U.S. fictional lore, Wolfsheim will only have money—that is, wealth without the cultural capital it affords white characters in the same economic position. Nonetheless, he will yield power over those around him through money in a manner that is deemed criminal by virtue of his ethnic difference. Wolfsheim is based on an actual historical figure, Arnold Rothstein, a gangster who "fixed" the World Series in baseball in 1919. When the narrator, Nick Carraway, first meets Wolfsheim, he regards him as an ethnic oddity: "A small flat-nosed Jew raised his large head and regarded me with two fine growths of hair which luxuriated in either nostril. After a moment I discovered his tiny eyes in the half darkness."[13] And when he realizes that he is the man that fixed the World Series, he expresses his outrage: "The idea staggered me. I remember of course that the World Series had been fixed in 1919 but if I had thought of it at all I would have thought of it as a thing that merely *happened*, the end of some inevitable chain. It never occurred to me that one man could start to play with the faith of fifty million people—with the single-mindedness of a burglar blowing up a safe."[14] His manipulation of the market, which was widespread in the 1920s, is a direct affront to the American way of life represented by its iconic pastime, and is thus, as a racialized ethnic outsider, tantamount to criminality. In a manner that accords with their social position, the criminal character of Gatsby's dealings is offloaded onto Wolfsheim just as the lower-class Gatsby is found guilty of the crimes committed by the aristocracy, in this case, Daisy Buchanan.

Gatsby's lovelorn delusions spur his efforts to present himself as a worthy suitor to a member of the privileged classes. His predicament is all too similar to that of the poor and lower middle classes sacrificed in the 2008 crisis who, conned by unscrupulous lenders, got in over their heads. The overleveraged were

Figure 7.2. Meyer Wolfsheim (Amitabh Bachchan), Nick Carraway (Tobey Maguire), and Jay Gatsby (Leonardo DiCaprio).

described in the mainstream press as unworthy recipients of credit who wanted too much. Such is Gatsby's cardinal weakness, succinctly presented by Daisy, as wanting "too much."[15] He represents the appropriation of the entitlements of the elite by the poor. He is greedy with Daisy's affections and her past, demanding that she declare that she never loved Tom Buchanan, which she is unable to do. He invades the intimate history and space of the Buchanan couplehood and attempts to take it over. His endeavors are suggestive of the revolutionary spirit of the "colored" against the white hegemony of Stoddard's cautionary text: imagined in postcrisis popular culture as the invasive and unstoppable forces of the walking dead, or the rising up of the racialized and trans/queer underclasses quarantined in prisons, or migrants marginalized as domestics and ancillary workers or incarcerated in detention centers and holding cells and who threaten to take over the home and the nation. These stories contain the kernel of their revolutionary potential concealed in their narratives. Women in prison stories evoke a female homosocial replete with various forms of deviance. Yet many prison tales offer a critique of the penitentiary and moments of complete refusal of the very idea of a debt to society, of a life of debt and indebtedness to institutions that perpetuate violence and otherwise do not serve their populations' interests. Likewise, zombie stories are legion because they imagine popular movements represented by the massified undead who rise up to invade the major institutions of capitalist culture—from shopping malls, military installations, prisons, the police, the government, and international organizations like the IMF. Even within storylines that submerge revolutionary spirit into normative formations—protomilitary heteropatriachal communities—there are moments, however fleeting, of transgression and liberation. For zombie stories, it might be the liberation from capitalist institutions, freedom from the indentured servitude of a life unto debt, or—as in the case of *Land of the Dead*—an allegory for socialist revolution. Zombie films like *Night of the Living Dead* provide antiracist storylines that critique and challenge white supremacy.

This strain of critique also emerges in Baz Luhrmann's spectacular revision of the "great American novel" for Hollywood. The glitzy spectacle of Jazz Age affluence is punctuated by hip-hop and jazz mixes curated and presented by hip-hop star Jay Z (Shawn "Jay Z" Carter), who also has a cameo in the film and is credited as executive producer. His status as mogul and major African American cultural producer is inflected in the storyline when he appears traveling alongside the Gatsby crew exhibiting accoutrements of equal extravagance. He displays his cultural capital with a vengeance as a challenge to the whiteness of the narrative as he places himself squarely in the spectacular framing of the story and, extratextually, as the shaper of its soundtrack. He creates a musical atmosphere that defies and challenges the racism in the original story that would render all peoples of color passive, silent, and subordinate. In doing so, he gives voice and visibility to those marginalized by racial capitalism. Jay Z's musical direction provides a powerful remedy for the forces of dehumanization in racial capitalism, one that is rendered in and beyond textual modes and that signals a refusal to be an object or coordinate in the story as a sign of racial difference or degeneration. The music links past and present musical forms to highlight the persistence of early forms of racism and eugenic discrimination. And this musical counterpoint sets the stage for a broader critique of capitalism.

We need new fictions and viable alternatives to racial capitalism, ones that question the foundations of an economic order in which some accede to humanity and others are objectified and instrumentalized. After the economic crisis, U.S. popular culture generated stories that put the capitalist social order in question by engaging the dialectics of personhood and dehumanization, normativity and deviance, freedom and imprisonment, and mobility and stasis—thus the prevalence of zombies, migrants, trans/queers, and prisoners. Many of these stories merely revise capitalism and reignite its appeal, offering outcomes that promise renewal and a return to financial and moral stability. Yet these postcrisis stories also contain moments of liberation from the coercive power of capitalism—moments that, if drawn together, might create an entirely new way of imagining the social order and, perhaps, encourage fantasies of liberation that might lead to their realization.

Notes

Introduction

1. Buchanan, *Suicide of a Superpower*, 428.
2. See Robinson, *Black Marxism*.
3. Žižek, *Violence*, 2.
4. Leech, *Capitalism*, 4.
5. Junod, "The Falling Man."
6. Freud, *Interpretation of Dreams*, 271–273.
7. See Fraser, *Weapons of Mass Distraction*.
8. Roubini and Mihm, *Crisis Economics*, 4.
9. Ibid., 270.
10. Ibid.
11. Ibid., 271.
12. Ibid., 275.
13. Lenin, *Imperialism, the Highest Stage of Capitalism*.
14. Federici, "From Commoning to Debt," 232.
15. Boyle and Mrozowski, *Great Recession in Fiction, Film, and Television*, xi.
16. Ibid., xxiii.
17. Lorey, *State of Insecurity*, 1.
18. Ibid., 2.
19. Žižek, *Living in the End Times*.

Chapter 1. Border Absurd

1. Deleuze and Guatarri, "Capitalism," 215.
2. Lyotard, "Energumen Capitalism," 232.

3. Sloterdijk, *Critique of Cynical Reason*, 5.
4. Giroux, *Public Spaces, Private Lives*, xii.
5. Davis, "Introduction: Notes on Black Humor," 14.
6. Quoted in ibid., 23.
7. Knickerbocker, "Humor with a Mortal Sting," 299.
8. Ibid., 305.
9. Blyth, *Austerity*, 2.
10. Davidson, "It's Official."
11. Newman, *Accordion Family*, xix.
12. Haugsted, "Showtime Scores," 38.
13. Bolonik, *In the Weeds*, 1.
14. Gillota, "'People of Colors,'" 972.
15. Jaramillo, "Narcocorridos," 1588.
16. Jeffords, *Hard Bodies*.
17. Howe, "Not Your Average Mexican," 87–88.
18. See Ramírez Berg, *Latino Images in Film*.
19. Pierson, "Breaking Neoliberal?" 21.
20. Pierson, "Introduction," 3.
21. Bolonik, *In the Weeds*, 74.

Chapter 2. Migrant Domestics and the Fictions of Imperial Capitalism

1. Roy, *Poverty Capital*.
2. Piketty, *Capital in the Twenty-First Century*, 2.
3. See Colby and Lettow, "Have We Hit Peak America?" 54–63.
4. Quoted in Mander, *Capitalism Papers*, 89.
5. Bello, "Globalization."
6. Parreñas, *Servants of Globalization*.
7. Marx, "Economic and Philosophic Manuscripts," 73.
8. Ibid., 74.
9. Forrest, "Households, Homeownership and Neoliberalism," 1.
10. Ibid., 3.
11. Ashton, "Troubled Assets," 73–90.
12. Wyly et al., "New Racial Meanings of Housing," 572–573.
13. Choy, *Empire of Care*.
14. Lanzona, *Filipino Worker*, 3.
15. Ibid., 9.
16. Sayres, *Analysis of the Situation*, 5.
17. Parreñas, *Servants of Globalization*, 27.
18. A. Tyner, *Made in the Philippines*, 1.
19. Rodriguez, *Migrants for Export*.
20. See Tyner, *Made in the Philippines*.
21. Tadiar, "Domestic Bodies," 172.
22. Greenspan, *Age of Turbulence*, 347.

23. See note 11 in Chakravartty and da Silva's "Accumulation, Dispossession, and Debt," 383.
24. I'm grateful to Genevieve Clutario for pointing me to this show.
25. Hurt, "Business."
26. Ibid.
27. Galindo, Prólogo, 10.
28. Federici, "From Commoning to Debt," 239.
29. Ananya Roy, *Poverty Capital*, 24.
30. Ibid., 27.
31. Ibid.
32. Graeber, *Debt*, 380–381.
33. See Fojas, *Islands of Empire*.
34. Manalansan, "Servicing the World," 215–228.
35. **Ahmed, "Melancholic Migrants," 127.**
36. Posner, *Failure of Capitalism*, 220–227.

Chapter 3. Zombie Capitalism

1. McIntosh and Leverette, "Giving the Living Dead," *Zombie Culture*, viii–ix.
2. Newitz, *Pretend We're Dead*, 2.
3. Ibid., 7.
4. Ibid., 1–2.
5. Davis, *Passage of Darkness*, 9.
6. See McNally, "Land of the Living Dead," 114–115.
7. Harman, *Zombie Capitalism*.
8. Graeber, *Debt*, 17.
9. Lazzarato, *Making of the Indebted Man*, 7–8.
10. Graeber, *Debt*, 379.
11. Ibid.
12. Ibid., 380.
13. Berne, *Games People Play*, 81.
14. Ibid., 81.
15. Lazzarato, *Making of the Indebted Man*, 7.
16. Nietzsche, *On the Genealogy of Morals*, 58.
17. Lazzarato, *Making of the Indebted Man*, 45.
18. Derrrida, "Of an Apocalyptic Tone," 3–37.
19. Dellamora, *Apocalyptic Overtures*.
20. Kermode, *Sense of an Ending*.
21. Graeber, *Debt*, 367.
22. Lazzarato, *Making of the Indebted Man*, 20.
23. Brown, "The Metastasis of Economic Hate," 807.
24. Graeber, *Debt*, 368.
25. Ibid.
26. Ibid.

27. Ibid., 6–7.
28. Ibid., 383.
29. Quoted in McNally, "Land of the Living Dead." 108.

Chapter 4. Queer Incarcerations

1. Ball, "Prison Life, Real and Onscreen," 2.
2. Rees, *Great Slump*, 22.
3. Ibid., 23.
4. O'Brien, *So I Went to Prison*, 67–68.
5. Rees, *Great Slump*, 17.
6. O'Brien, *So I Went to Prison*, 6.
7. Ibid.
8. O'Brien, *So I Went to Prison*, ix.
9. Ibid., 267–268.
10. Ibid.
11. Ibid., 105.
12. Henry, *Women in Prison*, 7.
13. Ibid., 20.
14. Davis, *Are Prisons Obsolete?* 66.
15. Henry, *Women in Prison*, 80–81.
16. Ibid., 81.
17. Caprio, *Female Homosexuality*, 76.
18. Ibid., 77.
19. Freud, *Three Essays*, 3.
20. Henry, *Women in Prison*, 49.
21. Giallombardo, *Society of Women*, 7.
22. Kerman, *Orange Is the New Black*, 49.
23. Alexander, *New Jim Crow*.
24. Sudbury, "Unpacking the Crisis," 13.
25. Kunzel, *Criminal Intimacy*.
26. Henry, *Women in Prison*, 90.
27. Ibid., 91.
28. Bryan, *Inside*, 83–84.
29. Deming, *Prison Notes*, 174.
30. Kerman, *Orange Is the New Black*, 180.
31. Ibid.
32. Bryan, *Inside*, 277–278.
33. Graeber, *Debt*.

Chapter 5. Sinkholes and Seismic Shifts

1. Henwood, "Foreword," x, ix.
2. Vincent, "What Are Sinkholes?"
3. Lewis, *Panic!* 3.

4. Ibid.
5. Tihansky, "Sinkholes, West-Central Florida."
6. Lee, "Florida's Expanding Sinkholes."
7. Quoted in Mander, *Capitalism Papers*, 7.
8. Warren, "Man Swallowed by Giant Sinkhole," 29.
9. Jonsson, "Florida Sinkhole Swallows Man."
10. AP, "Sinkhole Swallows Man."
11. Wines, "One Sinkhole Killed," 11.
12. Freud, "The Uncanny," 368–407.
13. Lacan, *Four Fundamental Concepts of Psychoanalysis*.
14. Searcy, "Car-Sized Sinkhole."
15. Bachelard, *Poetics of Space*, 6.
16. Ibid., 7.
17. Homes, *This Book Will Save*, 2.
18. Ellis, *Less than Zero*.
19. Homes, *This Book Will Save*, 3.
20. Ibid., 7.
21. Ibid., 30.
22. Ibid., 31.
23. Ibid., 35.
24. Ibid., 34.
25. Ibid., 85.
26. Ibid., 19.
27. Ibid., 358.
28. Ibid.
29. Ibid., 369 and 372.
30. Kanza, from PakistanTribe.com (accessed March 21, 2015).
31. Yacowar, "The Bug in the Rug," 90–107.
32. Aveni, *End of Time*, 3–4.
33. Brown and the TDAT Group, "Today Is the Time," 897.
34. Friend, "The Picture's Wrecked Again."
35. Ibid.
36. Ryan and Kellner, *Camera Politica*, 54–55.
37. Keane, *Disaster Movies*, 126.
38. Ibid., 96.

Chapter 6. Imperial Ruins and Resurgence

1. See Klein, *Shock Doctrine*.
2. Marchand and Meffre, *Ruins of Detroit*, 16.
3. Sugrue, "City of Ruins," 15.
4. Vergara, *New American Ghetto*, x.
5. See Grandin, *Empire's Workshop*; Fojas, *Islands of Empire*; and Hart, *Empire and Revolution*.

6. Ibid.
7. Vergara, *American Ruins*, 205.
8. Ibid., 206.
9. Ibid., 12.
10. LeDuff, *Detroit*, 3.
11. Ibid.
12. Ibid., 7.
13. Ibid., 1.
14. Ibid., 19.
15. Richardson, *Igniting the Caribbean's Past*, 6.
16. Rogers, *Halloween*, 10–12.
17. Ibid., 62.
18. Maciak et al., "Preventing Halloween Arson," 196–197.
19. Ibid., 197.
20. AP, "2 in Detroit Acquitted of Arson," 6.
21. LeDuff, *Detroit*, 49.
22. Ibid., 285.
23. Ibid., 285 and 286.
24. Herscher, *Unreal Estate*, 8–9.
25. Ibid.
26. Eisinger, "Is Detroit Dead?" 8.
27. Waller, *The Living and the Undead*, 3.

Afterword

1. Freeland, *Plutocrats*, 1.
2. Žižek, *First as Tragedy*, 12–13.
3. Freeland, *Plutocrats*, xiv.
4. Leonard and Negra, "After Ever After," 196–197.
5. Freeland, *Plutocrats*, 242.
6. Ibid., 4.
7. Ibid., 5.
8. Black, *War against the Weak*, xv.
9. Fitzgerald, *Great Gatsby*, 17.
10. Stoddard, *Rising Tide of Color*, vi.
11. Ibid., vi–vii.
12. Ibid., 13.
13. Fitzgerald, *Great Gatsby*, 74.
14. Ibid., 78.
15. Ibid., 139.

Bibliography

Ahmed, Sara. "Melancholic Migrants." *The Promise of Happiness*. Durham: Duke University Press, 2010.
Alexander, Michelle. *The New Jim Crow: Mass Incarceration in the Age of Colorblindness*. New York: The New Press, 2010.
AP. "2 in Detroit Acquitted of Arson in Fires at House Tied to Drug Deals." *New York Times*, Oct. 8, 1988, 6.
AP. "Sinkhole Swallows Man." *7Days*, Mar. 3, 2013.
Ashton, Philip. "'Troubled Assets': The Financial Emergency and Racialized Risk." *International Journal of Urban and Regional Research* 36:4 (2012): 73–90.
Aveni, Anthony. *The End of Time: The Maya Mystery of 2012*. Boulder: University Press of Colorado, 2009.
Bachelard, Gaston. *The Poetics of Space*. Trans. Maria Jolas. Boston: Beacon Press, 1994.
Badiou, Alan. *Philosophy for Militants*. Trans. Bruno Bosteels. London: Verso, 2012.
Ball, Aimee Lee. "Prison Life, Real and Onscreen." *New York Times*, Aug. 4, 2013, 2.
Bello, Walden. "Globalization and the New Slave Trade." *Manila Review* 2 (2013).
Berne, Eric. *Games People Play: The Basic Handbook of Transactional Analysis*. New York: Ballantine Books, 2004.
Black, Edwin. *War against the Weak: Eugenics and America's Campaign to Create a Master Race*. New York: Four Walls Eight Windows, 2003.
Blyth, Mark. *Austerity: The History of a Dangerous Idea*. Oxford: Oxford University Press, 2013.
Bolonik, Kera. *In the Weeds: The Official Companion Book to the Hit Showtime Series*. New York: Simon Spotlight Entertainment, 2007.

Boyle, Kirk, and Daniel Mrozowski, eds. *The Great Recession in Fiction, Film, and Television: Twenty-First Century Bust Culture*. Lanham, Md.: Lexington Books, 2013.

Brown, Katina, and the TDAT Group. "Today Is the Time to Take Environmental Action." *Nature* 432 (Oct. 21, 2004): 897.

Brown, Pamela. "The Metastasis of Economic Hate." *South Atlantic Quarterly* 112:4 (2013): 804–811.

Bryan, Helen. *Inside*. Boston: Houghton Mifflin Co., 1953.

Buchanan, Patrick. *Suicide of a Superpower: Will America Survive to 2025?* New York: Thomas Dunne Books, 2011.

Caprio, Frank S. *Female Homosexuality: A Modern Study of Lesbianism*. New York: Grove Press, 1954.

Chakravartty, Paula, and Denise Ferreira da Silva. "Accumulation, Dispossession, and Debt: The Racial Logic of Global Capitalism—An Introduction." *American Quarterly* 64:3 (2012): 361–385.

Choy, Catherine Ceniza. *Empire of Care: Nursing and Migration in Filipino American History*. Durham: Duke University Press, 2003.

Colby, Elbridge, and Paul Lettow. "Have We Hit Peak America? The Sources of U.S. Power and the Path to National Renaissance." *Foreign Policy* (July/Aug. 2014): 54–63.

Davidson, Adam. "It's Official: The Boomerang Kids Won't Leave." *New York Times Magazine*, June 20, 2014.

Davis, Angela Y. *Are Prisons Obsolete?* New York: Seven Stories Press, 2003.

Davis, Douglas M. "Introduction: Notes on Black Humor." *World of Black Humor*. Ed. Douglas M. Davis. New York: E. P Dutton and Co., 1967. 13–26.

Davis, Wade. *Passage of Darkness: The Ethnobiology of the Haitian Zombie*. Chapel Hill: University of North Carolina Press, 1988.

Deleuze, Gilles, and Félix Guattari. "Capitalism: A Very Special Delirium." *Hatred of Capitalism: A Semiotext(e) Reader*. Eds. Chris Kraus and Sylvère Lotringer. Los Angeles: Semiotext(e), 2001. 215–220.

Dellamora, Richard. *Apocalyptic Overtures: Sexual Politics and the Sense of an Ending*. New Brunswick, N.J.: Rutgers University Press, 1994.

Deming, Barbara. *Prison Notes*. Boston: Beacon Press, 1966.

Derrida, Jacques. "Of an Apocalyptic Tone Recently Adopted in Philosophy." *Oxford Literary Review* 6:2 (1984): 3–37.

Eisinger, Peter. "Is Detroit Dead?" *Journal of Urban Affairs* 36:1 (2013): 1–12.

Ellis, Bret Easton. *Less than Zero*. New York: Simon and Schuster, 1985.

Federici, Silvia. "From Commoning to Debt: Financialization, Microcredit, and the Changing Architecture of Capital Accumulation." *South Atlantic Quarterly* 113:2 (2014): 231–244.

Fitzgerald, F. Scott. *The Great Gatsby*. New York: Collier, 1992.

Fojas, Camilla. *Islands of Empire: Pop Culture and U.S. Power*. Austin: University of Texas Press, 2014.

Forrest, Ray. "Households, Homeownership and Neoliberalism." *Housing Markets and the Global Financial Crisis: The Uneven Impact on Households*. Eds. Ray Forrest and Ngai-Ming Yip. Cheltenham, U.K.: Edward Elgar Publishing, 2011. 1–19.

Fraser, Matthew. *Weapons of Mass Distraction: Soft Power and American Empire*. New York: St. Martin's, 2003.

Freeland, Chrystia. *Plutocrats: The Rise of the New Global Super-Rich and the Fall of Everyone Else*. New York: Penguin Press, 2012.

Freud, Sigmund. *The Interpretation of Dreams*. Trans. James Strachey. New York: Avon Books, 1998.

———. *Three Essays on the Theory of Sexuality*. Trans. James Strachey. New York: Basic Books, 1962.

———. "The Uncanny." *Collected Papers*. Vol. IV. Trans. Joan Riviere. London: Hogarth Press, 1956. 368–407.

Friend, Tad. "The Pictures: Wrecked Again." *New Yorker* 89:13 (May 24, 2004). www.newyorker.com/magazine/2004/05/24/wrecked-again (accessed July 14, 2015).

Galindo, María. Prólogo. *La pobreza, un gran negocio: Un análisis crítico sobre oeneges, microfinancieras y banca*. Por Graciela Toro Ibáñez. La Paz, Bolivia: Mujeres Creando, 2010. 1–10.

Giallombardo, Rose. *Society of Women: A Study of a Women's Prison*. New York: John Wiley and Sons, 1966.

Gillota, David. "'People of Colors': Multiethnic Humor in Harold and Kumar Go to White Castle and Weeds." *Journal of Popular Culture* 45:5 (2012): 960–978.

Giroux, Henry A. *Public Spaces, Private Lives: Beyond the Culture of Cynicism*. Lanham, Md.: Rowman and Littlefield, 2001.

Graeber, David. *Debt: The First 5,000 Years*. Brooklyn: Melville House, 2011.

Grandin, Greg. *Empire's Workshop: Latin America, the United States, and the Rise of the New Imperialism*. New York: Metropolitan, 2006.

Greenspan, Alan. *Age of Turbulence: Adventures in a New World*. New York: Penguin, 2007.

Harman, Chris. *Zombie Capitalism: Global Crisis and the Relevance of Marx*. Chicago: Haymarket Books, 2009.

Hart, John Mason. *Empire and Revolution: The Americans in Mexico since the Civil War*. Berkeley: University of California Press, 2006.

Haugsted, Linda. "Showtime Scores with Black-Humored 'Weeds.'" *Multichannel News*, Aug. 1, 2005, 38.

Henry, Joan. *Women in Prison*. London: White Lion Publishers, 1973.

Henwood, Doug. "Foreword: Dystopia Is for Losers." *Catastrophism: The Apocalyptic Politics of Collapse and Rebirth*. Eds. Sasha Lilley, David McNally, Eddie Yuen, and James Davis. Toronto: PM Press, 2012. ix–xv.

Herscher, Andrew. *Unreal Estate*. Ann Arbor: University of Michigan Press, 2012.

Homes, A. M. *This Book Will Save Your Life*. New York: Penguin Books, 2006.

Howe, Andrew. "Not Your Average Mexican: *Breaking Bad* and the Destruction of Latino Stereotypes." *Breaking Bad: Critical Essays on the Contexts, Politics, Style, and

Reception of the Television Series. Ed. David P. Pierson. Lanham, Md.: Lexington Books, 2014. 87–102.
Hurt, Harry III. "Business: A Path to Helping the Poor, and His Investors." *New York Times*, August 10, 2003.
Jaramillo, Deborah L. "Narcocorridos and Newbie Drug Dealers: The Changing Image of the Mexican Narco on US Television." *Ethnic and Racial Studies* 37:9 (2014): 1587–1604.
Jeffords, Susan. *Hard Bodies: Hollywood Masculinity in the Reagan Era*. New Brunswick, N.J.: Rutgers University Press, 1994.
Jonsson, Patrick. "Florida Sinkhole Swallows Man: Shocking Start to 'Sinkhole Season.'" *Christian Science Monitor*, Mar. 1, 2013.
Junod, Tom. "The Falling Man." *Esquire*, Sept. 2003.
Keane, Stephen. *Disaster Movies: The Cinema of Catastrophe*. London: Wallflower Press, 2006.
Kerman, Piper. *Orange Is the New Black: My Year in a Women's Prison*. New York: Spiegel and Grau Trade Paperbacks, 2013.
Kermode, Frank. *The Sense of an Ending: Studies in the Theory of Fiction*. London: Oxford University Press, 1967.
Klein, Naomi. *The Shock Doctrine: The Rise of Disaster Capitalism*. New York: Metropolitan Books, 2008.
Knickerbocker, Conrad. "Humor with a Mortal Sting." *The World of Black Humor*. Ed. Douglas M. Davis. New York: E. P Dutton and Co., 1967. 299–305.
Kunzel, Regina. *Criminal Intimacy: Prison and the Uneven History of Modern American Sexuality*. Chicago: The University of Chicago Press, 2008.
Lacan, Jacques. *Four Fundamental Concepts of Psychoanalysis: The Seminar of Jacques Lacan Book XI*. Trans. Alan Sheridan. New York: Norton, 1998.
Lanzona, Leonardo A. *The Filipino Worker in a Global Economy*. Makati City, Philippines: Philippine APEC Study Center Network and the Philippine Institute for Development Studies, 2001.
Lazzarato, Maurizio. *The Making of the Indebted Man*. Trans. Joshua David Jordan. Cambridge, Mass.: Semiotext(e), 2011.
LeDuff, Charlie. *Detroit: An American Autopsy*. New York: Penguins Books, 2013.
Lee, Jan. "Florida's Expanding Sinkholes Won't Deter Fracking." *Triple Pundit: People, Planet, Profit*, Feb. 9, 2015.
Leech, Garry. *Capitalism: A Structural Genocide*. London: Zed Books, 2012.
Lenin, Vladimir. *Imperialism, the Highest Stage of Capitalism*. Sydney: Resistance Books, 1999.
Leonard, Suzanne, and Diane Negra. "After Ever After: Bethenny Frankel, Self-Branding, and the 'New Intimacy of Work.'" *Cupcakes, Pinterest, and Ladyporn: Feminized Popular Culture in the Early Twenty-First Century*. Ed. Elana Levine. Urbana: University of Illinois Press, 2015. 196–214.
Lewis, Michael. "Introduction: Inside Wall Street's Black Hole." *Panic! The Story of Modern Financial Insanity*. Ed. Michael Lewis. New York: Norton, 2009. 3–8.

Lorey, Isabell. *State of Insecurity: Government of the Precarious*. London: Verso, 2015.
Lyotard, Jean-François. "Energumen Capitalism." *Hatred of Capitalism: A Semiotext(e) Reader*. Eds. Chris Kraus and Sylvère Lotringer. Los Angeles: Semiotext(e), 2001. 229–241.
Maciak, Barbara J., Madison T. Moore, Laura C. Leviton, and Mary E. Guinan. "Preventing Halloween Arson in an Urban Setting: A Model for Multisectoral Planning and Community Participation." *Health Education and Behavior* 25 (1998): 194–211.
Manalansan, Martin. "Servicing the World: Flexible Filipinos and the Unsecured Life." *Political Emotions*. Eds. Ann Cvetkovitch, Janet Staiger, and Ann Reynolds. New York: Routledge, 2010. 215–228.
Mander, Jerry. *The Capitalism Papers: Fatal Flaws of an Obsolete System*. Berkeley: Counterpoint, 2012.
Marchand, Yves, and Romain Meffre. *The Ruins of Detroit*. Göttingen, Germany: Steidl Publishers, 2010.
Marx, Karl. "Economic and Philosophic Manuscripts of 1844." *The Marx-Engels Reader*. Ed. Robert Tucker. New York: W. W. Norton and Co., 1978. 66–125.
———. "The Eighteenth Brumaire of Louis Bonaparte." *The Marx-Engels Reader*. Ed. Robert Tucker. New York: W. W. Norton and Co., 1978. 594–617.
McIntosh, Shawn, and Marc Leverette. "Giving the Living Dead Their Due." *Zombie Culture: Autopsies of the Living Dead*. Eds. Shawn McIntosh and Marc Leverette. Lanham, Md.: Scarecrow Press, 2008. viii–ix.
McNally, David. "Land of the Living Dead: Capitalism and the Catastrophes of Everyday Life." *Catastrophism: The Apocalyptic Politics of Collapse and Rebirth*. Eds. Sasha Lilley, David McNally, Eddie Yuen, and James Davis. Oakland, Calif.: PM Press, 2012. 108–127.
Newitz, Analee. *Pretend We're Dead: Capitalist Monsters in American Pop Culture*. Durham: Duke University Press, 2006.
Newman, Katherine S. *The Accordion Family: Boomerang Kids, Anxious Parents, and the Private Toll of Global Competition*. Boston: Beacon Press, 2012.
Nietzsche, Friedrich. *On the Genealogy of Morals and Ecce Homo*. Trans. Walter Kaufman. New York: Vintage, 1969.
O'Brien, Edna V. *So I Went to Prison*. New York: Frederick A. Stokes Co., 1938.
Parreñas, Rhacel Salazar. *Servants of Globalization: Women, Migration, and Domestic Work*. Stanford: Stanford University Press, 2001.
Pierson, David P. "Breaking Neoliberal? Contemporary Neoliberal Discourses and Policies in AMC's *Breaking Bad*." *Breaking Bad: Critical Essays on the Contexts, Politics, Style, and Reception of the Television Series*. Ed. David P. Pierson. Lanham, Md.: Lexington Books, 2014. 15–31.
———. Introduction. *Breaking Bad: Critical Essays on the Contexts, Politics, Style, and Reception of the Television Series*. Ed. David P. Pierson. Lanham, Md.: Lexington Books, 2014. 1–12.
Piketty, Thomas. *Capital in the Twenty-First Century*. Trans. Arthur Goldhammer. Cambridge: Belknap Press of Harvard University Press, 2014.

Posner, Richard A. *A Failure of Capitalism: The Crisis of '08 and the Descent into Depression.* Cambridge: Harvard University Press, 2009.
Ramírez Berg, Charles. *Latino Images in Film: Stereotypes, Subversion, and Resistance.* Austin: University of Texas Press, 2002.
Rees, Goronwy. *The Great Slump: Capitalism in Crisis 1929–1933.* New York: Harper and Row, 1970.
Richardson, Bonham C. *Igniting the Caribbean's Past: Fire in British West Indian History.* Chapel Hill: University of North Carolina Press, 2004.
Robinson, Cedric. *Black Marxism: The Making of the Black Radical Tradition.* Chapel Hill: University of North Carolina, 2000.
Rodriguez, Robyn Magalit. *Migrants for Export: How the Philippine State Brokers Labor to the World.* Minneapolis: University of Minnesota Press, 2009.
Rogers, Nicholas. *Halloween.* Oxford: Oxford University Press, 2002.
Roubini, Nouriel, and Stephen Mihm. *Crisis Economics: A Crash Course in the Future of Finance.* New York: Penguin, 2011.
Roy, Anandya. *Poverty Capital: Microfinance and the Making of Development.* New York: Routledge, 2010.
Ryan, Michael, and Douglas Kellner. *Camera Politica: The Politics and Ideology of Contemporary Hollywood Film.* Bloomington: Indiana University Press, 1990. 54–55.
Sayres, Nicole J. *Analysis of the Situation of Domestic Workers.* Manila: International Labor Organization, 2005.
Searcy, Matthew. "Car-Sized Sinkhole Shuts Down Franklin Street." Mar. 16, 2015. Wsiltv.com. np (accessed March 17, 2015).
Sloterdijk, Peter. *Critique of Cynical Reason.* Trans. Michael Eldred. Minneapolis: University of Minnesota Press, 1997.
Stoddard, Lothrop. *The Rising Tide of Color against White World Supremacy.* New York: Charles Scribner's Sons, 1922.
Sudbury, Julia. "Unpacking the Crisis: Women of Color, Globalization, and the Prison-Industrial Complex." *Interrupted Life: Experiences of Incarcerated Women in the United States.* Eds. Rickie Solinger, Paula C. Johnson, Martha L. Raimon, Tina Reynolds, and Ruby C. Tapia. Berkeley: University of California Press, 2010. 13.
Sugrue, Thomas J. "City of Ruins." In Yves Marchand and Romain Meffre, *The Ruins of Detroit.* Göttingen: Steidl, 2010. 9–15.
Tadiar, Neferti. "Domestic Bodies of the Philippines." *Sojourn: Journal of Social Issues in Southeast Asia* 12:2 (1997): 153–191.
Tihansky, Ann B. "Sinkholes, West-Central Florida: A Link between Surface Water and Ground Water." U.S. Geological Survey, Tampa, Florida, 1999.
Tyner, James A. *Made in the Philippines: Gendered Discourses and the Making of Migrants.* London: Routledge Curzon, 2004.
Vergara, Camilo José. *The New American Ghetto.* New Brunswick, N.J.: Rutgers University Press, 1995.
———. *American Ruins.* New York: Monacelli Press, 1999.

Vincent, James. "What Are Sinkholes, How Do They Form and Why Are We Seeing So Many?" *Independent*, Feb. 18, 2014.
Waller, Gregory. *The Living and the Undead: Slaying Vampires, Exterminating Zombies*. Urbana: University of Illinois Press, 2010.
Warren, Lydia. "Man Swallowed by Giant Sinkhole." *Sunday Mail*, Mar. 3, 2013, 29.
Wines, Michael. "One Sinkhole Killed, and Many Others Opened, but Experts Counsel Not to Panic." *New York Times*, Mar. 16, 2013, 11.
Wyly, Elvin, C. S. Ponder, Pierson Nettlin, Bosco Ho, Sophie Ellen Fung, Zachary Liebowitz, and Dan Hammel. "New Racial Meanings of Housing in America." *American Quarterly* 64:3 (2012): 571–604.
Yacowar, Maurice. "The Bug in the Rug: Notes on the Disaster Genre." *Film Genre: Theory and Criticism*. Ed. Barry K. Grant. New Jersey: The Scarecrow Press, 1977. 90–107.
Yousef, Kanza. "Beware! You Can Sink into the Earth." PakistanTribe.com. Mar. 21, 2015 (accessed March 21, 2015).
Žižek, Slavoj. *Violence: Six Sideways Reflections*. New York: Picador, 2008.
———. *First as Tragedy, Then as Farce*. London: Verso, 2009.
———. *Living in the End Times*. New York: Verso, 2010.

Index

affluence porn, 44
American Ruins (Vergara), 127, 131–33
An American Autopsy (LeDuff), 128–29
anthropocene, 105
apocalypse, 70–71
arrested development: boomerang kids and, 26–27; economic freefall and, 11–12
Arrested Development TV series, 11, 20; absurdity of capitalism, 19; background, 17–19; border wall storyline, 24; children's failure to launch, 26; economic austerity plan, 19–22; ideological shifts in second incarnation, 23–24; middle class lifestyle maintenance and, 16; political affiliations, 24–25; racialized social movements, 24; second incarnation, 23–27; ship of fools, 18
arson. *See* Devil's Night
austerity plan: *Arrested Development,* 19–22; retribution language, 22

Bachelard, topoanalysis of house, 109
bailouts, mortgage industry, 12
bankruptcy, 11–12, 125

Battle: Los Angeles film, 18
Beck, Glen, illegal immigrant borrowers, 53
Beloved (Morrison), 109
benevolent patronage, 58
Berne, Eric, social interactions and game analysis, 65–66
"Beware! You Can Sink into the Earth," 115
biblical storylines, disaster stories and, 118–19
biopolitics: debt society and, 85–86; self production and, 141; women in prison stories, 84
black humor, 11, 21, 28
Blackstone, 140–41
Blue Jasmine (film), 142–43
boom/bust model of capitalism, 52, 58–59. *See also* renewal beliefs
boomerang capitalism, 45, 52
boomerang kids, 26–27
border culture: *Arrested Development*, 17–25; *Breaking Bad*, 34–40; *Weeds*, 27–32
border economies, globalization and, 40
border symbolism, 11
border wall, *Arrested Development* and, 24
Boyle, Kirk, 9

166 · Index

Breaking Bad TV series, 11; extralegal activities, 33–34; Heisenberg's uncertainty principle, 36; *Jesse Pinkman*, 38; Latino characters, 34–35; Mexican character jobs, 31–32; middle class lifestyle maintenance and, 16–17; neoliberalism and, 35; Skyler White, 34; Walter's domination, 37, 39; Walter White, 33; white male entitlement, 32; white supremacists, 37–38

Bryan, Helen, *Inside*, 84

Buchanan, Patrick J., 1–2, 15

Bush, George W., 18, 45–46

Bush, Jeff, 107, 109, 122

business, female empowerment, 28–29

Caged film, 13, 84, 88–89

Capadocia TV series, 13, 84, 91–92

capital: economic growth and rate of return, 44; financialization of, 37; the Great Creditor, 67–68; pleasure of accumulation, 37; poverty capital, 42; social life of, 17–21; wage labor and accrual, 47–48

capitalism: boom/bust cycle, 12, 52, 58; Bush, George W., on, 46; crisis capitalism, 5–7; culture, effects on, 135–36; cynicism and, 19–20; debt capitalism, 7–15; disaster capitalism, 125; disaster films, 118–23; doomsday, Detroit and, 128; family and, 22, 25; financialized, 2; freefall, 3–5; Freeland on, 141; imperial capitalism, 7–8; madness of, 19; postcrisis stories and, 9–14; race relations, zombies and, 62–63; racial capitalism, 2–3, 65–66, 125; racialization, Detroit and, 125; speculative, 42; violence and, 2–3; Zombie Capitalism, 64; zombies as monsters of, 62

Caprio, Frank S., 90

children living with parents, 26

Choy, Catherine Ceniza, 50

Class with the Countess: How to Live with Elegance and Flair (de Lesseps), 56

climate change, 116–20

communal awareness, prison and, 96–98

communism, communal living and, 98

communitarian living in *The Walking Dead*, 77–78

consciousness, cynicism and, 20

corporate takeover of prisons, 92–93

Cox, Earnest Sevien, *White America*, 144

Cox, Laverne, 83, 93

credit cards, 71

credit industry, inclusionary discrimination and, 49

Cribs TV series, 43

crime, neoliberalism and, 35

crisis capitalism, 5–7

critique, political disillusionment and, 20

cultural signification, markets and, 52

cycles of renewal: boom/bust cycle, 12, 52, 58; Detroit, 125–26

cynicism, 11, 19–21, 28

Davis, Wade, 64

Dawn of the Dead film, 13, 63. See also zombie apocalypse; zombies

The Day After Tomorrow film, 104–5, 116–17, 120

debt: Berne's game analysis and, 65–66; climate change and, 116–17; discharge and social being, 66; disciplining the poor and, 54–55; future and, 70; Great Creditor, 67–68; illegal immigrant borrowers, 53; logic of, postapocalypse, 70; as mediated experience, 66; Nietzsche, 67–68; permanent, credit cards, 71; persistence, zombie apocalypse and, 68; racial capitalism and, 65–66; Siegel borrows to keep house, 51–52; sociality and, 65; to society, prison and, 81–82, 85–88, 102; Strike Debt, 66–67; and subjugation, 8; suicide and, 55; as viral contagion, 61

debt capitalism, 7–15

debt crisis of 1979: global debt and, 8

debt economy, 8, 65–68

Debt Resistors' Operations Manual (Strike Debt), 66–67

debt society: biopolitics and, 85–86

DeLaria, Lea, 83

de Lesseps, Alexandre, 42, 53–54

de Lesseps, Luann, 53, 56, 57, 142

Deleuze, Gilles, capitalism's rationality of the irrational, 19

Dellamore, Richard, on apocalypse, 70

Deming, Barbara, 96–97; *Prison Notes,* 84
Derrida, Jacques, on apocalypse, 70
Detroit: bankruptcy filing, 125; Devil's Night, 129–32; doomsday capitalism and, 128; historical legacies, 137–39; history, 134–35; homeownership, 124–25; racialized capitalism, 125; renewal beliefs, 132–34; Rome comparison, 127–28; ruin porn, 126–28; urban death, 124, 128
Detroit: An Autopsy (LeDuff), 125
Detroit Unreal Estate Agency, 133
Detropia documentary (Grady and Ewing), 125–26, 138–39
Devil's Night, Detroit, 129–32
disaster capitalism, 125
disaster stories, 12–13; biblical storylines, 118–19; capitalism's end, 118–23; climate change, viewers' opinions, 119–20; cultural crisis and, 121; *The Day After Tomorrow,* 104–5; ecological disaster specific, 117–22; Keane, Stephen, 117–18; redemption, 117; sinkholes, 12–13; Statue of Liberty and, 121; strong male leader, 121; *2012,* 104; types, 117; U.S. locations, 121. *See also* sinkholes
discrimination, inclusionary, credit industry and, 49
displacements, chain of, 46
dollhouse (Siegel estate), 48–50
domestic labor: work and home confines, 48. *See also* Filipina/Filipino workers
downward mobility: boomerang kids and, 26–27
Drew, Richard, photograph of falling man, 3–5
drug trade, 36–37

ecological disaster stories, 117–22
economic crises: disavowal, 53; environmental crisis and, 107; geological order and, 105–6; housing crisis and, 124–25; plutocracy and, 140–41; popular culture and, 8–10; sinkhole descriptions and, 107; *So I Went to Prison,* 85–88; white middle class and, 10–11
economic disparity: global taxation and, 43; Piketty on, 43. *See also* inequity

economic freefall, 7; stories, 7–14; women in prison stories, 84; zombie stories, 69
economic growth: rate of return on capital, 44
economic renovation stories, 52
economic system: white male body and, 37
economy of the self, 141
Ellis, Bret Easton, *Less than Zero,* 110
Emmerich, Roland: *The Day After Tomorrow,* 120; *Independence Day,* 121
Enron bankruptcy, 141
entanglement, Detroit's future and, 136
entitlements: shifting, 39–40; white males, 32
environmental crisis: disaster stories, 117–22; financial crisis and, 107; global capitalism and, 107; sinkholes as sign, 114–15
ethnic construct of whiteness, 31–32
European patrimonialism: neoliberal capitalism and, 53

Failure to Launch film, 26
falling body as trope, 3–4
family: capitalism and, 22, 25; children living with, 26; zombie stories, 75–76
Federici, Silvia, 8, 54
female empowerment in *Weeds,* 28–29, 32
feminized labor, 50
Filipina/Filipino workers: Chinese insurance commercial, 41–42; as free agents, 58; land purchase dreams, 47–48; low wages and perpetual migrancy, 50–51; as moral counterparts, 42; new slave trade and, 46; popular culture representation, 56; *The Queen of Versailles,* 42, 44–45; *The Real Housewives of New York City,* 42; state as advocates, 50; state facilitated export of labor, 50; Tadiar on, 50
film: *Battle: Los Angeles,* 18; *Blue Jasmine,* 142–43; *Caged,* 13, 84, 88–89; *Dawn of the Dead,* 13, 63; *Failure to Launch,* 26; *The Great Gatsby,* 145–49; Great Recession and, 8–9; *Jeff Who Lives at Home,* 26; *Only Lovers Left Alive,* 125, 134–39; *Snake Pit,* 89–90; *This is the End,* 18; *Touch of Evil,* 35, 63; *2012,* 18, 104, 115–16, 118–20; *World War Z,* 13, 62, 73–76, 74, 79
fire motif, 129–32. *See also* Devil's Night

folk culture: zombies and, 63–64
Frankel, Bethany, 141–42
free agents, migrant works as, 58
freedom, slavery and, 65
freefall: economic freefall, personal, 17; sinkholes and, 112–13. See also *Arrested Development* TV series
freefall capitalism, 3–5; culprits in media, 8–9; housing projects, 11–12; white middle class and, 10–12
Freeland, Chrystia, on plutocracy, 140–41, 143–44

game analysis and social interactions, 65–66
Gaspay, Marissa, 47; dollhouse and, 48–49
gender roles in *The Walking Dead*, 77
genre cycles, 117
geological order, 105–6
geopolitics of zombie apocalypse, 65
Gilbert, Dan, 134
Gilded Age, 43; Siegels and, 45
Gill, Michael Gates, *How Starbucks Saved My Life: A Son of Privilege Learns to Live Like Everyone Else*, 10
Giroux, Henry, on cynicism, 20–21
global capitalism: debtor-creditor relationship, 67–68; environmental crisis and, 107; Freeland on, 141; prison stories and, 101; racialized violence and, 42–43; zombie stories and, 69
global debt: debt crisis of 1979, 8
global economic market: boom and bust model, 52
globalization: boomerang kids and, 26; border economies and, 40; Filipina workers and, 46–52; migrants as free agents, 58; NAFTA and, 40; ruin porn and, 126; the state and, 50; white supremacist ideology and, 146
global taxation, 43
government control: economic precariousness and, 14
Graeber, David, 55, 64–65, 80
Grant, Madison, *The Passing of the Great Race*, 144
Great Creditor, 67–68
The Great Gatsby (film), 145–49
The Great Gatsby (Fitzgerald), 142–46

Great Recession: boomerang generation, 26–27; Grantville and, 60–61; *The Great Gatsby* revival, 146–49; housing projects, 11–12; mortgage industry bailout, 12; popular culture and, 8–10, 14–15; ruins and, 124–25; white middle class and, 10–11. *See also* postcrisis stories
Greenfield, Lauren, 44
Guattari, Félix, capitalism's rationality of the irrational, 19

Halloween, fire and, 130–31
Harman, Chris, *Zombie Capitalism*, 64
Henry, Joan, *Women in Prison*, 84
history, capitalism and, 135–36
homeownership: Detroit, 124–25; dollhouse on Siegel estate, 48; marginalized populations and, 49; neoliberalization of markets, 49; privation and, 48; wage labor and, 47–48
Homes, A. M., *This Book Will Save Your Life*, 105, 110–14
homosexuality, 90–93, 98–101
homosocial settings: prison, 89; sexuality, 90–93, 95; *Snake Pit*, 89–90
hope, zombie apocalypse, 79–80
house, symbolism, 109
housing crisis, Detroit and, 124
housing market: economy and, 12; timeshares and, 47
How Starbucks Saved My Life: A Son of Privilege Learns to Live Like Everyone Else (Gill), 10

IMF (International Monetary Fund), 6
immigrant borrowers, 53
immigration, *World War Z* and, 75
imperial capitalism, 7; boomerang, 45; debt economy and, 8; infantalization of others, 46, 50; paternal benevolence and, 45–46
Independence Day, 121
inequity: free market neoliberal capitalism and, 43. *See also* economic disparity
Inside (Bryan), 84
interest rates, debt crises and, 8

Jarmusch, Jim, *Only Lovers Left Alive*, 125, 134–39
Jeff Who Lives at Home (film), 26

Keane, Stephen, on disaster films, 117–18
Kerman, Piper: *Orange is the New Black,* 82–83; Women's Prison Association, 98
Kermode, Frank, meaning in apocalypse, 70–71
Knickerbocker, Conrad, 21
Krugman, Paul, zombie economics, 64

labor export economy: Filipino workers, 46
Lacan, Jacques, the Real, 108
Land of the Dead, social order, 77–79
Lanzona, Leonardo A., Jr., 50
Lazzarato, Maurizio, 8; Great Creditor of Capital, 67–68
LeDuff, Charlie: *An American Autopsy,* 128–29; *Detroit: An Autopsy,* 125
Lenin, Vladimir, imperial capitalism and, 7–8
lesbianism: gay for the stay in prison, 98–101; women in prison stories, 90–93
Less than Zero (Ellis), 110
Leverette, Marc, on zombies, 61–62
Lewis, Michael, "Inside Wall Street's Black Hole," 106
Lifestyles of the Rich and Famous, 44
Lock-Up: Extended Stay Maricopa County Jail TV series, 13, 84, 99–100
Lorey, Isabell: on governmental control, 14

Manalansan, Martin, on disaffection, 57
Marchand, Yves, 125; *The Ruins of Detroit,* 126
marginalized populations: homeownership, 49; pop culture and, 10; racialized/migrant workforce, 44–45. *See also* racialized communities
Marx, Karl, on privation, 48
Marxism, Zombie Capitalism and, 64
Mayan prophecy, 118–19; *2012,* 118–20
McIntosh, Shawn, on zombies, 61–62
Meffre, Romain, 125; *The Ruins of Detroit,* 126
melancholic migrants, 57–58
microfinance industry, 42, 53–55
middle class. *See* white middle class
migrant workforce, 44–45; disaffections, 56–59; feminized labor, 50; illegal immigrant borrowers, 53; infantilization, 50; low wages and, 50–51; melancholic migrants, 57–58; Philippines labor migration, 50

Mihm, Stephen, on crisis capitalism, 6
Modern Family TV series, 22
morality: Filipina counterpoints, 42; marijuana and, 29–30; neoliberalism and, 29–30; post-conventional, 29–30. *See also* women in prison stories
Morrison, Toni, *Beloved,* 109
mortgage industry bailout, 12
Mrozowski, Daniel, 9

NAFTA, neoliberalism and, 40
nativist language, 39–40
neoliberal capitalism: altruism in, 58; European patrimonialism and, 53; inequity and, 43; microloans and, 54; NAFTA and, 40; self production and, 141; war spending and, 76; zombie capitalism and, 64, 134
neoliberalism: *Breaking Bad* and, 35; cheap labor from former colonies, 44; conditioning the poor to, 54–55; crime and, 35; cynicism and, 20–21; drug trade and, 36–37; masculinity, 32; morality and, 29–30; NAFTA and, 40; Washington Consensus and, 2; white manhood and, 32–33; zombies and, 63–64
Newitz, Analee: zombies as monsters of capitalism, 62
Nietzsche, Friedrich, on debtor-creditor relationship, 67–68
Night of the Living Dead, 71–72, 72. *See also* zombie apocalypse; zombies
Noxon, Christopher: *Rejuvenile,* 27

O'Brien, Edna V., *So I Went to Prison,* 83–84
Occupy movement, 43, 124
O'Neal, Stan, 106
Only Lovers Left Alive film, 125, 134–39, *137, 138*
Orange Is the New Black TV series, 11, *98, 100*; debt and, 81–82; gay for the stay, 98–101; racial dynamics, 93–95; social dynamics and, 13; white character dominating new culture, 28; "You've Got Time" (Spektor), 82. *See also* Kerman, Piper

Parreñas, Rhacel Salazar, 50–51
The Passing of the Great Race (Grant), 144

penitentiary, meaning, 82
Peterson, Pete, 141
Petty, Tom, freefalling and, 5
Piketty, Thomas, economic disparity and, 43
plutocracy, 140–41, 143
the poor: debt and discipline, 54–55
poor communities: drug trade and, 36–37; incarceration and, 94–95. *See also* marginalized populations
Posner, Richard A.: boom/bust cycle, 58–59
post-conventional morality, 29
postcrisis capitalism, 61–63
postcrisis stories, 8–14
postracial order: *The Walking Dead*, 73; *World War Z*, 73–74
poverty capital, 42
power dynamics: postapocalypse, 69–70; women in prison, 90
prison: communal awareness and, 96–98; debt to society, 81, 102; gender differences, 91; privatization, 92–93
Prison Notes (Deming), 84, 96–97
privation, Marx on, 48

The Queen of Versailles TV show, 12, 42, 44–45; disaffection of workers, 57; Gaspay, Marissa, 47; home ownership and, 48–49; infantilization of Filipinas, 50; symbolism of Versailles, 52–53
queers, prison stories depiction, 13
Quiggin, John: zombie economics, 64

racial capitalism, 3; Detroit and, 125; European domination, 3; Robinson on, 2; social contract of debt and, 65–66
racial coding: zombies and, 62
racial drag in Chinese commercial, 41–42
racialized characters, 11; nativist language, 39–40
racialized communities: drug trade and, 36–37; eugenics and, 144–46; LeDuff in, 129
racialized violence: global capitalism and, 43; normalization of, 28
racialized workforce, 44–45
racism: credit industry and inclusionary discrimination, 49; incarceration and, 94–95

Randazzo, Tony, 107
the Real, 108
The Real Housewives of New York City, 42–43, 53–57, 141–42
refugees: disaster stories, 116–17; zombie stories, 74–75
Rejuvenile (Noxon), 27
renewal beliefs, 58–59; Detroit and, 133–34; imperial capitalism and, 45; plutocracy and, 142–43; racial violence and, 58; repressed discontent, 59
revolutionary spirit, 148–49
riches to rags stories, 52
The Rising Tide of Color against White World-Supremacy (Stoddard), 144
risk assessment, the poor and, 55
risk society, 141
Robinson, Cedric, on racial capitalism, 2
Roubini, Nouriel, on crisis capitalism, 6
Roy, Ananya: on microlending, 54; sites of poverty, 56
ruins: Detroit, 124–28
The Ruins of Detroit (Marchand and Meffre), 126

Sassen, Saskia, 50
Schartzman, Steven, 140–41
Secret Lives of the Super Rich, 44
Secret Millionaire TV series, 11
self production, 141
sexuality: homosocial settings, 90–93, 95; Nancy's business in *Weeds*, 29–30; *The Walking Dead*, 77; women's prison genre and, 84
Siegel, David and Jacqueline, 12, 42, 44–47, 51–52
sinkholes, 12–13, 105; "Beware! You Can Sink into the Earth," 115; Bush, Jeff, 107; commercial development and, 106, 108; consuming quality of, 109; ecosystem collapse and, 114–15; Florida, 106–8; freefall and, 112–13; geological order and, 105–6; insurance industry and, 107; intimate spaces and, 109–10, 113; language used to describe, 107–8; media on, 108; metaphor, 122–23; personal nature of, 109; prevalence, increase in, 114; punishment for human crime, 108;

regularity, 108; size descriptions, 109; *This Book Will Save Your Life* (Homes), 105; water demands and, 106, 108
slavery: fire motif, 130; freedom and, 65
Sloterdijk, Peter, on cynicism, 20
Snake Pit film, 89–90
Socialist Workers Party: Chris Harman, 64
sociality: debt and, 65
social order: debt economy and, 67–68; drug trade and, 36–37; game analysis and social interactions, 65–66; *Land of the Dead,* 77–79; *Orange Is the New Black,* 13; power dynamics after zombie apocalypse, 69–70; white male as representation, 32–33; zombie apocalypse and, 63–64; zombie story refugees, 74–75
So I Went to Prison (O'Brien), 83–88
speculative capitalism, 42, 44
Spektor, Regina, "You've Got Time," 82
the state: as advocates for Filipina/Filipino workers, 50; Filipino labor export and, 50; globalization and, 50; military in zombie stories, 75–77; *World War Z,* 75–76; zombie stories and white supremacy, 71–73
stereotypes, 35
Stiglitz, Joseph: freefall capitalism and, 3
stock market crash of 1929: falling bodies story, 4; *So I Went to Prison,* 85–88
Stoddard, Lothrop, *The Rising Tide of Color against White World-Supremacy,* 144
Strike Debt, 66–67
subjugation, debt and, 8
subprime: definitions, 46. *See also* microfinance industry
Sudbury, Julia, 94–95
suicide and debt, 55
systemic violence, Žižek on, 2–3

Tadiar, Neferti, on Filipina domestic workers, 50
TDAT (Tyndall Centre for Climate Change Research), 119
This Book Will Save Your Life (Homes), 105, 110–14
This Is the End (film), 18
time-shares, 47
topoanalysis, home and, 109

Touch of Evil film, 35
tribal *versus* racial, 93–95
TV series: *Arrested Development,* 11, 16–27; *Breaking Bad,* 11, 16–17, 31–39; *Capadocia,* 13, 84, 91–92; *Cribs,* 43; economic crises and, 9; house and home shows, 11–12; *Lifestyles of the Rich and Famous,* 44; *Lockup Extended Stay: Maricopa County Jail,* 13; *Modern Family,* 22; *Orange Is the New Black,* 11, 13, 28, 81–82, 93–95, 98–101; *The Queen of Versailles,* 12, 42, 44–53; *The Real Housewives of New York City,* 12, 42–43, 53–57, 141–42; *Secret Lives of the Super Rich,* 44; *Secret Millionaire,* 11; *Two Broke Girls,* 11; *Undercover Boss,* 10–11; *The Walking Dead,* 13, 60–62, 68–73, 77–81; *Weeds,* 11, 16, 27–32
Two Broke Girls TV series, 11
2012 film, 18, 104, 115–116; Mayan prophecy, 118–20

Undercover Boss TV series, 10–11
unheimlich, 108
unreal estate: Detroit and, 133–34
upper middle class: boomerang kids and, 26–27
urban death, 124, 128

vampire metaphor, 134–35
Vergara, Camilo, 125–27, 139
Vincent, James: geological deformations and economic crisis and, 105–6
violence: capitalism and, 2–3, 40; racialized, normalization of, 28; systemic, 2–3

wage labor, 47–51, 92
The Walking Dead TV series, 13, 62; communitarian living, 77–78; gender roles, 77; Grantville and, 60–61; hope, expressions of, 79–80; institutions in, 68–69; postracial order, 72–73; prison allegory, 80–81. *See also* zombie apocalypse; zombies
Washington Consensus, 2
Weeds TV series, 11, 27–28; interracial dynamics, 30–31; Mexican character jobs, 31–32; middle class lifestyle maintenance and, 16; sexuality, Nancy's, 29–30

White America (Cox), 144
white characters dominating new culture, 28; prison, 94–95; zombie apocalypse and, 69–70
white cultural capital, 28
white male entitlement in *Breaking Bad,* 32
white masculinity: economic system and, 37; neoliberalism and, 32–33; as social order representation, 32–33; Walter White and neoliberalism, 32–33
white middle class: economic crisis and, 10–11; lifestyle maintenance, 16–17. *See also* middle class
whiteness: as ethnic construct, 31; female empowerment and, 32
white privilege in prison stories, 94–95
white supremacy: in *Breaking Bad,* 37–38; zombie stories and, 71–73
Wines, Michael, 107–8
Women in Prison (Henry), 84, 89; homosexuality, 90–91
women in prison stories, 13, 148; accidental imprisonment, 84; biopolitics, 84; *Caged,* 84, 88–89; *Capacodia,* 84, 91–92; debt to society and, 102; friendships, 98–99; gay for the stay, 98–101; homosexuality, 98–101; homosocial life, 89; *Inside* (Bryan), 84; *Lockup Extended Stay: Maricopa County Jail,* 84, 99–100; power, forms, 90; *Prison Notes* (Demings), 84; queer reading, 84; queers, depiction, 13; *So I Went to Prison* (O'Brien), 83–84; white privilege, 94–95; *Women in Prison* (Henry), 84
Women's Prison Association, 98; Kerman, Piper, 83
workers, state debt and, 8
World Bank, 6
World War Z film, 13, 62; family portrayal, 75–76; hope, family and, 79; immigration policies and, 75; international organizations, 74; mood setting, 74; postracial order, 73–74; refugees, 74–75; the state, 75–76. *See also* zombie apocalypse; zombies

Yacowar, Maurice, disaster films, 117
"You've Got Time" (Spektor), 82
Yunnis, Muhammad, 54

Zency, Eric: financial crisis and environmental crisis, 107
Žižek, Slavoj, 15; risk society, 141; systemic violence and, 2–3
zombie apocalypse: communitarian living, 77–78; credit cards advent and, 71; debt, logic of, 70; debt and future, 70; debt and social life, 65; debt's persistence beyond death, 68; disorienting shift, 70–71; eradication of money, 69; geopolitics, 65; neoliberalism and, 63–64; panic about economic disaster and, 64–65; postcrisis stories and, 13; power dynamics, 69–70; refugees, 74–75; social dynamics and, 63–64; U.S. military, 75–77; white patriarch, 69–70. See also *Dawn of the Dead; Night of the Living Dead; The Walking Dead; World War Z*
Zombie Capitalism, 64
zombie economics, 64
zombies, 78; Davis, Wade, on, 64; disruption of U.S. racial order, 62; evolution in *Land of the Dead,* 78–79; folk culture and, 63–64; Leverette, Marc, 61–62; McIntosh on, 61–62; metaphors, 61–62; as monster of the recession, 80; race relations and, 62–63; racial coding and, 62; the state and white supremacy, 71–73
zombie stories, 148–49; global capitalism and, 69

CAMILLA FOJAS teaches in media studies and American studies at the University of Virginia. Her books include *Border Bandits: Holywood on the Southern Frontier* and *Islands of Empire: Pop Culture and U.S. Power.*

The University of Illinois Press
is a founding member of the
Association of American University Presses.

University of Illinois Press
1325 South Oak Street
Champaign, IL 61820-6903
www.press.uillinois.edu